DONALD STONE, JR., the author of this book
in the French Literary Backgrounds series,
is Assistant Professor of French, Harvard
University. He is also the author of *Ronsard's Sonnet Cycles: A Study in Tone and
Vision*, and the editor of *Four Renaissance
Tragedies*.

France in the Sixteenth Century

A Medieval Society Transformed

by
DONALD STONE, JR.

Prentice-Hall, Inc. A SPECTRUM BOOK Englewood Cliffs, N. J.

FRENCH LITERARY BACKGROUNDS SERIES

General Editor, Victor Brombert,

Yale University

© 1969 by

PRENTICE-HALL, INC.,

Englewood Cliffs, New Jersey

Library of Congress
Catalog Card Number: 69-11352

Printed in the United States of America

Current Printing (last digit):

10   9   8   7   6   5   4   3   2   1

PRENTICE-HALL INTERNATIONAL, INC. (LONDON)

for

J.C.S.

Preface

This book is designed to introduce students to the history and literature of the French sixteenth century. It does not claim to be either impartial or complete in presenting this phenomenon, but hopes rather to stimulate the student to examine and test the views expressed through his courses and reading. Also, since certain writers of this century are clearly more important and more representative than others, I have chosen to discuss them in some detail instead of devoting minimal descriptions to a wider range of authors. My intention was to insure that the student receive at the outset an awareness of the complexity of these great minds and, ultimately, of the period he is about to study.

As footnotes were to be avoided in the preparation of the text, I have provided in the bibliography a listing of specific as well as general material used in the elaboration of my ideas.

I am indebted to W. G. Moore, who read portions of the manuscript, and especially to Victor Brombert, who provided me with this opportunity to delve more deeply into the mysteries and marvels of the sixteenth century in France.

D.S., Jr.

Kirkland House
Cambridge, Mass.
December 31, 1967

Contents

France
in the
Sixteenth Century

Introduction

In this modern age, it is becoming more and more impossible to follow closely and to understand the shifting nature of world or even national politics. The continuous interaction of innumerable forces, the rise and fall of prominent faces, and the multiplicity of interpretations we are offered to explain each significant event overwhelm us and tax our powers of analysis. Indeed, someone has said that if the best minds of today were asked what Zeitgeist dominated our time, they would unquestionably reply that there is none and that our age is characterized by chaos and transition.

It is hard to believe that such convictions would not apply to virtually all periods of history or that an understanding of the scope of events could be arrived at more easily in the past than today; and yet, despite the even greater distance between ourselves and earlier centuries, we tend to feel freer about defining the worlds which have preceded us. Perhaps we tacitly believe that they were simpler societies, that we have some superior ability to discern the true course of events now that all is artifact. Such pretension on our part can only destroy our very intention, which is to give a faithful, intelligent, and sympathetic rendering of the period in question.

This volume will deal with a period in French history that has been called both the Renaissance and the sixteenth century. Only the second term is fact. The first is an interpretation, and, in point of fact, few moments in the development of the French people have been so persistently subjected to the pretension of omniscience as the sixteenth century. It has been succinctly defined, patiently separated from preceding centuries, endowed with a prevailing Geist, and related to the Italian Renaissance, which, in all things, appears the inspiration for a new mode of life. The sixteenth century has also been considered as the very opposite—the persistence of a pre-existing culture that continued to evolve. As might be expected, the second view was a reaction to the first and based, in its way, upon equally simple assumptions. The student who is just beginning his inquiry into the nature of the sixteenth century in France would do well to note both pitfalls and avoid (as this study will attempt to do) either position.

If we think for a moment of the France of the seventeenth century, we imagine Louis XIV at Versailles, entertaining his host of nobles. They fawn, they flatter his every whim. He rewards them with a program of dancing and fireworks. The vast expanses of the allées of Versailles are lit. Jewels, silks, and lace adorn the guests. The entire scene highlights Louis' claims to wealth, power, and prestige—claims that a French king of the fifteenth century could hardly make.

The Hundred Years War nearly ruined the French monarchy. At the same time, the monarchy was the only institution capable of uniting the country against the English. It continued to strengthen itself after the cessation of hostilities, but the kings were far from the munificence or the power of Louis XIV. When Charles VIII married Anne de Bretagne in 1491, it was she who decorated Amboise with tapestries and furniture. In his minority the same King had his position saved for him by his older sister Anne of Beaujeu, who fought off with words and arms a number of powerful nobles eager to seize the throne.

If we know the salon Molière depicts in his *Critique de l'Ecole des Femmes*, we have heard seventeenth-century aristocrats discuss taste and the rules of Aristotle. This is hardly the same aristocracy which throughout the fifteenth century staged jousts and tournaments in order to preserve the chivalric ideal at all costs. Not only had the nobility of Louis XIV acquired cultural pretensions, but the court tended to replace the monastery and the university as the center of artistic life. The world of Villon or Gerson or Fichet was the Montagne Sainte Geneviève. Molière and Racine thrived on the stimulus of Paris and Versailles.

However brief, these comparisons reflect startling shifts in the civilization of France between the fifteenth and seventeenth centuries. In that they represent a series of transformations which include the movement from a church-oriented culture to one centered in the cities and courts, from an ethos based on chivalry and a feudal mentality to an interest in art, self, and the cultivation and perfection of both within this earthly sphere, these transformations suggest a development from what we term the medieval world to the modern age. At either pole—the fifteenth and seventeenth centuries—we can easily recognize the institutions by which the respective periods can be defined, and we must assume that the sixteenth century provided the essential moment of transition. During this era the older forms and institutions declined, and others rose to take their place. This is the drama of the sixteenth century, its excitement, its fascination, but also its complexity.

To say that the years 1500–1599 were for France, England, or Spain a period as complex as our own already conveys a patronizing attitude. A more fruitful approach would be to recognize at the outset that the years covered by this volume were subject to the same multitude of economic, political, and social problems as any moment in civilized history. Secondly, we must realize that for this reason the scholar cannot be too circumspect in his remarks. The world he attempts to analyze existed in a distant past. The ties, such as language, are patently deceptive. Medieval French often has the advantage of being sufficiently different from the modern language to require extensive study and glossaries. The temptation to assume that Middle French can, with a slight modernization of spelling, approximate the language of today must always be resisted.

When we attempt to understand the cultural milieu, we find that, rather than being deceptive, it is simply foreign to the modern educational experience. Our own training does not even approximate that of the writers of the sixteenth century. Who among us can claim to have acquired the knowledge of antiquity which Daurat inculcated in the young poets of Coqueret? When we read the Bible, does it occur to us to seek out the lengthy commentaries that to Rabelais or Lefèvre d'Etaples were inseparable from a study of the basic text? We have a general knowledge of mythology, but since we have not read Boccaccio's *Geneologia deorum* or similar books by Gyraldi, Conti, and Cartari, how can we be sure that our conception of certain mythological figures, beasts, and objects corresponds to the views of those who consulted such texts? Still, all is not lost. If we are aware of the dangers inherent in interpreting this distant period, if we are ever more eager to acquaint ourselves with the documents of the day, then a crucial period in Western history will open before us.

1

The Problem of the Renaissance

THE MAJOR VIEWS

The idea of a rupture between the fifteenth and sixteenth centuries is not a modern construct. Without using the specific word "Renaissance," several writers of the time referred to their culture as a moment of rebirth in literature, culture, and general knowledge and contrasted this culture with the ignorance of the preceding age. Rabelais, in Gargantua's letter to Pantagruel, wrote, "*Maintenant toutes disciplines sont restituées*" (1532). Ronsard, in his ode "A sa Lyre" (1550), maintained:

> *Heureuse lire honneur de mon enfance,*
> *Je te sonnai devant tous en la France*
> *De peu à peu, car quant premierement*
> *Je te trouvai, tu sonnois durement,*
> *Tu n'avois point de cordes qui valussent,*
> *Ne qui répondre aus lois de mon doi pussent.*
> *Moisi du tens ton fust ne sonnoit point,*
> *Mais j'eu pitié de te voir mal empoint;*
> *Toi qui jadis des grans Rois les viandes*
> *Faisois trouver plus douces & friandes:*
> *Pour te monter de cordes, & d'un fust,*
> *Voire d'un son qui naturel te fust,*
> *Je pillai Thebe', & saccagai la Pouille,*
> *T'enrichissant de leur belle dépouille.*

The humanists also clearly stated that a touchstone of this rebirth was their superior acquaintance with the literature and languages of antiquity. Ronsard's allusion ("*Je pillai Thebe', & saccagai la Pouille*") refers to Pindar and Horace, with whose aid the poet had transformed French poetry. Rabelais, in criticizing the jurists of his day, pointed

4

specifically to their inability to understand the laws since "*ils n'avoient congnoissance de langue ny Grecque, ny Latine, mais seullement de Gothique et Barbare; et toutesfoys les loix sont premierement prinses des Grecz . . . et secondement sont redigées en latin le plus elegant et aorné qui soit en toute la langue Latine.*" Such a view of the sixteenth century and of the period that preceded it remained uncontested for many centuries, not because objective research upheld this position, but because the centuries following 1599 shared the prejudices of the humanists, or fond of creating their own prejudices, they were convinced, by new biases, of the necessity to sanction such a dichotomy between the ignorant Middle Ages and the enlightened sixteenth century.

The era of Molière and Racine, the so-called Classical age, with its admiration for the works and canons of antiquity, was not likely to reverse the views of the preceding century. The same may be said of those who wrote just before and after the Classical age. However much Malherbe (1555–1628) decried the insufficiencies of Ronsard, just as Ronsard had deprecated his own predecessors, the great reform he wished to institute patently belonged in the line of many of the Pléiade's innovations. The later years of the seventeenth century produced the famous *Querelle des Anciens et des Modernes* during which, it is true, certain Frenchmen advanced and defended the idea that French was no longer inferior to Latin or Greek and that reliance upon Virgil or Homer for the creation of new works was not necessary, but it was this very concept of progress and perfection in letters, applied to the history of civilization in general, which prevented the eighteenth century from turning against the primacy of antiquity over the Middle Ages.

Proud of their culture, the *philosophes* of the eighteenth century tended to conceive of history in terms of periods of advances and sophistication (like their own) or of great intellectual darkness. They felt a definite affinity with classical times and scorned the Middle Ages for what the *philosophes* considered a near fatal setback in the development of human knowledge. This assumption led them to repeat many of the criticisms hurled against the Middle Ages by the humanists and poets of the sixteenth century. In their opinion, medieval scholars possessed inferior minds because they considered as factual theories which, by that time, had been disproved. Moreover, these scholars used corrupt and fraudulent texts on which to base their discussions. The whole period was the victim of superstition and credulity, which were associated with the religiosity of the Middle Ages. While the rational, anticlerical mind of the Enlightenment saw immediate parallels between its own era and the sixteenth century, to push back into the medieval period was to enter into contact with the very opposite of what it held sacred. As a result, a review of the relative merits of the Middle Ages and the sixteenth century could not be made until society decided to question the guiding principles of reason, progress, and enlightenment.

Such a questioning of values came with the Romantic movement, which broke openly with Classical canons of ordered creation and a *beau idéal* to praise instead the irregular, the unsophisticated, even the grotesque. Certain of its historians dismissed advances made by science and society as the determining factor in the evolution of man in favor of a more mysterious force—the Volksgeist (the collective personality of a people). What they were revolting against, in fact, were those prejudices that for so long had made the Middle Ages appear inferior to the sixteenth century or to the civilization of classical times. The Middle Ages came into its own and occupied for the Romantics the place that antiquity had once held for the humanists or the *philosophes*. The "simplicity" of the Middle Ages became a touching example of that mysterious Volksgeist which moved a whole world, produced majestic cathedrals, and maintained a long unity of religious sentiment.

The transmutation of values that the Romantics wished to effect must ultimately be seen in the light of the long dominance of Classical aesthetics over French literature. But whatever caused the Romantics to glorify the Middle Ages and to pit the grotesque against the Classical rules, their revolt made it increasingly impossible to dismiss summarily medieval history and culture as insignificant excrescences. The humanists in sixteenth-century France may have felt that the culture they inherited was valueless, but it became more difficult for an historian of art, literature, or institutions to believe that such an attitude was fair or that the newness of poetry or thought of which the humanists boasted was truly new.

BURCKHARDT

To complicate matters further, in 1860 Jacob Burckhardt, a Swiss historian, published *The Civilization of the Renaissance in Italy*. This book, though more than a century old, is today still a classic. The criticisms it has merited are more than offset by the contribution that Burckhardt made toward a definition of the vast subject announced in his title.

The immense impact of this book can be best appreciated when one considers how Burckhardt described the Italian Renaissance. It was for him the moment when man discovered his individuality. Throughout the Middle Ages, man was conscious of himself only in relation to two institutions of which he was a part—the Church and the feudal system. Between the fourteenth and fifteenth centuries man became aware of himself outside these impersonal phenomena. The despotic form of government in many Italian city-states, with its lack of protection for the rights of the individual, and the incessant warring forced this realization upon him since man could now count on himself alone. Despotism drove him to revolt. If he met with success, he was a victor; if he failed, he knew exile. Whatever the case, a sense of the self was aroused.

Burckhardt also formulated the portrait of "the Renaissance man." An individual of wide talents, the Renaissance man thirsted for glory and for glory in the modern sense of the term—self-aggrandizement, not the devotion of the medieval soul. Burckhardt gave to antiquity a large role to play in this development of a new personality which, he was convinced, possessed an essentially pagan nature. Antiquity was for him a force that fiercely rivalled the Christian ethic.

One need go no further in a presentation of Burckhardt's ideas to show how much *his* Renaissance has become *the* Renaissance. Individualism, thirst for personal glory, paganism, disregard for the medieval vision of life, such is the manner in which countless manuals of literary history present the Renaissance. Though scholars may argue about specific points in *The Civilization of the Renaissance in Italy*, no voice has succeeded in penetrating so far and wide as Burckhardt's. Students should recognize, however, to what degree their impressions may be grounded on the theories of a single man and should seek exposure to a fuller range of attitudes concerning this most complex phenomenon. The necessity for such exposure is all the greater since Burckhardt's study came at a critical moment. No sooner had the Romantics newly explored the world of the Middle Ages than Burckhardt arrived to codify and establish an interpretation of the Renaissance founded upon a discontinuity between the Middle Ages and the period that followed it.

The reaction against Burckhardt has come from many and varied quarters. It has tended to discuss mainly the origins and nature of the Renaissance.

In the later half of Burckhardt's century, Ernest Renan and Emile Gebhart studied medieval mystics, especially St. Francis of Assisi. Without breaking with Burckhardt's theories, Renan praised St. Francis for being free from medieval scholasticism. Gebhart and others pursued Renan's points to conclude that in St. Francis' simple, intense faith, the Renaissance began to take form. Prominent among those who saw the origins of the Renaissance in pre-existing national cultures was the

Frenchman Louis Courajod. Between 1887 and 1896 this historian of art delivered a series of lectures at the Louvre on Renaissance art. He remarked that the salient features of Renaissance painting—realism and naturalism—could be found in French art of the fourteenth century. From France this tradition moved to Burgundy in the following century and then to Italy. With the Italian Wars (1494–1559), France came into contact with an evolved form of a style born on French soil, and the circle was completed. France, not Italy, was responsible for Renaissance art! If Professor Courajod's thesis was not widely accepted, it did set forth the intriguing concept that a culture other than the world of Italy might have been instrumental in the development of the Renaissance, and, most important, he found that a rich and important culture existed in the fourteenth century, in the Middle Ages.

The revolt of the medievalists against Burckhardt has been an unending process. It continues today with a momentum that would have thrilled the Romantics. Typical of the tenor of the revolt is Charles Homer Haskins' *The Renaissance of the Twelfth Century* (1927). "The Great Renaissance," wrote Haskins, "was not so unique or so decisive as has been supposed." With such remarks, as well as his carefully worded title, this historian hoped to bring about for the twelfth century a full recognition of its humanistic efforts (no longer the exclusive property of Burckhardt's Renaissance) and to devalue the persistent use of "Renaissance" to designate a post-medieval phenomenon. Etienne Gilson has not hesitated to do likewise.

> Si donc l'on admet que, par delà l'Humanisme de la lettre et de la forme, il y a un humanisme de l'esprit, avec tout ce qu'il implique de confiance dans la stabilité, la valeur, l'efficacité de la nature et de l'homme, on ne peut plus méconnaître qu'en assimilant Aristote, le moyen âge assimilait l'hellénisme même dans ce qu'il a d'éternellement valable et opérait une révolution bien plus profonde que celle de l'art d'écrire, une révolution dans l'art de penser,[1]

he wrote in a book of essays published in 1932 and so joined other Catholic medievalists in rescuing the Middle Ages and scholasticism from many centuries of slight. It was a reaction based on religious and philosophical convictions, much as Courajod's national pride gave impetus to his revision of the origins of Renaissance. However passionate (versus scholarly) some reactions proved to be, the need to reassess the Renaissance could not be long ignored.

---

[1] Etienne Gilson, *Les Idées et les Lettres* (Paris: J. Vrin, 1932), p. 190.

THE RENAISSANCE IN THE NORTH

Although Burckhardt dealt principally with Italy, he did not refrain from discussing the passage of Italian culture to other countries, such as France. "We may as well be spared the complaints over the early decay of medieval faith and civilization," he said. "Had they been strong enough to hold their ground, they would be alive to this day." Burckhardt wasted no words in offering a picture of the Renaissance outside Italy, not unlike the views of Rabelais or the *philosophes*. Medieval culture, fallen into decay, was easily replaced by the more vital Italian culture, which struck the imaginations of western Europeans and spurred them on to imitate Italy and break with the past. It is not difficult to see how such a position could be adapted to the study of literature, and in France Gustave Lanson became the significant link.

Sorbonne professor and director of the Ecole Normale Supérieure, Lanson once wielded vast powers in the French academic world. His adoption of Burckhardt's views in his *Histoire de la Littérature française*, published in 1894, brought to the domain of French literature not only Burckhardt's ideas but a prestige no less great than that enjoyed by Burckhardt in the world of history.

The influence of Burckhardt on Lanson appears in the very first sentence of that part of the *Histoire* dealing with the sixteenth century: "*La fécondité du moyen âge semblait tout à fait épuisée à la fin du XVᵉ siècle.*" As the old order declined, suddenly Charles VIII decided to march on Italy (1494), and the new civilization overwhelmed the French.

> La rencontre de la France et de l'Italie se fit dans les dernières années du XVᵉ siècle. . . . C'est l'armée de Charles VIII, toute la noblesse, toute la France, qui se jette sur l'Italie. . . . Cinq ou six fois en une trentaine d'années, le flot de l'invasion française s'étale sur la terre italienne, et se retire sur le sol français: vers 1525, la pénétration de l'esprit, de la civilisation d'Italie dans notre esprit, notre civilisation, est chose faite, et notre race a fécondé tous les germes qu'elle portrait en elle.

However we may question Lanson's fidelity to the phenomenon he was describing, there is no questioning his fidelity to Burckhardt. For this reason, the reactions to Lanson's views paralleled the reception of *The Civilization of the Renaissance in Italy*.

Henri Chamard's *Les Origines de la poésie française de la Renaissance* (1932) took a close look at the relationship between Renaissance poetry and French medieval traditions to conclude that neither *l'esprit gaulois* nor *l'esprit courtois* had completely died away. When Abel Lefranc began publishing a critical edition of Rabelais, who, for Lefranc, was indubitably an atheist, Etienne Gilson retorted with his article "Rabelais franciscain" (1924). Again we are dealing with a significant title. Gilson wished to accentuate Rabelais' religious training, his acquaintance with the theology of the period, his profound orthodoxy in spite of his humor, which Gilson also reset in historical perspective to show that it was more naughtiness than nastiness. Krailsheimer's *Rabelais and the Franciscans* (1963) made the same points. As early as 1947, A. H. Schutz suggested that Ronsard may have been influenced by French medieval poetry. A. Noyer-Weidner had a comparable point to make in an article published in 1958.

There are many tempting features in Lanson's theory. It brings Italy and France together as a firm continuum of cultural advancement. It provides a fine interrelating of literary history and external events (the Italian Wars). Most important, it divides the movement of French letters in a manner that has long appealed to the French mind. There is no denying the greatness of the seventeenth century and particularly of its Classical period. As a literature, it offers differences as great as those social and political differences between the seventeenth century and the Middle Ages outlined in the Introduction. In a search for the origins of this great literature, the possibility of going back beyond 1500 seemed impossible. By the same token, the sixteenth century's interest in antiquity, in style and form, and its disdain for the traditions of the Middle Ages provided clear signs that the significant break came about 1500.

The annexation of sixteenth-century literature by devotees of Classicism meant both reducing the literature of 1500–1599 to the status of a preparatory period for the brilliant age to come and institutionalizing Burckhardt's view that the sixteenth century began with a new spirit. This new spirit came from Italy and bore the unmistakable traits of Renaissance paganism and individualism. Thus, while a few professors endeavored to demonstrate the continuity between the fifteenth and sixteenth centuries, the majority devoted their skills to examining the classical and Italian sources of French literature after 1500 and to discerning signs of revolt against the accepted forms of thought and belief in favor of new views derived from Italy, Rome, and Greece, as if, as Burckhardt suggested, nothing of consequence remained of the Middle Ages to influence Ronsard or Rabelais and their contemporaries. Yet if cultures do die, they can hardly be said to expire neatly with the passing of one century and the arrival of another. In addition, whatever importation of Italian culture took place after 1494, it did not fall upon a world comparable to the Italy that Burckhardt had studied. However much France enjoyed with Italy the growing importance of towns and commerce during the later years of the fifteenth century, France was not a country of small city-states. Weakened by wars, it did not have the wealth of Italy, the patrons, the large commercial class which, by virtue of the hegemony of the city-state, had meshed with the nobility to produce a ruling élite of great riches and great culture. In France, the nobles enjoyed life on their estates, their hunts, and their privileges. They read little and scandalized the Italians with their poor manners and their ignorance. The bourgeois plied his trade and fought the guilds and nobles whose rights interfered with his business.

Regarding its cultural heritage, France in 1500 had little in common with the Italy of 1300. Old but true is the observation that the culture of antiquity never entirely died in Italy, whereas the greatest accomplishments of the Middle Ages belonged to France. Her cathedrals and her universities still stood to testify to the force of French medieval civilization. This world, as it was represented by the scholastic teaching at Paris, had nothing to gain from assimilating new ideas from without and certainly proved its feudal cast more than once during the fifteenth and sixteenth centuries by attempting to retain the rights it possessed against the encroachment of royal power. France's medieval inheritance was considerable and enduring. For that reason, a brief glance at those areas of activity which continue in uninterrupted evolution from the fifteenth to sixteenth century may help us to understand the meaning of Charles VIII's descent into Italy and the impact it supposedly had upon the following century.

THE MEDIEVAL INHERITANCE

The Monarchy

There is no major historian today who would deny that, in the fifteenth century, the ruling houses of France, Spain, Austria-Burgundy, and England emerged as institutions possessing land and means quite beyond those of their predecessors. What remains unclear is the extent of their power and the implications behind the process by which the various royal houses rose to prominence.

As the fifteenth century opened, the French kings were beset by the English, the Burgundians, lack of money and hope. By the end of the century the English and the Burgundians had ceased to be a problem. Under Louis XI alone the royal domain was enlarged by the addition of Guyenne, Provence, Anjou, Maine, and a part of Burgundy. Louis XII brought to the Crown Brittany and Orléans, and Francis I, Angoulême. A meeting of the Estates-General in 1439 enacted measures which in effect, though not word, laid the foundations for a standing army as well as a tax (*taille*) to pay for that army. Normally, in many regions of France, the king had to obtain the permission of provincial assemblies before tithing. By 1451 Charles VII had found a way of circumventing the local assemblies. With greater peace in the country and increased revenues from the royal domain, the King was able to do away with the regular *taille* and maintain his army on the special *taille des gens de guerre* alone. The tax load was, in fact, so reduced that when the King asked that the money to support his soldiers be paid without consulting the provincial estates, the towns were willing to pay immediately. No assemblies were convoked. The King had his money, and the assemblies, no voice.

The king also came to enjoy extensive powers over the Church. Many historians point to Francis I's Concordat with Rome (1516) as a sign of the Crown's new strength. When Pope Leo X agreed to permit the King to name archbishops, bishops, abbots, and priors, he was granting Francis I powers long exercised by the French monarch in defiance of the local chapters' right to elect their own masters. The Concordat expressly passed over the right of election. Little wonder that the Venetian ambassadors to Francis' court wrote he could tax his subjects as much as he wanted and less wonder that certain historians, Robert Mousnier and Alfred Pollard in particular, should place France among the "new monarchies" that arose in the fifteenth century. France, moreover, was by far the richest of the emerging nations. It possessed more people than all its rivals combined. Its natural resources and farmlands gave France a potential that Spain and Austria swiftly recognized. The numerous pacts signed by Spain, the Italian states, Austria, and even England against France following the outbreak of the Italian Wars testify to the immediate threat which Charles VIII and his successors created for their neighbors. That these pacts could deter but never destroy the French threat was another measure of the country's strength.

At the same time, one must consider how new this monarchy was and whether the Venetian ambassador was a faithful source of information. Mousnier and Pollard have been seriously challenged in their claims of absolute power for Francis and his line. The problem of medieval privileges enjoyed by towns, nobles, universities, and local assemblies simply did not disappear. The Venetian ambassadors may have thought that Francis I could tax as much as he wanted, but history records quite a different situation for both his predecessors and his successors.

Of equal interest is an understanding of the process by which the kings of France and the other "new monarchies" added to their estates. The celebrated phrase used to describe the politics of Austria, *"Bella gerant alii: tu, felix Austria, nube"* ("Others wage war, thou, Austria, marry"), accurately describes the situation in France as well. The French monarchy was always favored by the Salic Law, which excluded succession through the female line, and by the principle of escheat, which provided that the domains of extinct houses had to revert to the Crown. Through careful planning and some uncanny luck, everything began to fall into the hands of the kings by the fifteenth century. It was because of escheat that the Crown acquired Guyenne, Maine, Anjou, and Provence under Louis XI. When Charles VIII married the heiress to Brittany, he promised to respect the autonomy of the duchy, but Anne promised to marry his successor if she survived Charles. Charles VIII had no sons, and the Crown passed to his cousin Louis XII, who promptly divorced his wife and married Charles's widow to hold Brittany within the royal domain. The annexation became inevitable when Claude de France, one of Louis' daughters, married Louis' successor, as was the King's intent. Louis XI even married his deformed child to the heir of Orléans to insure that the marriage would not be consummated; he succeeded. These were boons to the Crown, and while the kings could not leave everything to fortune, the "new monarchies" did not invent escheat, nor did they institute the dynastic politics of marriage. They merely began to reap substantial benefits from their strategy.

Louis' marriage to Anne de Bretagne parallels the marriage of Ferdinand of Aragon and Isabella of Castile, the grandparents of Charles V, who was the son of Philip of Hapsburg (himself the son of Maximilian I and Mary of Burgundy) and Joan of Castile (daughter of Ferdinand and Isabella). The marriage of Philip and Joan effectively began the Hapsburg empire, uniting as it did Spain, Austria, and Burgundy. It took place in 1495, the year after Charles VIII came to Italy, and was an obvious effort not only to insure the succession in Spain but also to surround France by a united kingdom hostile to it.

There was also nothing new in basing war upon the same principles of dynastic politics, and the formal basis of Charles VIII's descent into Italy was dynastic rights. When the land and titles of Anjou escheated to the French Crown, the King also inherited the Angevine claim to the kingdom of Naples. (Moreover, the Duke of Orléans, pretender to the Crown, was bound by marriage to the ruling family of Milan. When Louis, Duke of Orléans, became Louis XII, the French kings had two claims to Italian territory, and Francis I forgot neither.)

Today we would look in amazement upon an attempt by France to occupy and rule Italy. The geography is all wrong. But the concept of natural boundaries and aggrandizement up to these boundaries is a very modern concept. France began to employ it systematically only with the seventeenth century. In the fifteenth century and until the Peace of Cateau-Cambrésis in 1559, which France was too exhausted and harried to break, the kings pursued the old policy of dynastic claims and war for gain. It is hard to say how seriously Charles VIII took his claim to the kingdom of Naples, but there is no doubt that he coveted the riches of the Italian city-states. The cost of the war, the treachery of those city-states, and the difficulties of ruling from such a distance were no deterrent.

To be entirely fair to Charles, it should be noted that the inevitable shift in trade from the Mediterranean to the Atlantic following the discovery and exploitation of the New World had not yet taken place, and the recent annexation of Provence gave France access to Mediterranean ports. Moreover, he was asked to come to Italy. A woman's pride had been hurt and demanded revenge. Isabella of Aragon, married to the Duke of Milan, found herself refused the first place in the court by Beatrice d'Este, wife of Ludovico the Moor, uncle of the Duke and actual ruler of the Duchy. Isabella complained to her father, the King of Naples, who implied that he would attack Milan. Ludovico chose to protect himself by becoming an ally of the King of France, who was asked by Ludovico to help him (and conquer Naples in the bargain). A move in keeping with the oldest diplomatic games, Ludovico's appeal to Charles does, nevertheless, denote a departure from former Italian tactics. The Italian city-states were no longer able to deal with their own affairs satisfactorily. For some time, the diplomacy of the cities had maintained a successful system of checks and balances as alliances were formed, broken, and re-formed to prevent any one state from dominating the peninsula. France's entry into Italian politics also signaled a widening of horizons in European politics.

Soon Ludovico and others saw what fools they had been to bring a foreigner into their midst. To gain strength, they dealt with France's rivals outside Italy—Spain and Austria. Thus the diplomatic horizon widened ever more and precisely at that moment when the new states of Castile-Aragon and Austria-Burgundy were strengthening their positions. The dominance of Italy in the affairs of western European history was at an end. Spain, Austria, England, and, above all, France must receive more and more of the attention that historians could give to Italy in previous centuries. But the changes took time, and meanwhile the medieval mentality in politics and government held sway.

Humanism

It is not possible to speak of the fifteenth and sixteenth centuries in France without using the word "humanism." The meaning of this term is hardly fixed, and like many "ism's" of literary history, it should be used with care. The dictionaries make of humanism either a vast term ("a preoccupation with human interests and ideals") or a precise one ("the philological, historical, and philosophical studies of European scholars from 1400–1600"). There is a definite point at which these descriptions meet, since those studies are generally considered as denoting a turn from scholastic theology and the world of abstractions to the problems of man's role and aspirations here on earth, but little is to be gained from attempting to use the word without defining it clearly. For this study, humanism will mean "an interest in classical letters and in scholarship with respect to classical and biblical texts," and the humanist will be defined as "a man who studies these letters and languages and pursues such scholarship."

The origins of those currents of French humanism important for the sixteenth century go back to the 1350s when the Faculty of Theology at the University of Paris adopted as its official doctrine the Nominalism of William of Occam. Occam did not formulate the Nominalist position. He merely effected the revival of an old debate in scholastic thought dating approximately from the eleventh century. The source of this debate appears to be a single sentence in Porphyry's introduction to the *Categories* of Aristotle as translated into Latin by Boethius: "*Mox de generibus et speciebus illud quidem sive subsistant, sive in solis nudis intellectibus posita sint, sive subsistentia corporalia sint an incorporalia, et utrum separata a sensibilibus an in sensibilibus posita et circa haec consistentia, dicere recusabo.*" [2] The major distinction on which Porphyry refused to pass judgment concerns the nature of universals—do they really exist or are they simply constructs of the mind? The Nominalists held that they are concepts existing only within the mind. The Realists maintained that these universals had a definite existence outside the mind. In the first great period of scholastic thought (the eleventh and twelfth centuries), the former view was formulated by Roscellinus, the latter by William of Champeaux.

---

[2] Next, regarding genera and species, I shall refuse to say this: whether they exist or whether they have been placed simply in our minds alone, whether they are tangible substances or intangible and either separate from the senses or posited in the senses and existing with them.

Because of these different conceptions of universals, Realists and Nominalists were inevitably separated from each other in their view of life and religion. Believing that universals had a true reality, the Realists were the more spiritual group and more easily disposed to understanding and appreciating such crucial elements of doctrine as the Trinity. Since the Nominalists insisted that universals were simply names attached to particulars after the fact (whence Nominalism, from the Latin *nomen*— name), they could hardly be expected to possess the spiritual élan of their rivals. Indeed, with their fundamental aversion to abstraction, the Nominalists of the later Middle Ages ushered in an inductive, empirical approach that helped lay the foundations of modern science.

Scholasticism entered its second great phase with Albertus Magnus (1193–1280) and St. Thomas Aquinas (c. 1227–1274). Although they gave less attention to the debate over universals, they were nonetheless recognizable Realists. Among St. Thomas' achievements was a masterful union of reason and faith. He began with the Aristotelian idea that everything was meant to fulfill its function. Man, possessing reason, was therefore intended to use that reason, even to know God. If man would but look about him, he would see an ordered universe and recognize that there must be a prime mover, a God. Reason and faith could not be incompatible; they taught the same truth.

Nominalist reaction began with Duns Scotus and flowered with his student William of Occam. In the works of the former, the reaction centered upon a distrust of reason, thus moving squarely against the meticulous efforts of the great Realists to establish a harmony between faith and reason. Duns Scotus distinguished between those doctrines of theology that can be proven and those that must remain articles of faith. Occam pursued these attitudes to the point of implying a formal split between philosophy, on the one hand, and theology, on the other, an essential distinction that paved the way for scientific investigation as we know it today. Unfortunately for the development of scholastic teaching in France in the fifteenth century, few seized the more constructive implications of Occam's teaching.

Because the Nominalists feared that any great emphasis on reason could prove dangerous to the faith, they placed, as did Duns Scotus, the articles of faith beyond the scope of reason and narrowed the domain of rational investigation. Biblical studies stagnated since dogma had to be accepted, not proven, and at the same time a more restricted use of reason produced only interminable demonstrations of logical proofs. The great age of scholastic philosophy was over, and even within the Nominalist movement the more sensitive and mystical souls felt the decline. Caught between theology as blind acceptance and philosophy

as logical debate, they sensed a spiritual need that was no longer fulfilled. Out of their discontent emerged the most interesting and important French humanists of the fifteenth and ultimately of the sixteenth century.

Prominent among the partisans of a new spirit in France at the
beginning of the fifteenth century were Pierre d'Ailly (c. 1350–1420)
and two of his students, Jean Gerson (1363-1429) and Nicholas de
Clamenges (c. 1360–1437). All three held important posts (Ailly and
Gerson were chancellors of the University of Paris, Clamenges, professor
at the Collège de Navarre); all passed through a Nominalist indoctrina-
tion but, in the end, exalted other forms of religious sentiment. It
never occurred to Pierre d'Ailly to prove the existence of God by other
means than faith and tradition, yet he could not deny the power of
mystical ecstasy to help the mind receive the truths of revelation. Gerson
and Clamenges went even further. They recognized the limits of reason,
but for matters of faith, they balked at blind logical acceptance. Religion
was not a science, but a way of life. Mysticism was the finest means of
attaining that life. In simple, affective contemplation, the soul felt God
and opened to Him. As professors, Gerson and Clamenges insisted that
Nominalist education ignored this intuitive realm and with its logical
demonstrations prepared the mind at the expense of a feeding of the
soul.

That Pierre d'Ailly's students surpassed him in upholding a mystical
approach to religion doubtless stemmed from their contact with certain
new sects located in the Low Countries. Ailly's mysticism came from
St. Bernard and Robert de Saint Victor. Gerson and Clamenges knew
the Brethren of the Common Life and the canons of Windesheim, who
were later to influence Erasmus. Gerson was once even thought to have
been the author of the famous *Imitation of Christ*, composed by Thomas
à Kempis, a brother of one of the founders of the Brethren. In this
work such passages as the following indicate the depth and quality of
feeling among this new group of mystics:

> The Kingdom of God is within you, saith the Lord. Turn thyself to
> the Lord with thy whole heart, forsake this wretched world, and thy
> soul shall find rest. Learn to despise all outward things, devoting thy-
> self to spiritual things only, and thou wilt perceive the Kingdom of
> God come unto thee. For the Kingdom of God is peace and joy in the
> Holy Spirit, the which is not given to the wicked. Christ will come
> unto thee, and give thee His consolation, if thou prepare for Him in
> thy heart a worthy dwelling place. All His glory and beauty are from
> within, and there He findest delight.

Mysticism is only one of several bonds which unite Jean Gerson and Nicholas de Clamenges. Both men were enamoured of good Latin and consciously strove to write as elegantly and correctly as possible. In addition, Ailly and his students were quite active in the affairs of the Church. All upheld the powers of a Council over the pope and agitated for reform. Within the University of Paris, Gerson in particular attempted educational revisions that would diminish the importance of scholastic logic in favor of a more spiritual approach. In none of these activities was Gerson successful, but the admixture of educational, linguistic, and spiritual reform revealed a pattern of interest that would run throughout French humanism and would determine many ideas of the Reform movement to come.

Gerson died in 1429, and the next name of importance is that of Guillaume Fichet, who was born in 1433. The hiatus suggested by these dates can be traced directly to the devastating effect of the Hundred Years War.

Life in France during the Middle Ages had never been easy. The "Black Death" (plague), introduced into Europe in the fourteenth century, broke out in repeated waves that often decimated a local population. Constant cultivation of the land with little use of fertilizing material and no improvement in farming methods to compensate for exhausting the soil resulted in ever-dwindling production. The economy, always fluctuating because it was tied to the flow of gold and silver, offered little insurance against disaster. The Hundred Years War merely aggravated these hardships. By hiring mercenaries, the kings rendered war more and more destructive. When the mercenaries could not be paid or when peace was established, they stayed to pillage the countryside and carry off the meager crops produced. Desperate for money, the Crown devised new means of taxing its subjects. It even changed the face value of coins and thus contributed yet another element to the economic chaos. If, during these years, the serf who survived the wars, the famine, and the plague often won his freedom and greater privileges in exchange for the invaluable work he was willing to do, the slow demise of serfdom can be counted among the very few advances in France at this time.

Caught up in the same forces that were ruining France, the University of Paris compromised its status further by turning away from the constructive work of such minds as St. Thomas and Gerson and indulging vigorously in endless bickering over rights and status. While discipline and pedagogy were nearly forgotten, the Gallican clergy demanded that the provisions of the Pragmatic Sanction of 1438 be enforced. (The Pragmatic Sanction, a form of "constitution" for the French church based on the work of the Council of Basel, was intended to protect the French clergy against the king and the pope.) Since the Pragmatic Sanction could work only if king and pope were willing to abide by it —something they quite obviously were loath to do—the struggle proved long and bitter.

The Hundred Years War ended in 1453. Gradually, as trade increased and the economy achieved greater stability, France experienced a new prosperity which made possible, in particular, the establishing by Guillaume Fichet in 1470 of a printing press at the Sorbonne. Within three years, the press had published Sallust, Florus, Valerius Maximus, the *De officiis* of Cicero, the *Elegantiae* of Lorenzo Valla and Fichet's own *Rhetorica*. The *Rhetorica* was written to reveal to France the philological work being done in Italy, work which Fichet had learned about in Avignon. In religious matters this man points up the cross-currents of the scholastic world. A humanist, Fichet, too, deplored the poor Latin of his contemporaries; he greatly admired Plato with the same interest in a new spiritualism that motivated Gerson and Pierre d'Ailly. At the same time, Fichet was a Realist and actively worked against the Nominalists, who in 1470 accused a Realist, Pierre du Ruisseau, of heresy. Not only did they eventually lose the case, but powerful forces began to rise up against them. The Nominalists were as suspect for their political leanings as for their religious biases. The Pope had not forgotten that Gerson and Ailly had once upheld the rights of the Councils over the Holy See. Such an attitude was embarrassing also to the French king, Louis XI, who hoped at this time for a rapprochement with Rome. On March 1, 1474, the King decreed that the Realist doctrine be taught in the Faculties of Art and Theology "comme plus utile que celle des nouveaux docteurs . . . nominalistes." The Nominalists prepared a brilliant defense, and on April 30, 1481, the King revoked his ban.

Fichet left Paris in 1472 for Italy and never returned. He left behind a small but dedicated group of scholars who welcomed the Greek Hermonymos and later the Italian scholars Andrelini, Aleandro, and Emili.

After Fichet's departure, humanist activity in Paris was directed by Robert Gaguin (1433–1501). Gaguin had travelled in Italy and grouped about himself a number of French scholars eager to imitate the Italian humanists. They, too, regretted the sterility of the scholastic curriculum and looked, on the one hand, to the elegance and beauty of classical Latin and, on the other hand, to the thought of antiquity, its mysticism, and its asceticism to counteract the atmosphere which surrounded them. Any description of their attitudes would, therefore, suggest dissatisfaction with and separation from the practices of the day. Already Italy appears to be an influence in French thinking. The Renaissance and the Reform seem only moments away.

In fact, nothing could be further from the truth. Some of the issues of these great upheavals may have been in the making, but violent change, predicated on an attack against the Church, could hardly describe the intentions of the humanists just mentioned. When Gerson and Pierre d'Ailly stressed the rights of the Councils over the pope, it was in reaction to the Great Schism, which they saw as a tragedy for the Church. They hoped to correct and thus revive, not destroy, that institution, just as their reservations about debates of logic arose from a pedagogical and spiritual fear that their students were not being taught to feel the intensity of Christian faith. We must not forget that the sixteenth century witnessed a Counterreform as well, and it is perhaps easier to describe Gerson and Gaguin as forerunners of the Catholic Counterreform than as nascent Protestants.

No evidence exists to intimate that these humanists hoped to effect changes in any way other than from within the existing Church. However much they revelled in the correctness of Ciceronian Latin, they did not suggest that man was fundamentally good and original sin, a Christian myth. They may have been dissatisfied with aspects of Nominalist pedagogy, but they did not propose that such traditional commentaries on the Bible as the *Livre des Sentences* be dropped from the curriculum and replaced by a study of the Bible alone. Often of Nominalist persuasion, they were tempted by mysticism and used antiquity to complete their education, not to revolutionize it or to ridicule unmercifully the system in use. That that system should prove inadequate to so many demonstrates to what degree scholasticism had definitely entered into a decline, and there is no doubt that such unrest is important. But the Church had known unrest before and survived. The Reform became a reality only when a solution to such unrest could no longer be found within the framework of existing institutions. Similarly, the desire for change became the Reform only when basic practices and dogma of the Church were the object of criticism. Neither stage was reached in the fifteenth century. The work of men like Gerson, nearly submerged by the effects of war, was slow in returning to life. However successful were Fichet and Gaguin in attempting to bring Italian humanism to France, their group remained small, surrounded by a hostile system that grew progressively more conservative and satisfied with its own methods and views. These facts have tempted such critics as Sainte-Beuve to write of the fifteenth century as "*un désert*," a Burckhardtian attitude which tends to accentuate the upsurge of the sixteenth century and to denigrate what preceded. Such an attitude is no longer convincing. The modest gains of Fichet and Gaguin were gains. Their work had a definite impact on the nature of sixteenth-century humanism and must be given full credit for such. How crucial was their stimulus can be shown by the works and lives of the great humanists who bridged the two centuries in question: Lefèvre d'Etaples and Desiderius Erasmus. Contemporaries, these men shared much, yet differed profoundly. Both studied Latin and Greek with the clear intention of enhancing their ability to deal with the original texts of the Bible, but what Erasmus read and enjoyed in the process did not make the same impression on Lefèvre. In the biting wit of Lucian, Erasmus found a spirit so close to his own that he used Lucian extensively in writing *In Praise of Folly.* Lefèvre found Lucian irreverent and fled him as he fled the sensuality of Catullus. While Erasmus devoted much time to exegetical works, others of his titles, such as the *Adages* and *Colloquies,* were addressed to a public beyond the universities. In time Erasmus was read throughout western Europe by those learned doctors and aristocrats who admired his urbane and pithy style. By the same token, he alienated his more pious contemporaries, who rightly sensed that Erasmus shared neither their intense (and intolerant) religion nor their limited appreciation of antiquity.

The two humanists also received different educations and exhibited throughout their lives the traits of their beginnings. Erasmus was taught by the Brethren of the Common Life and therefore escaped the scholastic training which Lefèvre underwent in Paris. While the French humanist gradually became interested in the mystical currents of earlier days, now reinforced by the writings of such distinguished Italians as Pico de la Mirandola, Ficino, and Nicholas of Cusa, Erasmus journeyed to England. In 1499 at Oxford, he met Richard Charnock and John Colet, who had begun a course on the Epistles of St. Paul. Colet had studied in Italy and learned to prize the methods of philological investigation used by Lorenzo Valla. His work with St. Paul was designed to do more than establish the best text, however. Colet had come to believe more and more in a religion that would be simple, pure, untrammeled by rite and clergy, a religion of faith such as could be drawn from the Epistles. The influence of Colet on Erasmus cannot be denied. While Erasmus never responded to the mysticism of the Dutch Brethren, he most decidedly sympathized with their simple piety. He was already familiar with Valla and, after the stimulus offered by Colet, began a long definition of his own beliefs. The *Adagia* (*Adages*) of 1500 showed how attached Erasmus was to classical antiquity; the *Enchiridion militis christiani* of 1504 revealed his other side: a faith founded on Scripture. The following year, publication by the venerable Valla of his *Annotationes in Novum Testamentum* decided Erasmus to edit, translate, and comment upon the New Testament. The writing of *Moriae encomium* (*In Praise of Folly*), published in 1511, was to intervene between the conception and execution of this vast project, which did not see completion until 1516. A far cry from what modern studies would call a definitive edition, Erasmus' publication was nonetheless significant since it gave a clear statement of the author's views on scholarship and theology. Erasmus banished the scholastic commentaries and insisted that theologians had to know history, philosophy, the biblical languages, and Valla's philological techniques. Most important perhaps was his willingness to accept the word of the Scriptures over established dogma. Humanism was beginning to tread on hallowed ground.

Lefèvre, too, devoted himself to the study of the Bible, inspired by Erasmus' *Enchiridion*. In his *Quincuplex psalterium* he commented upon five Latin versions of the Psalms. In 1512 he did with the Epistles of St. Paul what Erasmus had done for the New Testament. But his observations did not coincide with those of Erasmus. Erasmus accentuated the simplicity, the piety of the primitive Church. He was impatient with the obscure passages, the histories, and the legends. Lefèvre never lost his mystical orientation or his scholastic training. He joined Erasmus in condemning much of the earlier scholastic commentary and in upholding the Scriptures as the sole source of dogma but saw in the Scriptures much that Erasmus rejected. When Lefèvre explicated biblical texts, he not only preserved the four levels of scholastic inquiry (historical, allegorical, anagogical, and topological) but visibly revered the Bible for its obscurity and mystical richness that could support and fill a four-level critical approach. As a result, Lefèvre saw symbols and justifications for contemporary practices everywhere. His St. Paul upheld the cult of the Virgin, the efficacy of good works, and the cult of the saints. He accepted St. Paul's views on grace, but did not tread the path that would lead Luther and Calvin to formulate a theory of predestination. He had no difficulty approving the doctrine of the Immaculate Conception.

Humanism, then, is no less a complex phenomenon than the evolution of the monarchy. So much points ahead as if to justify Burckhardt's theories. Erasmus and Lefèvre had an impressive classical learning. They dared examine biblical texts and criticize pre-existing commentaries and interpretations. Italy definitely provided stimulus for the movement. The spread of Nominalism after Albertus Magnus and Aquinas marked a decline that could have been possible only if scholastic circles no longer shared the high spiritual and intellectual aims which prompted these great minds. Gerson's conciliar views may have derived from a pious reaction to the Great Schism, but in his fight for the Councils against the pope, he was seconding the sort of movement which culminated in the formation of the Anglican Church in England and the Concordat of Francis I, who went as far as he could in having his power over the French church recognized without making the complete break with Rome effected by Henry VIII. So much points ahead but so little sustains a theory of rupture with the past.

It is true that Italy was now a marked influence on French thinking, but the attraction of Pico or Ficino had a precedent in French thinking that went back to Gerson at least. If the new mystical sources were Italian, the interest in mysticism owed little to the Italy of Burckhardt. It is true that humanist exegeses were more daring than the criticisms made by previous scholars of the Latin and learning of their contemporaries, but there was a fundamental difference between the approaches and attitudes of Lefèvre d'Etaples and Erasmus, and Lefèvre was the Frenchman. He was the mystic; he managed to reconcile, as French humanism had long done, a spirit of reform and allegiance to certain beliefs which placed him more within than without the framework of the existing Church.

Many French reformers of this period sought above all a return to the Bible and to the simplicity of the primitive Church. They did not associate nor want to associate these sentiments with fixed doctrines or institutions. Their views, often called "Evangelism," cast much light on why France eventually remained a Catholic country and emphasize through their roots in early French humanism why the Renaissance in France cannot be separated from the world that preceded it.

THE LITERARY TRENDS

The most conspicuous literary flowering at the end of the fifteenth century was produced by a group of poets known as the Grands Rhétoriqueurs. *Rhétoriqueur* here means simply poet; *poète* and *poésie* were not widely used before the sixteenth century. The term *rhétoriqueur* was not gratuitous. The period considered oratory and poetry but variations on the single art of persuasion. They differed in the form and means used, but no other distinctions seemed essential. Therefore, in the treatises of the day, poetry was termed *la deuxième rhétorique* to set it off from oratory, and chapters on *la deuxième rhétorique* dealt exclusively with rhyme schemes and form. As a consequence, that the works of the Grands Rhétoriqueurs demonstrate what today appears to be an inordinate interest in rhyme, rhyme schemes, and forms should be of little surprise.

The Rhétoriqueurs worked where they could find patrons with whom they and their works became inextricably connected. Octavien de Saint-Gelais was aided by Louise de Savoie (mother of Marguerite de Navarre and Francis I). Jean Lemaire de Belges, guided by another Rhétoriqueur, his godfather Jean Molinet, passed from patron to patron until, in 1527 with the death of Molinet, he became the official poet of the House of Austria. Jean Marot began as secretary to Anne de Bretagne and retained the post until her death. It was such essential patronage that produced an avalanche of *pièces de circonstance*. Saint-Gelais sang of the liberation of Louis d'Orléans and the marriage of Anne de Bretagne. One of Lemaire de Belges' most popular works, "L'Epître de l'amant vert," was inspired by a pet parrot of Marguerite d'Autriche. When Jean Marot followed the court to Italy as royal historiographer, he composed a "Voyage à Gênes" to record his feelings. Guillaume Crétin's "Complainte sur la Mort de Guillaume de Brissipat" adds yet another favorite genre to those practiced regularly by the Rhétoriqueurs in response to their official duties.

In addition to the poems they wrote to praise or lament their patrons and their exploits, the Rhétoriqueurs indulged in endless moralizing. They made much of their learning, as Jean de Meung had done before them, and peppered their works with a plethora of proverbs. Religious poems in praise of the Virgin and a particular treatment of nature also characterized these poets. Patently interested in imitating the garden of Guillaume de Lorris, they filled poem after poem with gardens of singing birds or sweet-sounding brooks described in detail and in diminutives.

The *Roman de la Rose* provided technical as well as thematic material for the Rhétoriqueurs. They loved allegory—the longer and the more ingenious, the better. "Voyage à Gênes" is a lengthy allegory decrying the ambitious. Octavien de Saint-Gelais' *Le Séjour d'Honneur*, written in four books, is also typical of the genre. The poet, tired of inactivity, is seized by *Sensualité* who guides him to the "mer de Joie-Mondaine" (inhabited by cadavers) and then on to "L'Isle Vaine-Espérance." Despite *Mme Grâce-Divine*'s attempts to convince him to abandon the trip, he persists. Next he enters the "Forêt des Aventuriers" but laments because the time of great adventure is no more. At last he discovers the "Séjour d'Honneur" (the court). Unfortunately Long-Age obliges him to leave. As he weeps for his lost youth, *Dame Raison* shows him that true happiness can be found only in heaven. The poet ends his days in the house of *Entendement*.

The work reveals in itself the political (praise of the court), moral (the final lesson), and poetic (the description of the beauties of the court and the garden) preoccupations of the Rhétoriqueurs. Its extreme length points up their love of virtuosity, which also drove them to sow their works with anagrams, puns, and rhyme schemes of the most elaborate sort such as the *rimes batelées*, where the rhyme is reproduced at the following caesura (*"Que n'avons-nous Juvénal et Horace?/ Que n'est or' à ce un second Perse en vie . . ."*) and *rimes léonines*, where the caesura and final syllable rhyme (*"Mais voirement, ami Clément/ Tout clairement dis-moi comment . . ."*).

We must not conclude from this that these poets were silly, insensitive men. Their works were, by and large, meant to be taken seriously but within an aesthetic framework that defined poetry as the second rhetoric. Because poetry was tied to the art of persuasion, the Rhétoriqueurs were constantly concerned with the excellence of their vehicle. In believing that complexity and ingenuity were directly related to the success of their poetry, they showed only how much they were of their time and how much poetry, too, participated in what Huizinga has called "the evil of superfluity."

Such luxuriant and excessive ornamentation bears no little resemblance to the unending verbiage of Nominalist demonstrations. They possessed the same love of technique and form over content, the same concern with an exposition that adorned the idea rather than preparing or advancing it. Even the religion of the time bears witness to this trend toward ornamentation and flamboyance.

> Pierre d'Ailly, in *De Reformatione*, deplores the ever-increasing number of churches, of festivals, of saints, of holy-days; he protests against the multitude of images and paintings, the prolixity of the Service, against the introduction of new hymns and prayers, against the augmentation of vigils and fasts. In short, what alarms him is the evil of superfluity.[3]

Huizinga goes on to give ample evidence of his failure to effect any reforms.

It is becoming fashionable to point to aspects of Rhétoriqueur poetry that reveal the influence of late fifteenth century humanism. We know now that Charles d'Orléans wrote a long Latin poem entitled "Canticum amoris." The poets in Lemaire de Belges' temple of Venus

---

[3] J. Huizinga, *The Waning of the Middle Ages* (New York: Doubleday & Company, Inc., 1956), p. 153.

speak French, Tuscan, and Latin. Lemaire de Belges himself paraphrased two sonnets of Serafino d'Aquila, a Petrarchist not unknown to the Pléiade. It is always important to note, however, to what use this inspiration was put. Charles d'Orléans's "Canticum amoris" presents a dialogue between the poet and his soul about the necessity to flee worldly pleasures and embrace the pleasures of heaven, all carefully enumerated in the poem. The Saint-Gelais who wrote the *Séjour d'Honneur* also translated Ovid's *Heroides* (1497), but when Charles VIII died the next year, he composed a long lament in the form of a dream (the *Roman de la Rose* again!). The Rhétoriqueurs knew Petrarch and Boccaccio as well as the Bible, from which they imitated in particular the book of Proverbs. Yet, if we may judge by their treatment of these Italian humanists, the French poets looked upon them in much the same light as they did the book of Proverbs. Although the narration is often rich and the moral incidental in Boccaccio's *De Claris Mulieribus*, which tells of the lives of the great women of the past, the book became a manual for the contemplation of Fortune's wheel. Where Boccaccio had seen passions and human drama, these poets saw a moral lesson. The *Triomfi*, in which Petrarch sings of Laura again through a series of triumphs (Love over men, Chastity over Love, Death over Chastity, and so forth), were treated as sermons, and François Robertet, a patron of the Rhétoriqueurs, reduced them to six neat rondeaux. With regard to style, exposure to the greats of antiquity merely accentuated the ornamental bent of the period. Latinisms, mythology, and erudite allusions joined with diminutives, sweet-singing birds, and babbling brooks to decorate the extravagant growth that is the poetry of the Rhétoriqueurs. The new was caught in the clutches of the old, just as Lefèvre d'Etaples' spirit of reform belonged more properly with the protestations of Pierre d'Ailly and Gerson than with the schismatic views that conviction and circumstances brought Luther to adopt. Lefèvre had no desire to split the Church when commenting on St. Paul. Similarly, the Rhétoriqueurs hardly treated Petrarch and Boccaccio, Ovid and Virgil as vehicles for a revolution in poetry.

Still both phenomena came to pass. The pages to follow relate the slow and complicated process by which these changes occurred.

2

ᚠrancis I

(1515-1547)

ITALY

Louis XII died on New Year's day, 1515. The throne was his *étrenne* to Francis of Angoulême. We do not know if the new King made any New Year's resolutions, but judging by his future acts, he was determined to succeed in one particular thing: the conquest of Italy. Before the year was out, he had descended into Italy with an impressive invading force.

As the Italian states were no more capable of uniting against a common enemy in 1515 than they had been previously, Francis I, like Charles VIII and Louis XII before him, first knew stunning victories. He arranged the Concordat with Pope Leo X and in 1519, when a Holy Roman Emperor had to be elected, threw himself into the intrigue, attempting to buy votes at exorbitant prices only to meet firm opposition from the previous Emperor's choice, his grandson Charles. Maximilian's wishes were eventually recognized, and Charles became Charles V, ruler of Germany, Burgundy-Flanders, Naples, and Spain. Francis I had been caught in a hostile vice, a fact that must have influenced the electors more than his money. They had more to fear from a union of France and Germany than from Charles V's elevation. Such a union could only have made the French Emperor strong enough to impose his wishes on the electors (his vassals), whereas with Charles's election the rising star of France was checked and her King received a worthy rival.

Italy became their battleground. As a Spanish prince, Charles V, too, had claims to Naples. As Holy Roman Emperor, he alone could grant investiture over his fiefs of Milan, Mantua, and Monferrat, now in, now out of France's hands. Small battles on the Flemish and Spanish borders during 1523 proved indecisive, and when an attack by Imperial troops on Marseilles failed (June, 1524), Francis I felt the time ripe for a new invasion of Italy. He crossed into Italy in October, marched to Milan, and subsequently laid seige to Pavia. The defenders held out for three months. Then, in January, an Imperial army attacked the French. The battle was fierce and catastrophic. Francis I saw his finest men cut down and was himself captured by the enemy. He wrote to his mother, Louise de Savoie: "Of all I possessed only my honor and my life are safe," which time has erroneously reduced to "All is lost save honor."

Francis I's imprisonment in Madrid and those events which surrounded the negotiations undertaken by Louise de Savoie, Marguerite de Navarre, Henry VIII, and Charles V read like a complicated melodrama—and with reason. Pavia had been a dramatic moment. France seemed doomed. As regent, Louise attempted to give a contrary impression: France was still capable of resisting Imperial occupation. England, like the Pope and other Italian rulers, had mixed feelings over Charles's victory. The Italians had no love for an Emperor who was now ostensibly powerful enough to rule them with a firm hand. Henry VIII wanted France partitioned with a sizable portion going to him. The Emperor temporized, and the longer he hesitated, the more Henry chafed at helping so strong a figure. Charles kept well informed of the shifting sentiments toward him. He also knew how precarious his situation was, depite the conclusiveness of his victory at Pavia. The Protestants in Germany posed a constant threat; his coffers were never full enough. As a result, on January 14, 1526, Charles V made peace with Francis I and signed the Treaty of Madrid. Its terms were harsh. France restored all of Burgundy to Charles. Francis I renounced his rights to Naples, Milan, Asti, and Genoa; he agreed to aid the Emperor in a crusade against the Turks, who pressed Charles's eastern frontier. He abandoned his suzerainty over Flanders and Artois; he agreed to pay Charles's debts to Henry of England and to marry Charles's sister Eleonora. Still, France was free to live and fight another day. And so she did.

As soon as Francis I was safely on French soil, he repudiated the Treaty of Madrid, saying that as a prisoner, he had been forced to meet Charles's demands. He made warm overtures to the Pope and to those Italian states that continued to have second thoughts about Pavia. Their common sentiments produced the Holy League of Cognac. The papal armies began to assemble; one of Charles's generals sacked Rome, and Francis I immediately dispatched an army to Italy to sustain poor Pope Clement VII, shut up in his Castle St. Angelo for safety's sake. The campaign eventually failed. Marguerite d'Autriche, Charles's aunt, and Louise de Savoie, tired of the wars, brought about in 1529 a treaty known as the Ladies' Peace or the Peace of Cambray. In essence, the terms were those of the Treaty of Madrid, except that France retained Burgundy. Thus, there were concessions from both sides, proof not only of the difficulties, financial and military, of France and the Empire, but of the skillful maneuvering by England and the Italian states to prevent a disturbance in the balance of power. Francis I, of course, never gave up. He sent troops into Italy in 1535 and again in 1544, but these were mere sorties compared to earlier invasions. He died soon after Henry VIII (1547), a tired and disappointed man.

However foolish, egotistical and even foolhardy Francis I was in pursuing the Italian Wars, history has long pardoned him and chosen to remember his reign as a new era in France. To understand and adjudicate this traditional view of Francis I, we must examine the King's relationship to the arts and the world of humanism.

FRANCIS I AND THE ARTS

When art historians speak of the Renaissance in France, they refer to a mass importation of Italian culture as distinguished from any previous contact between France and Italy. The two countries in the fifteenth century had not lived in complete isolation. The humanists have already demonstrated that fact. In the realm of art, such distinguished painters as Fouquet and Perréal had travelled across the Alps and been exposed to Italian art long before 1515. Still, not only were the results unimpressive, but few works of the period suggest that Italian art forms had made a strong impression on the French mind. The same may be said of new architecture before Francis I.

In 1493–1495 Charles VIII brought to Amboise some Italian artists to aid in the completion of the château, begun, however, much before their arrival. Louis XII was to do the same some years later with Blois. In both cases the existing structures were scarcely altered by the Italians. Amboise's great tower and battlements are, in conception and execution, those of a medieval fortress. There and at Blois the Italians left their mark through decoration, placed about the windows, on the walls, and columns in the form of a proliferation of medallions, masks, fruit, putti, and flowers. The modest nature of this contribution of the Italians summarizes rather well the relationship between France and Italy at the turn of the sixteenth century. Indeed, so modest were the innovations and so dominant were the pre-existing forms that art historians have termed the painting of this time *l'art de la détente*. The term attempts to convey the lack of innovation, the dominance of a quiet style such as we see in the Maître de Moulins' "Virgin in Glory" (c. 1498–1499). The painting depicts Mary and child surrounded by angels with the donors on side panels. Every face radiates sweetness and serenity. There is no attempt at drama or dramatic movement in the composition. The body position, the stance of the Virgin, all betray the artistic interest in creating a picture devoid of stress. Such conservatism has been traced in part to the patrons of the day, who showed little interest in change, but, having examined the literature and scholarship of the closing years of the fifteenth century, we know that the old ways had not disappeared from any major aspect of French life at that time. New elements were constantly coming to bear, but whether in the form of Italian ornamentation or Italian literature, they effected no marked changes. Even the success of Italian decoration has been attributed to the French enjoyment of Flamboyant Gothic, an indigenous, highly decorative form.

It is in the light of such facts that Francis I's reign appears so remarkable, for in the domain of art and architecture, the new King did effect a revolution. It was he who brought to France the Italian artisans, painters, and styles that constitute the Renaissance of the arts in France. His efforts were not uniformly successful, but where they took root, they determined the nature of France's artistic production for years.

Prior to the defeat at Pavia, the French court led a nomadic life through the Loire valley, which Francis I loved so much. He hoped to create for that court the munificence in architecture and painting he had seen in Italy. To this end he brought Leonardo da Vinci to France. The great man came, painted a bit, and promptly expired. Another Italian, Del Sarto, arrived just before Leonardo died. He spent all of Francis I's generous salary and fled. The King had little initial success with painters. His glory during those early years of his reign found expression in the beautiful châteaux of the Loire country.

Azay-le-Rideau, Chenonceaux, Chambord, and part of Blois exalt the success of Francis' endeavor. They also reveal the basic traits of France's first Renaissance style in architecture. The medieval fortress was maintained as the formal base around which the familiar ornament was worked—loggie, staircases, pilasters, decorated with garlands, fruit, and the like. For those who have seen the corner towers at Azay-le-Rideau it will be clear that decoration could affect even the basic structure. These tiny towers cannot be compared to those at Amboise. They are tourettes, derivatives of the former style and far more ornamental than protective.

The predominance of decoration was perhaps inevitable. At the time France turned toward Italy, the detail, the arabesque held sway among its artists, and a singular resemblance between the ornamentation of the Italian style and French Flamboyant Gothic made much of Italian art readily acceptable to the French. When, somewhat later, Francis I renewed his efforts to secure painters for his court, he wrote to those cities he was most acquainted with, that is, to cities other than Venice, whose Tintoretto or Veronese towered above the talents Francis eventually brought to Paris. Still, art historians are quick to note that changes in Italian styles did not escape the French. Before the close of Francis I's reign, the Italian Bramante had brought his country's architecture back to classical models. Similarly, Chambord does not resemble in all respects other Loire *châteaux*. It is an architectural mass constructed along broad horizontal lines. If its roof abounds in chimneys covered with ornamentation, the architects had nonetheless conceived of a whole rather devoid of purely ornamental appurtenances and remarkably symmetrical. The towers, more massive than those at Azay-le-Rideau, strongly resemble their medieval ancestors. Yet they are also part of an overall design which looks ahead to another period in French architecture. The new style was still derived from Italy, but by its interest in architectonic form versus ornamentation, it properly belonged to an Italy of classical inspiration.

This new style emerged in the late 1530s. St. Michael's in Dijon, begun in 1537, shows the transition. Already the arches above the doors appear more Romanesque than Gothic. Above the tympana and along the arches decorative effects abound. As the building progressed, the heavy decoration disappeared. The architecture is simpler and highly symmetrical. The pilasters are in the main unadorned. The style was definitively announced by the château at Ancy, begun in 1538. Nothing suggests even the vestiges of a *château-fort*. The building is even simpler than Chambord in conception. The corner towers are square, the roof, without decoration. The division into three stories is sharply outlined, thus accentuating the square mass as contrasted with the vertical frills of earlier French *châteaux*.

Ancy was designed by an Italian, Sebastiano Serlio. Another important Italian name of the period is Il Primaticcio, renamed Le Primatice by the French. His presence in France is explained by Francis I's second campaign to bring Italian artists to his court. This time, the King reaped a bountiful success.

After Pavia and Madrid, Francis I returned to France, but not to the Loire valley. He had found a new love, the Ile-de-France and especially Fontainebleau. To create for himself a splendid environment, he wrote to Michelangelo and to Giulio Romano, student of the deceased Raphael. Michelangelo sent Francis I his promising protégé Il Rosso (Le Rosse), who arrived in France in 1531. Two years later, Romano's pupil arrived. It was Il Primaticcio. Their arrival marked the founding of the first Ecole de Fontainebleau, the most important school of painting in France during the sixteenth century.

Il Rosso set to work decorating the wing of the Fontainebleau château to be known as the Galerie François I. At a moment when architecture was about to abandon its emphasis on decoration, Il Rosso literally covered every inch of the walls in the château with ornamentation. The lower surface was panelled and decorated in large bursts of design with shields, garlands, and crossed swords; the upper surface contained a fresco. The inspiration here was Il Rosso's master, Michelangelo, but the pupil did not stop with the paintings. The area surrounding the frescos had to be filled. Il Rosso chose stucco as his medium and proceeded to adorn all remaining surfaces with putti, fruit, and so forth. The result is not unimpressive, but whatever one's tastes, this gallery affords ample evidence of the penchant for decoration among the Italians who came to Fontainebleau. It should be added that the subjects treated by Il Rosso in the Galerie François I and by Il Primaticcio in his room, the Galerie d'Ulysse (begun around 1541), were taken from mythology and classical literature. These paintings may explain, in part, the surprising familiarity of the court with mythological subjects, to which the love poetry of the century bears witness.

When, in 1540, Il Rosso committed suicide, Il Primaticcio inherited his position as chief artist to the King. To refresh his inspiration, he returned to Italy until 1542 and brought back to France a series of molds made from many of Rome's most famous (and most classical) statues, including the "Laocoön" and "Apollo Belvedere." The gesture had an important influence not only on Il Primaticcio's own works but on many traits of French painting and sculpture to come.

Despite Il Rosso's death, Il Primaticcio had still to share the limelight, unofficially, until 1545 with a renowned Italian called Benvenuto Cellini. Cellini finally departed, convinced that he was not sufficiently appreciated in France, but not before he had created an exquisite bronze nymph—the nymph of Fontainebleau. The nymph, nude, reclines; to her right is the head of a stag around which she places her arm. The pose along with those forms brought from Italy by Il Primaticcio were to be repeated again and again by artists of this century.

What are the principal traits of the Ecole de Fontainebleau? The Galerie François I accentuates its love of decoration. In painting Il

Rosso and Il Primaticcio strongly revealed the orientation of their masters. The former, trained by Michelangelo, painted boldly. His figures are dynamic and nervous; his composition, often improbable. (See his "Pietà," for example.) Il Primaticcio, trained in Raphael's school, is far more serene. He was fascinated by the human body, but as a classical study in line and form. His "Ulysses and Penelope" has an academic coldness—the faces are expressionless—that contrasts sharply with Il Rosso's agitated figures. Since each painter founded his own atelier in France, the two styles continued to exist in their imitators. Jean Cousin's "Descent from the Cross" has all the movement of Il Rosso's works just as the Maître de Flore's "Birth of Love" reproduces Il Primaticcio's interest in the human form. (The canvas is equally important for the minute decoration of Venus' bed and the reclining position of the love goddess, so reminiscent of Cellini's nymph.)

Whatever the differences between Il Rosso and Il Primaticcio, neither had much in common with the Maître de Moulins and l'art de la détente. Whether dealing with a religious or classical subject, their attitudes toward composition (in the case of Il Rosso) and form (for Il Primaticcio) would not easily appeal to the same mind that appreciated the Moulins Virgin. As a result, it is tempting to wax metaphysical about Francis I's importation of these new artists, to talk of a new Weltanschauung, a new aesthetic, and new values, to suggest that contact with Italy at last bore fruit. The truth is probably less exciting and certainly less metaphysical. That the French nobility was impressed with Italy is certain; so, too, was the attraction of Italian wealth and pomp for the French kings. As Charles VIII demonstrated when he brought Italians to complete his château at Amboise, Italy, elegant castles, and being king had already acquired a definite set of associations. Francis I was acting accordingly, only on a grander scale. His early victories in Italy, his Concordat with the Pope, not to mention his own personality made greatness on the Italian scale seem imminent. His hope for election in 1519 shows how far such aspirations could reach. When he failed to become Holy Roman Emperor, he is said to have taken defeat in stride, yet defeat could only exacerbate his desire to make of the French court what Italy had already become. To imitate the Italian despots and their brilliant entourages was not necessarily to divest oneself of the past, to change vision or aesthetics, however. Doubtlessly Francis I's efforts did effect over the span of time a change in tastes, but there is every reason to believe that Italy's lesson for Francis I was a practical one: great rulers surrounded themselves with artists and lived in magnificent palaces.

FRANCIS I AND THE REFORM

When Guillaume Budé, in presenting his *De Asse* (1515) to Francis I, called the new King "*Genie de la France,*" [1] he most certainly was speaking as an interested person. He devoutly hoped that Francis I would interfere in the functioning of the intellectual world and use his power to further the aims of those humanists who sought reform within the Church and its ancillary institutions. In 1530 Francis I took a decisive step in that direction and founded the *lecteurs royaux*: three professors, one each for Greek, Hebrew, and mathematics, supported by the Crown to give public lectures on their subjects. The intent was patent and far-reaching. Greek and Hebrew were both necessary for a truly critical approach to the biblical texts. Since they were available only within an educational system controlled by the Church, the spirit of free inquiry could not flourish. The *lecteurs royaux* made these languages available in a form that excluded any interference from the Church.

Francis I did still more for the humanists. Centuries before he mounted the throne, two bodies were recognized as defenders of order in the state. The Faculty of Theology had an international reputation as arbiter in questions involving the faith. It saw itself and others saw it as not only obliged to ferret out heresy wherever it might hide itself, but as possessing the power to pronounce on suspected writings as truth or error. In this way the Faculty protected the faithful against dangerous ideas and preserved the integrity of established doctrine. The Parlement of Paris, an outgrowth of the old *curia regis*, originally assisted the king in affairs of justice. By the fifteenth century, it had become so independent that the justices heard cases in which the king was defendant or plaintiff. While in practice a court, the Parlement could not escape the realization that religious dissension threatened the state as surely as any act of sedition. It and the Faculty soon joined forces to preserve the status quo.

In 1521 the King was warned by Budé that Lefèvre d'Etaples had been called before the Parlement of Paris. Francis I stopped the case. In 1523 Berquin, who had translated Erasmus and Luther, was shut up in the Conciergerie after being condemned by the Faculty of Theology. The Faculty then proceeded to examine Lefèvre's works. The King had Berquin transferred to the Louvre, where he would be safe, and told the Sorbonne to leave Lefèvre in peace. In 1533, when the Faculty placed Marguerite de Navarre's "Miroir de l'âme pécheresse" among

---

[1] "The Guiding Spirit of France."

the books forbidden to the faithful, Francis I intervened in favor of his sister. He forced the professors to vote and sign a repudiation of their own attack. Such brave, decisive acts would seem to suggest that Francis I's commitment to protecting certain French humanists against their enemies was firm and enduring. They amply justify a view of the King as the patron of change. At the same time, even the most clear-cut facts can be misleading. What Francis I intended in aiding Budé's friends, to what degree he hoped to foster significant intellectual changes in his kingdom are very moot points. These interventions, even the founding of the *lecteurs royaux*, cannot be interpreted in isolation. And the story of the early Reform in France, as well as of Francis I's politics, includes a host of surprises.

In the early years of the sixteenth century, few events were more significant in the intellectual world than the trials of a German, Johannus Reuchlin. An excellent humanist, knowledgeable in Latin, Greek, and Hebrew, Reuchlin studied the *Talmud*, the *Cabbala*, and other Jewish texts in search of new light on Christian documents. His work earned for him the animosity of several fellow-Germans who found shocking any recourse to rabbinical literature in the context of Christian scholarship. Attacked directly in 1509, Reuchlin upheld the utility of an exegesis of the *Cabbala* and the *Talmud* for an intelligent understanding of the Bible and even asked that chairs of Hebrew be established in the universities. His enemies obtained, in 1513, a condemnation of his works by the Inquisition of Mainz. The Faculty of Theology at Cologne voted likewise in March, 1514. By April, the case was before the University of Paris.

Lefèvre d'Etaples knew of the controversy even before his own university had been asked to try the humanist. Reuchlin, once a student in Paris, had written Lefèvre the preceding year to plead his case. Though Lefèvre himself had not worked with the Jewish documents, he was predisposed toward Reuchlin on many counts. The Italian mystics whom Lefèvre so admired had a distinct respect for the *Cabbala*. The French humanist knew of Reuchlin's erudition and of his solid knowledge of Hebrew. Most important, he recognized immediately that at the heart of Reuchlin's case lay a struggle between proponents of traditional methods of inquiry and the new school of humanist study to which he, Reuchlin, and Erasmus belonged. Reuchlin lost his case before the University of Paris, even though Lefèvre fought for him. The debate split the Faculty, and the two camps, once formed, remained hostile throughout the years to come. By precipitating differences, the Reuchlin case also created or solidified new bonds. At the time of the trial, Lefèvre had not made any particular effort to study the works of Erasmus. He nevertheless knew of Erasmus' principles and had to suffer himself the growing mistrust of his contemporaries vis-à-vis his edition of St. Paul. He rejoiced when the Dutchman announced an edition of the New Testament to be published in Basel and publicly praised Erasmus. The die was cast. Whatever the original intentions of Lefèvre and even Erasmus, circumstances such as the Reuchlin case were forcing a cleavage between the old and new methods. However much Lefèvre and Erasmus may have wanted to work within the established Church, it seemed increasingly ill-disposed to accept them into the ranks of the faithful.

In the years to follow, Lefèvre did little to make himself more acceptable to the Church. In 1517 he attacked the traditional view that Mary, sister of Lazarus, Mary Magdalene, and the woman Mary, delivered from devils (Luke viii 2), were three separate persons. By basing his view on the Scriptures, he proclaimed once again the primacy of Scripture over dogma. Even more compromising was his participation in the *groupe de Meaux*. Under the direction of Guillaume Briçonnet, a small band of reformers decided to transform the diocese of Meaux into a model of the primitive Church, whose simplicity and purity they had so long acclaimed. They began in 1518, modestly at first, but gradually Sunday sermons became commentaries on the Bible. The cult of the saints was de-emphasized as well as indulgences and other general efforts to extract money from the people. In the spring of 1521, Lefèvre was asked to join the group. A year later he published his *Commentarii initiatorii in IV Evangelia*, which exhorted others to seek the same reforms.

That the work at Meaux should arouse criticism was inevitable. The tragedy behind Lefèvre and Briçonnet's situation stemmed from an infiltration of Luther's works and ideas into France at this very moment. The similarity of views escaped no one. When the Parlement of Paris condemned all writings by Luther in 1521, the position of such men as the reformers of Meaux became untenable. It was virtually impossible for them to say that they were opposed to the concepts of the German Reform movement; at the same time, the intransigence of the conservative scholastics made it clear that the *groupe de Meaux* did not agree with the Church, either. Briçonnet's choice in this situation is revealing. He publicly denounced Luther in October, 1523. To act otherwise would have meant a break with the Church that he and others were not prepared to make. The work at Meaux continued nonetheless. Lefèvre's publications show that the menace of being linked to Luther could not weaken his conviction that reform was needed.

What the threat of Lutheranism could not accomplish, the King's captivity did. On March 24, 1525, the case of the reformers at Meaux was brought before the Parlement of Paris. Lefèvre fled to Strasburg to return only with the arrival of the King from Spain. He discovered that the reforms effected at Meaux had been swept away. Berquin was arrested again, and this time could not be saved. He was hanged and burned in the spring of 1529. Marguerite de Navarre offered Lefèvre a post in her entourage at Nérac to protect him from the mounting storm of protest created by his works. Without ever taking sides in the religious debate, he worked there until his death in 1536. Lefèvre's life is the story of dedication to an ideal. That such dedication was to achieve dramatic consequences was the fault of history, not Lefèvre d'Etaples. His crusade at Meaux (which, it should be noted, he did not initiate) was a purely religious undertaking. Unlike Luther or Calvin, Lefèvre had no political ambitions. A mystic and a sincere believer, he wished to save souls, not to lead them. Caught in his later years between the dogmatic Church and the revolutionary Luther, he merely maintained his ideal of the purity of the primitive Church and the right of the scholar to free examination of the sacred texts. Briçonnet's condemnation of Luther was, on a less exalted plane, the expression of a similar reticence before the issues of religious unrest. Such reticence must ultimately characterize the attitudes of the most important of French humanist-reformers. As liberal as they appeared to their enemies in Paris' Faculty of Theology, they were still unwilling to repudiate their Church or to abandon the hope that she would reform herself.

Burckhardt labelled the spirit of the Italian Renaissance "pagan" and was criticized for this. Regarding France in the early days of the sixteenth century, such a declaration is more unthinkable than debatable. Etienne Dolet, it is true, held views that were interpreted as pagan and pantheistic, but he was an exception. Erasmus, even Lefèvre, could cast aside a popular cult or a fanciful interpretation of the Scriptures, but such objectivity did not make them pagans or atheists. In a situation where unrest and complaint existed long before Erasmus read Lucian or Lefèvre learned of Valla, the impact of foreign influence will always be hard to measure. Contact with classical culture made Erasmus worldlier and both Erasmus and Lefèvre more exacting in their judgments, but on examining their lives, one wonders whether any doubts they may have had about their faith did not come from the Church itself—often so brutal and uncompromising in its attitudes—rather than from any contact with antiquity or Italy. Similarly, that most reformers came to believe in a goal of simple faith and institutions quite unlike those of the existing Church reflected ultimately the influence of St.

Paul more than that of antiquity, and we cannot forget that the interest in antiquity and its languages was consciously tied to a scholarly pursuit of textual perfection and inspiration within the sphere of a religious crusade.

Of distinct importance in the thinking of the reformers was the increased sense that criticism of the old order must be permitted. What was established was not necessarily best. Changes must be allowed. Here antiquity may have played a role by revealing, as did St. Paul's Epistles, that thought and belief were not always as the pope or the Sorbonne had decreed; still, as the Religious Wars were to prove, those who fought for change were rarely any more tolerant toward their critics than those who detested change. Old thoughts and new thoughts received very similar emphasis. The same could be said of Francis I's politics.

In 1534, a group of fanatical reformers set up throughout France and particularly at Amboise, where the King was residing, large placards attacking the Mass. Francis I was outraged and ordered that the culprits and their sect be prosecuted. This event, known as the *Affaire des Placards*, traditionally dates the end of Francis I's sympathy with the Reform movement. The golden moment of royal patronage and protection had come to a close; the age of persecution had begun. The assumption here is that all was peaceful prior to the *Affaire des Placards* and that however much the reformers were beset by the Sorbonne, Francis' interest in the movement was sufficient to keep it out of harm's way. Such an assumption has little grounds to support it.

The reckless action in 1534 marked an explosion of resentment created by years of persecution that the King did not stop and for which he was often directly responsible. In 1523 Berquin may have escaped the stake, but Jean Vallière did not. If the death of Joubert in 1525 can be explained by the King's absence from France, the repression of 1524 and the burning of two Lutherans in Paris and Rouen two years later cannot. In truth, Francis I's attitude toward the Reform was never stable. It was even of questionable sincerity. Francis never abandoned his political ambitions and was astute and determined enough to use all means at his command, even the Reform, to pursue his goals.

In his struggle with Charles V, Francis I employed diplomatic as well as military strategy. Specifically, he tried to use to his advantage whenever possible the dissatisfaction of Henry VIII, of certain German Protestant nobles, and, more particularly, of the Pope with the Emperor. An alliance with the Pope gave Francis I a friendly force in Italy. An alliance with the German Protestants would weaken Charles's support from within his own country. At the same time this unity of purpose against Charles V was based on a flagrant contradiction in religious profession. As a result, each time Francis I found that he could lure the Pope into aligning with him against the Hapsburg, he stepped up persecution of the reformers to prove his good faith to the Holy Father. When he was attempting to secure the allegiance of the German Protestants, he had to show signs of a different sort, that is, of an enlightened policy toward the Reform. Thus, in 1524 and 1526, the wave of repression coincided with a rapprochement between Francis I and the Pope, whereas the liberalism of the 1530s corresponded to a new diplomacy, directed toward German Protestants and a unification of the warring parties under the aegis of Francis I.

With the duplicity of the diplomat must be reckoned the dilemma of the monarch. The spread of Lutheranism and other Reform views did not take place without incident. As early as 1524, signs were put on the doors of the cathedral of Meaux calling the Pope an antichrist. The same year at Lyons artisans were so stirred by the new ideas that a royal edict called for the expulsion of foreign merchants "*herectiques ou aultres*" from the city. More important, Luther was rapidly displaced by Zwingli as the influential voice in French Protestantism. Official documents and opponents of the new faith retained the word "Lutheran," but it was often a misnomer and used indiscriminately to describe any partisan of ideas hostile to the Church.

Much more strict than Luther, Zwingli defined true religion as complete obedience to the word of God as expressed in the Scriptures. While Luther accepted what the Scriptures did not specifically forbid, Zwingli accepted only what the Scriptures admitted and espoused. Little wonder that to the people of the day Protestantism appeared to be, in Imbart de la Tour's expression, "*un nihilisme.*" The recurrent mutilation of religious statues, like the Peasant's Revolt (1524–1525), which engulfed nearly a third of Germany, or the unrest at Lyons, was proof positive that Protestantism was synonymous with destruction and disturbance, whereas the Protestants felt that they were bringing about the return of a decadent Church to its pure, primeval state.

The pressure on Francis I to eradicate this movement was enormous. The King himself could hardly ignore the civil crisis growing within his realm. Marguerite de Navarre, given her religious convictions, pleaded for reconciliation, and so did certain of the King's counselors. While Protestantism had been more successful in some regions than in others, the centralization of French government did not permit a solution such as was to be found in Germany where each small, independent state adopted the religion of its ruler. The alternative to reconciliation in France was extermination—a foreshadowing of the mentality that produced the Religious Wars. Francis I rejected so violent a measure. Did he act out of sympathy for the Reform? Such a tactic was also contrary to his diplomacy. Francis I needed the support of his whole country to combat Charles V. He wanted to lead Europe, not divide it. Hence, a policy of reconciliation, with Francis I at the helm, was to solve his foreign and domestic difficulties.

Already, in 1527, Francis I had concluded an alliance with Henry VIII. Three years later in Henry's divorce case, Francis I gave all his support to Henry, who, after all, was repudiating Catherine of Aragon, the aunt of Charles V. Such support of a monarch about to break with the Pope needed a gesture toward the Holy Father to soften the blow. Francis I proposed to the Pope that his second son Henry marry Catherine de Medici, the Pope's niece. The Pope was flattered but did not give in to Francis I easily.

The idea of a reconciliation did not occur to the French King alone. Charles V had recently proposed that the work be done by a church Council. Francis gasped. A Council would displace him as the arbiter between Catholics and Protestants. Francis I must have gasped even louder in 1533 when Pope Clement VII announced a Council! Still, he would not be undone and arranged to discuss these issues with the Pope at Nice. It was at Marseilles that they actually met. The King talked rapidly, and Clement listened. Francis I won the round handily. Not only were Henry and Catherine de Medici married at Marseilles, but there would be no Council. Francis I would negotiate the reconciliation.

Guillaume and Jean Du Bellay represented Francis I among the Germans. They met with unparalleled success until the *Affaire des Placards* threatened to compromise everything. Again Francis I would not be undone. While persecuting their religious brethren in France, Francis I pursued with the German Protestants his plans for a reconciliation. He wrote them to explain that repression was necessary to preserve order in the kingdom and maintained the hope that Melanchthon, a distinguished Protestant theologian living in Wittenberg, would come to Paris to debate with the Faculty of Theology and establish the basis for an entente. Unfortunately, the Elector of Saxony would not grant Melanchthon leave to go to France (the hand of Charles V), and in the years that followed, all further negotiations proved that both sides were not nearly so eager for agreement as Francis I. Clement VII died at this point. The new Pope, Paul III, had decided liberal leanings. A Council was proposed, but the Germans considered that any Council held outside Germany would not be truly free to debate the issues involved. So ran the discussions.

Even though the preceding is but the briefest sketch of Francis I's reign, there is no denying the complexity of the period. If we perceive new trends and conflicts, they were hardly sweeping reforms which washed away the feeble remains of an earlier culture. Italy and antiquity had their role to play, a role that may well define for some a renaissance in France, but it will not be a Burckhardtian renaissance of pride and paganism. The fierce new vigor derived from religious convictions, not a quest for earthly glory. In a sense, Francis I does appear as an aspiring renaissance monarch. He glorified himself with a lavish court, patronized the arts, spent great sums, and pursued vast schemes. But history was good to him. It offered him the fulfillment of a hope that his predecessors could only nourish in dreams. Italian politics no longer worked successfully. National states, among them France, had come into being through a series of often fortuitous events. Without the potential that history afforded, he would have been but another feudal monarch playing the part of king.

History has much to tell us as well about the fortunes of the Reform movement at this time. We know that attacks upon the Church did not begin in France with Lefèvre d'Etaples. They flourished before and after the Hundred Years War. Yet only with the reign of Francis I did humanism seem akin to open revolt and criticism, a serious threat. A Renaissance spirit, it would seem. But history has also changed the drama's backdrop. Attempts by the Church to reform herself were not satisfactory. The kings would not relinquish any significant privileges they possessed, and the popes were locked in an increasingly violent struggle to remain a temporal power. Even great French prelates of the day, such as George d'Amboise, minister to Louis XII, devoted their energies to self-aggrandizement and to political intrigue. As the political tide began to turn in favor of the new national states, the Church could only devote more and more energy to its temporal position and inflame its critics all the more. In the absence of significant reforms, the kings were only too happy to champion the cause of the mal-contents. When Budé wrote ringing praises to Francis I in 1515, he must have envisaged religious as well as cultural progress. Ostensibly a book about money, the *De Asse* also contains violent denunciations of Pope Julius II's conduct. Francis I, Henry VIII, and the German princes played their parts well, and all went as far as they could in using the Reform to best political advantage. Their achievements are impressive and give to the Reform an air of success it deserves, but not necessarily for reasons of a new vision. Feudal kings and princes had long wished to rival the pope. Suddenly, history had caught up with their desires; the kings began to have their way.

THE WORLD OF LITERATURE

The brilliance of Francis I's reign extends well beyond the arts. Some of the most curious and most interesting works of sixteenth-century prose and poetry appeared at this time. Products of men and women born in the preceding century, they demonstrate sufficient awareness of Italian and classical literature as well as of the religious unrest to raise the same question of interpretation just examined with regard to art and politics. Are we witnessing a renaissance?

An answer in the realm of literature will not be simple as here, too, the exact value of antiquity, of scholarship, and of protest for these writers is not easily grasped. But again it is attitudes and not only the fact of familiarity with foreign and ancient letters that must be considered. Charles VIII's descent into Italy was a revolutionary event in cultural history only if the kind of contact with Italy it has symbolized was accompanied by the desire to turn away from the inherited traditions. The late Erwin Panofsky wrote regarding changes in the arts in Italy: "It was for the Italian Renaissance to reintegrate classical form with classical content, and it was by this reintegration that the classical images—first salvaged then split asunder and finally recomposed—were really 'reborn'." [2] We may well begin to answer our own question by seeking to learn whether France, in the years of Francis I's patronage, accomplished a similar reintegration of the new cultures it was discovering.

Marot (1496–1544)

Clément Marot's life was a full one, dominated by princes, poetry, and prisons. Since his father, Jean Marot, a Grand Rhétoriqueur, occupied a post in the household of Anne de Bretagne and at her death became *valet de la garderobe* to Francis I, Clément had easy access to the court. He also possessed a ready wit, a ready pen, and a skill at turning phrases and making compliments, traits which won for him quite early the title and function of *valet de chambre* to Marguerite

---

[2] Erwin Panofsky, "Renaissance and Renascences," *Kenyon Review*, VI (1944), 222.

d'Alençon, soon to become Queen of Navarre. In 1526 Jean Marot died, and Clément became *valet de chambre du roi*. His fortune was assured, or so it would seem. Clément had already known once the walls of the Châtelet prison, and he was destined to experience misfortune again.

His first arrest (March, 1526) has been called the work of a jealous lady who denounced Clément for having eaten meat during Lent. It is also true that while in Marguerite's service, Clément had come into contact with the new ideas of Lefèvre, of Briçonnet, of Marguerite, and other reformers. Perhaps the jealous lady did invent her story (the offense, however, was considered worthy of hanging in this intolerant era), but the fact remains that Marot had listened seriously to the group of reformers whom Marguerite protected and who tended more and more to discard ceremony and practice in order to seek a new spiritual bond with God. If Marot was not guilty in fact, he may well have been guilty in spirit.

In 1527 he helped a prisoner escape his guards and spent several weeks in the Conciergerie. In 1532 he was again accused of having eaten meat during Lent. Each time Marot found friends to rescue him. He also found inspiration for his pen. For example, on the occasion of his first arrest, Marot composed for Lyon Jamet an *épître-fable*, his most famous *épître*, in which the tale of the lion and the rat is retold. Not only did Jamet's name lend itself to a marvelous pun, but the story of mutual assistance had most immediate connotations for the imprisoned Marot.

A second prison poem written in 1526 is the *Enfer*, which reveals another side of the poet's talent. The *épîtres* are generally light and witty, designed to please as well as to convince. The *Enfer* is a satire against his judges and his prison. The following verses render Marot's tone. The poet has just described the lawcourts, their injustices, the grasping nature of the magistrates:

> *Et si tu quiers raison*
> *Pourquoy Proces sont si fort en saison,*
> *Sçaiche que c'est faulte de charité*
> *Entre Chrestiens. Et à la verité,*
> *.Comment l'auront dedans leur cueur fichée,*
> *Quand par tout est si froidement preschée?*
> *À escouter voz Prescheurs, bien souvent*
> *Charité n'est que donner au Couvent.*

The tone is bitter; the subject reminiscent of innumerable attacks upon contemporary religion made by the French reformers. The *Enfer*, for obvious reasons, remained unpublished for many years.

With the exception of an attack of the plague and the renewed accusation by the Parlement of Paris in 1532, Marot knew a peaceful, flourishing career between 1527 and 1534. The extent of his renown may be derived from two publications, *Les Opuscules et petitz Traictez de Clement Marot* (c. 1531) and *Petit traicté contenant plusieurs chantz royaulx, Balades et Epistres, faictes et composees par Clement Marot* (1532). Neither work is a faithful edition of Marot's works. The texts are corrupt; the content includes poems that Marot never wrote. It was this attempt by two enterprising editors to exploit Marot's popularity that induced him to bring out in 1532 an edition of his early works. The volume, entitled *L'Adolescence clementine*, naturally did not include the *Enfer*, and in the case of other poems, Marot discreetly omitted lines too frank and compromising. When the *Affaire des Placards* occurred, the poet knew that such precautions would be of no avail, however.

Marot fled, first to Marguerite's court, then to the court of Renée de France, Duchess of Ferrara. He was able to return to France by the end of 1536, but the religious question pursued him as it did his country. Publication of the *Enfer* (1539) and his *Psaumes de David* (1541)—for which he had been willing to depart from the Latin text of the Vulgate to prepare his translation—could hardly have served to silence his enemies. In 1542 Francis I signed new decrees against Lutheranism. Marot left France never to return. He found refuge in Geneva, but his mode of living was ill-suited for the austerity that Calvin had established there. He wandered on to appear finally in Turin, where in September, 1544, he died.

By virtue of Marot's position at the courts of Marguerite de Navarre and Francis I, he was obliged to produce the usual *pièces de circonstances*, epithalamia, commemoration of battles, and so forth. Dependent on patronage, Clément also contributed much energy to the asking of money and favors (*"l'élégant badinage"* as Boileau phrased it). The quantity of incidental material in Marot's works is phenomenal; it should not be allowed to overshadow his major works, however. They are important if only because they offer a curious variety and a faithful representation of the literary activity in France at the beginning of the sixteenth century.

Son of a Grand Rhétoriqueur, Clément Marot practiced the themes and the technique of his father's generation. His very early poem, the "Temple de Cupido," was inspired by works of Jean Lemaire de Belges and Molinet. His "Petite Epistre au Roy" is a 26-line tour de force in which Marot builds all his rhymes around variations on the word *rime*. The ballade, the rondeau, and the chanson were clearly his favorite forms in the early years. There are 14 ballades plus a chant royal, 67 rondeaux, and 42 chansons to ten épîtres in the *Adolescence clementine*. But Marot also translated Ovid's *Metamorphoses*, Virgil's first eclogue, and a few sonnets of Petrarch. Of the 67 rondeaux Marot wrote in his lifetime, 50 were composed before 1527. For his elegies and épîtres, the proportions are just the reverse. These suggestions of a shift in literary trends away from medieval practices make it essential to determine the poet's intent.

Marot never hid the fact that his knowledge of Latin was meager. In the 1536 prologue to his translation of Ovid (which Marot called *La Métamorphose*), he inserted a telling parenthesis: "*gettay l'oeil sur les liures Latins, dont la grauite des sentences, & le plaisir de la lecture (si peu que ie y comprins) m'ont espris mes espritz.*" Marot is actually revealing more here than the fact that his Latin was poor. He makes clear that Ovid's great poem is as interesting for "*la grauite des sentences*" as for "*le plaisir de la lecture.*" The attitude has more in common with Erasmus' *Adages*, Molinet's *Roman de la Rose moralisé*, or the medieval *Ovide moralisé* than with a desire to restore classical letters to prominence. In the same prologue Marot also justified this translation by noting

> tel list en maint passaige les noms d'Apollo, Daphne Pyramus, & Thisbee, qui à lhystoire aussy loing de lesprit, que les noms pres de la bouche: ce que pas ainsi n'iroit, si en facile vulgaire estoit mise ceste belle Metamorphose: Laquelle aux Poetes vulgaires, & aux paintres seroit tresprofitable.

No revival of antiquity here, just a handbook of fables and *topoi*.

Marot's love poems and his translations of Petrarch demonstrated that in French courtly society a taste for idealized love poetry had not been lost. But neither was the current of *esprit gaulois*. Try as he might to please his audience with the elevated tones of despair and adoration, Marot retained a far simpler view of love, one in which the physical triumphed rapidly over the aesthetic. The ritualistic art of loving became a mere game whose prize was the *dernières faveurs*. In the elegies, often rather prosaic and filled with the worn personifications of the *Roman de la Rose*, Marot's attempt to attain a courtly style is particularly striking. It could be compared to the technical innovations to be found in his rendering of the Psalms. Certain of his new strophic patterns even found their way into the works of the Pléiade! Are these to be considered as new literary breakthroughs? In truth, there is little reason to believe that such efforts were inspired by any curiosity which probed more deeply than Marot's rather superficial and traditional treatment of the *Metamorphoses*. Technical experimentation was a trademark of the Rhétoriqueurs. Efforts to elevate poetic style had roots in the distant and not-so-distant past of the fifteenth century.

Like so many personages of his time, Marot reveals a definite awareness of the classical and Italian influences we associate with Renaissance letters, but this awareness had not overcome the attitudes or the preoccupations of the preceding century. Among Marot's courtly elegies, the most patent example of a Petrarchist theme is that of the erotic dream (Elégie VI). When Marot took on the theme of the golden age,

> Au bon vieulx temps un train d'Amour regnoit,
> Qui sans grand art, et dons se demenoit,
> Si qu'un bouquet donné d'amour profonde,
> C'estoit donné toute la Terre ronde:
> Car seulement au cueur on se prenoit.
>   Et si par cas à jouyr on venoit,
> Sçavez vous bien comme on s'entretenoit?
> Vingt ans, trente ans: cela duroit un Monde
>   Au bon vieulx temps.
>   Or est perdu ce qu'amour ordonnoit,
> Rien que pleurs fainctz, rien que changes on oyt.
> Qui vouldra donc qu'à aymer je me fonde,
> Il fault premier que l'amour on refonde,
> Et qu'on la mene ainsi qu'on la menoit
>   Au bon vieulx temps.

his work is amusing, exaggerated ("*Vingt ans, trente ans: cela duroit un Monde/ Au bon vieulx temps*"). The rondeau's point does not even touch on the sense of nostalgia for an ideal past but is destined to explain why the poet remains hostile to love (vv. 12–13). Antiquity in the poem, like the pretty names in Ovid's *Metamorphoses* and like Italian decoration, is little more than artistic embellishment.

Marguerite de Navarre (1492–1549)

Gustave Lanson once called this remarkable woman "*la plus complète expression de la Renaissance française.*" He was doubtlessly referring to her knowledge of several languages, both classical and modern, to her imitation of Boccaccio in the *Heptaméron*, to her interest in Plato whom she knew through Ficino, and finally, perhaps, to her patronage of Lefèvre d'Etaples, Marot, and other great minds of the day. Lanson's remark is, therefore, not only a compliment to Marguerite, but a definition of the Renaissance, a very Burckhardtian definition. Nevertheless, of the works Marguerite composed in verse, not one reveals a departure from medieval modes or medieval subjects. In 1547 Marguerite gathered together a number of her poems and plays and published them in a collection entitled *Les Marguerites de la Marguerite des princesses.* The volume contained her long work "Le Miroir de l'âme pécheresse," other poems called "Discord . . . de l'Esprit et de la Chair," two *oraisons* ("De l'Ame fidèle" and "A Nostre Seigneur Jésus Christ"), several *chansons spirituelles*, four comedies taken from the Bible ("De la Nativité de Jésus Christ," "De l'Adoration des Trois Roys," "Des Innocents," "Du Desert"), a farce called "De Trop, Prou, Peu, Moins," another comedy, and several more poems including "La Coche," where three women discuss which of them has been made the most unhappy by Love. Clearly this is no place to look for the pagan spirit of the Renaissance.

The collection can boast of no sonnet by Marguerite. Her favorite verse form was the decasyllabic line, not the alexandrine. She showed no interest in alternating masculine and feminine rhymes. Her main source, she willingly acknowledged, was the Bible, and for the "Miroir de l'âme pécheresse," she listed beside each verse inspired by the holy text the biblical book and chapter. For all her knowledge of classical tongues, Marguerite seems even less of an avant garde poet than Marot. "La Coche," with its debate among highborn ladies who eventually go before the king to decide their case, has strong roots in the *amour courtois* tradition, but there are no Petrarchist sonnets and tender elegies to reflect new poetic trends in the courtly vein. Plato, through Ficino, represents the most prominent classical influence. But Marguerite belongs in the line of Gerson and Lefèvre d'Etaples, pious, mystical souls who turned to Plato as a source of religious inspiration. The very titles of Marguerite's poems demonstrate that her studies have scarcely turned her from an intense belief in God. There was a protest spirit in her, as with Lefèvre. Speaking to God in "Le Miroir," she admits

J'ay tous ces biens remis en oubliance;
Souvent vous ay ma promesse rompue,
Car trop estoit ma povre ame repue
De mauvais pain et damnable doctrine.

The Sorbonne knew what it was about in condemning Marguerite's poem. Still, such scorn for the Church seemed only to make her seek with greater insistence the good bread and the divine doctrine to feed her soul. In these poems revolt admitted to no solution outside the realm of established beliefs or institutions. One of Marguerite's long poems in the collection is entitled "L'Histoire des satyres et nymphes de Dyane," a fine classical *topos*, or so one would think. But in a short introduction Marguerite exposed her subject as an example of how "*Ignorance,*"

> *receu du coeur des hommes,*
> *Au plus profond ha engendré grands sommes*
> *D'inventions, moyens, subtilitez,*
> *Deceptions, feintes, habilitez,*

such that desire robs man of peace and rest. We have not left Marguerite's moralizing universe.

The same may be said of her plays. In addition to the biblical dramas included in the *Marguerites*, the Queen of Navarre wrote a series of plays only recently edited as a group by V.-L. Saulnier and entitled "*théâtre profane.*" The title should not lead the reader astray. The plays are *profanes* only in that their subjects are not derived from the Bible. Each work is an allegory. Each illustrates in its way moral and religious truths that Marguerite held dear. "Le Malade," for example, presents a series of individuals whose reaction to the "illness" of the protagonist symbolizes the significant human recourses when a man must face the "illness" of his mortal and imperfect being. The wife advises him to seek out the "*guérisseurs,*" the doctor praises his science, but the chambermaid, cursing her master's preoccupation with his body, tells him that onl⟶ "La foy [le] fera maintenir/ Et sain et joyeulx en tout temps." Similarly, in "L'Inquisiteur" Marguerite opposes the worldly, learned magistrate and a group of little children. The Inquisitor scolds them for playing games when they should be acquiring knowledge. They answer, as the chambermaid might have done, that joy comes from God, not learning. Besides allegory, Marguerite quite evidently enjoyed the debate as a vehicle for expressing her ideas.

She used both in her biblical plays even where her source furnished little or no justification. For the inn scene in the *Comédie de la Nativité*, Marguerite has Joseph and Mary refused by three successive innkeepers who symbolize pride, pleasure, and the absence of charity. After the shepherds have left the babe, Satan appears to tempt them and to challenge them. "*Venez à moy, nous ferons bonne chere,*" says Satan. "*Foy n'a en vous, creance, ne fiance/ Dont mieux me plaist repoz de conscience,*" answers one of the shepherds. "*La poureté point le corps ne nous blesse,/ Car nous sçavons d'ou vient nostre noblesse,*" answers another. The emphasis again is on the favorite Evangelist concepts of faith as a simple joy and love, an inner contentment that needs neither riches nor learning.

These aspects of Marguerite's plays the Queen borrowed from the medieval theatre of her day. The *Roman de la Rose* brought allegory to the theatre as well as to poetry. Scholastic education, so firmly oriented toward the debate as a basic pedagogic device, too, eventually made itself felt in medieval drama of the fifteenth and sixteenth centuries. The *Mystère du Vieil Testament*, written around 1450 and played as late as 1542 by the Confrères de la Passion, follows the fall of Adam and Eve with an interminable debate set in Heaven. The main characters are *Miséricorde* and *Justice*, who argue before God the case of man's first disobedience. As with Marguerite's plays, the debate has a definitely didactic purpose—the discussion explains why man must leave the garden of Eden and why his earthly life cannot be perfect—but the length of the scene also points to an evident interest among contemporaries in the process of argumentation. The appearance of Satan on the stage and the bergerie which closes the *Comédie de la Nativité* are also stock elements in medieval drama dealing with the birth of Christ. Finally, as is the case throughout medieval theatre, Marguerite's works have no acts and do not use the alexandrine but principally decasyllabic or octosyllabic verse and stanzas composed of eight, ten, and sometimes twelve verses.

Marguerite's intimate ties with the medieval theatre are all the more revealing since the early years of the century showed an increased interest in the theatre of antiquity. Erasmus translated Euripides' *Hecuba* and *Iphigenia in Aulis*. George Buchanan, the noted Scottish humanist, translated Euripides' *Medea* and *Alcestis*. These are enterprises that must be examined with all the care and caution demanded by the entire humanist movement. When Erasmus discussed his translations, for example, he spoke only of the arduous effort of converting Greek into Latin and once called his translations "an exercise in Greek," the language he wanted to master in order to study the Bible. When Buchanan wrote his own tragedy *Jephthes sive votum*, he did not hesitate to invent for the basic plot furnished him by the Bible a long scene between Jephthah and the high priest that is simply a debate on vows. This great humanist, too, could not resist the indigenous techniques of the day. Still, *Jephthes*, written between 1539 and 1544 when Buchanan was professor of Greek at Bordeaux, does have a chorus that effectively divides the play into acts. For the portrait of Jephthah, his daughter, and his wife, Buchanan dipped into Euripides and Seneca, whom the humanists knew even better because of the language, state, and availability of his texts.

Naturally, Marguerite was not writing a tragedy. But as Théodore de Bèze will show some years later, it was quite possible to produce a comedy (that is, a play that ends well) with a Satan and simple people using simple language, and still owe a strong debt to Graeco-Roman drama. Marguerite's learning does not seem to have inspired her in the least to effect such a mixture of traditions. Perhaps her Evangelist distrust of learning counterbalanced her "Renaissance" interests. In any case, her verse works make Lanson's dictum appear not only excessive but naïve.

To speculate about the negative influence of Marguerite's religious ideas on her humanism is not an idle pastime. Emile Faguet once insisted that the terms *Renaissance, Humanisme,* and *Réforme* did not mean the same thing and could designate, in the case of *Humanisme* and *Réforme* quite antonymous movements. He defined *Renaissance* as *"la résurrection des idées antiques,"* *Humanisme* as *"le goût de l'art antique,"* and *Réforme* as *"la renaissance du christianisme primitif."* His intention was to explain the very definite antipathy between certain reformers and tendencies within the humanist movement. Pious, simple, overtly moralistic, some reformers had little use for the more earthy side of antiquity. We have already mentioned Lefèvre's reaction to Catullus. With regard to Marguerite, we see that the question had its philosophical and religious overtones as well. Her commitment to a simple faith that detests pride and mistrusts learning led her very early to decry man's "cuyder," that is, his self-confidence. God demands humility, even humiliation, and in her famous "Miroir" Marguerite willingly refers to herself as *"chienne"* and *"ordure."* This is hardly the newly discovered pride that the Renaissance is said to possess. In addition, for such a religious person, this earthly life could not compete seriously with the attraction and deliverance of death. *"Vie m'est mort; car par mort suis vivante./ Vie me rend bien triste et mort contente,"* she says in the "Miroir," sentiments that point up the justness of Faguet's distinctions and demonstrate to what degree a humanist spirit, when accompanied by the moralizing of the Reform, could be subservient to this religious intent. Reading the ancients, tasting the works of Italy might renew one's interest in man and life, but when Marguerite observes, still in the "Miroir,"

> Ame regarde en quel lieu tu t'es mise, (. . .)
> Autour de toy as la terre remplie
> De ton immunde et orde infection,

we need not wonder long if such was their immediate effect on this woman.

François Rabelais (1494?–1553?)

Of all those who wrote major works of literature in France during the reign of Francis I, Rabelais is undisputedly the greatest. He is also both the best known and the least understood, a paradox that renders Rabelais the very symbol of this complicated epoch. His name, given an adjectival status, can be used to portray a brand of humor, a style, even a basic attitude toward life without there arising the slightest possibility of a misunderstanding. Similarly, as everyone knows that "rabelaisian" means "bawdy," "robust," so the ensemble of Rabelais' work signifies the most fundamental traits of the Renaissance sensibility. His energy, his appetite, whether for food, for drink, or for words, depict the dynamism of this new age. His anticlerical bent far outstrips the protests of the Reform and attacks, it has been said, some of the most cherished ideas of the Christian faith. The motto of the Abbaye de Thélème, *"Fay ce que vouldras"* is but one of the many signs in Rabelais' work of his break with tradition, conventions, and authority. A doctor, he dared to practice dissection and, in his pages on education, refused to neglect the exercise of the body in favor of the preparation of the mind. He attacked the jurists and the doctors of the Sorbonne for their ignorance; he displayed throughout his writings a remarkable erudition and love for antiquity.

We know very little about Rabelais' life, but many of the facts we do possess would substantiate this view of Rabelais as a new spirit, a Renaissance spirit. He was born at or near Chinon in the old province of Touraine. His father was a man of some importance, a bourgeois and lawyer. Precisely when Rabelais received his education remains a mystery. He most likely was taught according to the old methods and views. In March, 1521, he was at the Franciscan monastery of Puy-Saint-Martin and in correspondence with the great Hellenist Guillaume Budé. His order did not look favorably on Rabelais' studies and confiscated his Greek books. Though they were later returned, Rabelais had already decided to change orders and moved to the Benedictine abbey at Maillezais to be the secretary of Geoffroy d'Estissac. Between 1527 and 1530 he is lost from sight. His activities appear to have been among the most varied since a decade later the Pope was asked to legitimize two young children sired by Rabelais. In September, 1530, he was in Montpellier and was studying medicine. The following year he proved again that his was an independent mind by commenting Galen from the original Greek text.

By 1532 Rabelais had migrated to Lyons, where he secured a lucrative post as doctor at the Hôtel-Dieu. He published, in the same year, the first volume of his famous novel, entitled *Les Horribles et Espouventables Faictz et Prouesses du tres renommé Pantagruel, roy des Dipsodes.* It was signed Alcofrybas Nasier, the anagram of François Rabelais. The Sorbonne condemned the book within a year. Rabelais also travelled to Rome with the Cardinal Du Bellay, only to return to Lyons in 1534, where he published his second volume, *Gargantua*, today the first volume in all editions of the novel. From this point on, his life becomes increasingly vague. He was absolved by the Pope for having forsaken his monk's habit. In 1542 he published at Lyons an expurgated edition of the *Gargantua* and *Pantagruel*, but the Sorbonne condemned this edition, too. In 1546 the *Tiers Livre* was printed. This time Rabelais used his own name. It was immediately condemned. Rabelais remained in close contact with the Cardinal Du Bellay and perhaps travelled with him again. In 1548 an incomplete edition of the *Quart Livre* appeared at Lyons, probably because of Rabelais' continual lack of money. The complete manuscript was not published until 1552. It, too, was speedily condemned, but through a refusal of the Crown to intervene on the side of the Sorbonne, the book continued to be sold. Of Rabelais' last years, almost nothing is known. In 1562 an episode entitled "L'Isle Sonnante" appeared under the name of Rabelais. The *Cinquième Livre,* including the "Isle Sonnante" passage, was printed two years later. Rabelais was an original and daring thinker. He knew many of the most advanced minds of his day and quarrelled regularly with the most conservative. He never hesitated to be unconventional either in word— even the printed word—or deed.

While the image of a ribald Rabelais lives on, over the years the scholars' view of this writer has changed immensely. He has been brought closer to his period and further and further from the simple portrait of a *carpe diem* pagan. As early as 1924, Etienne Gilson protested against Abel Lefranc's attribution of "unorthodox" and "atheistic" to certain of Rabelais' ideas. Lucien Febvre's monumental *Le Problème de l'incroyance au XVIᵉ siècle: La Religion de Rabelais* demolished the Lefranc thesis once and for all. The same Lefranc once labored many years to prove that the voyage of the *Quart Livre* was inspired by Jacques Cartier's expedition to the New World, and others noted that the volume concerned with Panurge's marriage was published in 1546, only a few years after the outbreak of the *Querelle des Femmes* in 1541–1542. The *Querelle*, whose issues pitted feminists against antifeminists, had a long history dating from the debate at the time of Gerson and Christine de Pisan on the *Roman de la Rose*. The continued interest in a courtly love tradition (as evidenced by some of Marot's works) and the wave of Neoplatonism that accompanied the mysticism of certain French reformers gave new life to the debate. In 1541–1542 two poets, La Borderie and Antoine Héroet in their "L'Amie de la Cour" and "La Parfaite Amie," brought it to a head. La Borderie's poem attacked Platonic love; Héroet staunchly defended it. The *Tiers Livre* was said to be Rabelais' contribution to this quarrel.

Today, these theories, too, have receded into the background as critics recognize a complexity in this work that far outstrips the geography of the Cartier voyage or a debate on the nature of woman. Such a realization has paralleled the increased attempt to capture the meaning of Rabelais' words for his contemporaries. "*Fay ce que vouldras*" sounds very much like "Do what you want," but it could also be translated "Do what you will," a nuance that immediately brings the remark into the realm of a debate on free will—something that learned readers of Rabelais' time were more attuned to than their modern counterparts. Reconstructing the context in which Rabelais wrote is no easy task; yet work by Gilson, Screech, and Krailsheimer proves that we cannot understand Rabelais adequately without expending this effort.

It should not be surprising to one familiar with the problems of France under Francis I to learn that Rabelais' message is closely related to such questions as Evangelism and the Reform movement, faith and free will, and justification by works. To what degree his message brings unity to the novel is a recurrent subject of discussion. The novel came into being over a long period of time. In addition, the content and tone of the volumes tend to vary in such a way as to make one wonder if Rabelais even intended to give the novel anything but the most superficial continuity. Because *Pantagruel* proved so successful, Rabelais added a *Gargantua* to relate the life of Pantagruel's father, much as medieval poets elaborated on the earliest *chansons de geste* by developing the antecedents of the main heroes, such as Charlemagne. These are the books devoted to the giants, their appetites, their wars, and their education. In *Pantagruel* Panurge is introduced and his pleasures and pastimes related in very scabrous and rowdy detail. Already with *Gargantua* certain changes can be noted. Panurge is absent and the bawdy content, seriously reduced. In its place, we find the war with Picrochole (much more developed than the war of the Dipsodes and Amaurotes of the previous volume) and the construction of the Abbaye de Thélème, the "anti-monastère." The *Tiers Livre* discusses Panurge's problem: should he marry or not. His consultation of diverse characters who are to advise him occupies the major portion of the volume and is framed by Panurge's praise of debts and Rabelais' praise of the plant Pantagruélion. The whole book is preceded by an unusually long prologue. The giants qua giants and their remarkable feats are quite forgotten in the *Tiers Livre*. Pantagruel and Gargantua are present but reduced in size and function. The robust humor gives way to consultation of Homer and Virgil, enigmas and learned arguments, the meaning of which continues to be debated. As Panurge is dissatisfied with the advice he receives, Pantagruel decides that they should embark on a trip to the oracle of the Dive Bouteille. Their voyages fill the *Quart Livre* and the *Cinquième Livre*. Form and content, then, would suggest a strong bond between the first two and last two volumes. On the other hand, the preoccupation with Panurge and the announcement of a voyage at the end of the *Tiers Livre* ties this volume to the two which follow. If such overlapping material proves, for some critics, that Rabelais intended his novel to have a definite unity, the text leaves no doubt that throughout the novel Rabelais returned to certain preoccupations of importance to him, even while varying the context and the expression of his ideas as time passed.

In the beginning Rabelais read familiar medieval tales of chivalry and in particular *Les Grandes et Inestimables Croniques du grant et enorme geant Gargantua*, whose material would furnish him with the format of his first two volumes. His evident interest in popular legends (the name of Pantagruel and its meaning seem to come from a little devil mentioned in the *Mystère des Actes des Apôtres*) marks Rabelais as a humanist of the same vein as Marot. However learned Rabelais may have been, he did not write in Latin as did Budé and Erasmus. He certainly knew more than Marot and was more accomplished in his Latin and Greek, but the lure of the popular and the simple was as strong in him as in Clément. They both show (as do Marguerite's plays) that humanism and medieval traditions could coexist very easily at this time. Indeed, much of Rabelais' "Renaissance" enthusiasm and love of words, puns, and enigmas he shared with the Rhétoriqueurs and ultimately with the *soties* of the Middle Ages.

His involvement with the religious and intellectual currents of his day was no less great than his awareness of France's indigenous literary traditions. In his first volume to be printed such an involvement is not immediately clear. Comedy, literary pastiches, good-humored satire, these appear to have been Rabelais' overriding preoccupations.

Sometimes the comedy is manifest as when Pantagruel meets the Limousin who speaks a mixture of French and Latin to show off his learning. At the Library of St. Victor Pantagruel finds a collection of books with hilarious titles. Some are absurd and produce a comic effect by uniting the serious and the pedestrian: *Bragueta juris* (*The Codpiece of the Law*). Others reveal already the signs of Rabelais' involvement with the Reform. When authors' names are given, they often designate notorious enemies of the Reform (Béda, Jacob Hocstraten, Hardorun). The titles attributed to them [*Ars honeste petandi in societate* (*The Gentle Art of Farting in Company*), *De Optimitate triparum* (*Of the Excellence of Tripe*)] belie any bitterness on Rabelais' part. It is 1532; the King is with the reformers. Their opponents are more satirized than attacked. (Béda was known for his inordinate love of tripe.) Caricature of differing forms had a lasting appeal for Rabelais, but his intentions do not always come through as directly as in the description of the Library of St. Victor. Our ability to seize the element of caricature is in direct proportion to our knowledge of the norm from which the author chooses to deviate. We all know that a serious library does not contain works like *Ars honeste petandi in societate*, but unfortunately we are not aware today of all the literary traditions Rabelais and his public knew well.

The very first chapter of *Pantagruel* recounts his hero's origins. The description begins with the creation and passes on to an interminable genealogy of Pantagruel's ancestors. In the original edition, Rabelais explained that he had chosen to write this kind of introduction because such was the practice of all good historiographers, including Saint Luke and Saint Matthew. Abel Lefranc seized upon this chapter as one of the numerous instances in which Rabelais showed his disrespect for religion and its sanctity. A caricature of the Bible, the story of the creation, the genealogy of Christ, what better proof of Rabelais' impiety! At the same time, it should be noted that Rabelais insisted that this is the technique of all good historiographers. And, indeed, medieval specula regularly began their narration of contemporary events with the creation. In opening his book this way, Rabelais adhered to a long (and recognized) tradition. He was taking a *topos* as familiar to his readers as the content of a normal library is to us today. He transformed this *topos* exactly as he transformed the catalogue of the Library St. Victor. It became exaggerated, incredible, in short, comic. There may be something unorthodox (in the eyes of the Sorbonne at least) in his suggestion that the Evangelists were historiographers, and their names did disappear from subsequent editions of *Pantagruel*. However, the suggestion would be in keeping with the ideas of certain reformers who were hardly atheists. There may be a grain of seriousness in this opening chapter, but not the kind seen by Lefranc, who did not want to appreciate to what extent the *topos* employed by Rabelais is not restricted to the Bible and to what extent Rabelais' treatment is funny, very funny.

The notion of an element of seriousness immersed in a quantity of laughter defines rather well the proportions of levity to philosophizing in

Pantagruel. Here Panurge appears in all his mischievous splendor. He is a born raconteur and a fiendishly impish young man. There is the case of Humevesne and Baisecul; there is a war but sprinkled with bawdy stories and a mysterious love note. And yet from time to time, almost imperceptibly, Rabelais changes his style. The amusing stories or words or titles lapse. A new note is sounded.

In the midst of the hilarious episode of the visiting Englishman who comes to debate with Pantagruel, but without uttering any words, Pantagruel accepts the challenge with most solemn sentiments, among them: "*Or demain je ne fauldray me trouver au lieu et heure que me as assigné, mais je te prye que entre nous n'y ait debat ny tumulte et que ne cherchons honeur ny applausement des hommes, mais la verité seule.*" The simple, grave language moves far away from the general comic level of the book. It pinpoints for a second the attitude of the giant toward scholastic debate and reveals Rabelais' giants to be minds of the opposition, hostile to those established ways which the humanists had been criticizing for some time. Gargantua's famous letter to his son would seem to belong to just such a revolt of the humanists. Here the father contrasts the dark and ignorant age of his own education with the progress reaped by the humanists. This letter has been called a satire of the humanists' paean of their own advances. Perhaps. Perhaps, too, Gargantua's desire to see his son as "*un abysme de science*" is an impossible, gigantic wish. But, then, we are dealing with giants. Whether this chapter represents a serious outpouring of Rabelais' exuberance for learning or a hearty (but not destructive) laugh at the expense of the over-enthusiastic, it still documents the period's awareness that changes were occurring and situates the giants on the side of innovation.

The giants are enlightened men. They dislike artifice (the Limousin); they dislike unnatural constraints. (When Pantagruel breaks his chains and smashes his cradle, Gargantua imposes no punishment on his son.) They seem pleasure-loving but are ready to defend their principles (the war with the Amaurotes). They seek truth in their learning and seek learning only in its most vibrant form, but they know that the ultimate truth lies with God: "*Aye suspectz les abus du monde; ne metz ton cueur à vanité, car ceste vie est transitoire, mais la parolle de Dieu demeure eternellement.*" These words are among the last that Gargantua addresses to his son in his letter, which, without heaping upon this life the scorn that we find in Marguerite's poetry, still leaves no doubt about its ultimate value.

With such a view Rabelais again established a bond with his own society. It is so easy to be impressed by the drinking, the swearing, the satire, and the stories, to contrast this lust for life and humor with

Marguerite's "*Vie me rend bien triste*," and to conclude that Rabelais has lost that intense religiosity which characterizes much of the French Reform movement. Lucien Febvre has asked in all seriousness to what degree it was possible at this time for one to cast off religion. We are not at a point in history when church and state are firmly separated. The religious bent of contemporary education was unavoidable, and Rabelais was specifically prepared for holy orders. As we have seen, the important questions of the day related to basic religious issues. These questions conspired to give intellectuals a greater insight into their faith and to promote the examination of it in the light of criticism, which, it should be remembered, revolved around different ways of believing, not belief and a refusal to believe.

Before a battle with Loup Garou, Pantagruel prays. He makes a promise to God:

> *S'il te plaist à ceste heure me estre en ayde, comme en toy seule est ma totale confiance et espoir, je te fais veu que par toutes contrées tant de ce pays de Utopie que d'ailleurs, ou je auray puissance et auctorité, je feray prescher ton sainct Evangile purement, simplement et entiere-ment, si que les abus d'un tas de papelars et faulx prophetes . . . seront d'entour moy exterminez.*

The reader immediately recognizes in this promise the reformer's bias for a study of the Bible that bypasses the scholastic subtleties and ignorance. What surprises is this religious commitment by one of the giants. It is, however, but another example of their concern with truth and learning and of the serious dimension that lurks behind Rabelais' good fun.

Pantagruel has no sooner made his promise than a voice from Heaven says, "*Hoc fac et vinces*" (Do this and you will conquer). The phrase recalls the sign that appeared to Constantine, "*In hoc signo vinces*," but a new interpretation has been advanced by M. A. Screech, according to which Rabelais is referring to a phrase from St. Luke, "*Hoc fac et vives*" (Do this and you shall live). A lawyer has asked what he must do to achieve eternal life. "What is written in the Law?" responds Christ. When the lawyer says, "Thou shalt love the Lord thy God with all thy heart, and with all thy soul, and with all thy strength, and with all thy mind; and thy neighbor as thyself," Christ speaks the sentence quoted above. The resemblance between Christ's words and those of the heavenly voice cannot be denied. The biblical passage in question had great import in Rabelais' day. The Protestants had attacked the efficacy of good works and insisted that salvation depended on faith alone, as St. Paul suggests (Galatians ii 16). Catholics, wishing to fight fire with fire, seized upon this passage from St. Luke to show that Christ specifically said that by deeds one could contribute toward achieving eternal life. As is so often the case in Rabelais, the author's exact intent in the passage of Pantagruel's prayer can always be debated. That the giant promises to do something and is granted his wish intimates, nevertheless, that Rabelais did not agree with Luther on a cardinal point.

Faith, action, education, reform, all these aspects of *Pantagruel* reappear in *Gargantua*. The prologue that accompanies the new volume begins "*Beuveurs tres illustres*." The perspective does not seem to have changed since *Pantagruel*, and yet with *Gargantua* the explosive laughter of the earlier book recedes as had the aspirations of many reformers by 1534. Although *Gargantua* predates the famous *Affaire des Placards*, the duplicity of Francis I's politics had already taken its toll. The same year that the king forced the Sorbonne to revoke its condemnation of Marguerite's "Miroir" (1533), he sent commissioners into the duchy of Alençon to inform on the heretics. Rabelais' reaction was both cathartic laughter and determined self-justification. The pivotal chapters of *Gargantua* reaffirm the humanist's stand against the antiquated and emptyheaded approach to knowledge practiced by the Sorbonne, the Evangelical love of peace and good will, the French reformer's continued hesitancy to accept all of Luther, and finally, Rabelais' general praise of good sense, a healthy body, a simple, efficacious religion, and a cultured, critical mind.

The prologue to *Gargantua* reflects the degree to which Rabelais' attention is more than ever divided between the serious and the entertaining qualities of his book. Through a series of images including that of a bone, eyed by a dog and finally cracked open for its delicious marrow, Rabelais insinuates that the volume is deceptive in appearance. Light and empty on the surface, it may well contain, like the bone, a "*sustantificque mouelle*." At the same time Rabelais laughs at his own suggestion, saying that when he wrote the book, he gave it no more time that it took to eat and drink. The author concludes on a familiar note, "*Or esbaudissez vous, mes amours*," but not before having planted in our minds the thought that this may be a richer work than it (and its author?) suggest. Typical of the problems facing us in Rabelais, the sincerity of this about-face in the prologue can probably never be satisfactorily "proven" or "disproven." The veracity of Rabelais' insinuations lies in the chapters of *Gargantua*, where, in fact, Rabelais has placed considerable "*sustantificque mouelle*."

Education, war, and free will are the precise subjects around which Rabelais grouped his observations. The first is treated in great detail, as the reader witnesses Gargantua's training now at the hands of the "*sophistes*" and then under the tutelage of the enlightened Ponocrates. In the former case, Rabelais insisted again on the hopelessness of a scholastic education. Gargantua studies outmoded and incorrect grammars, learns to prove absurdities and to memorize so well that he can recite a text backward. His religious schooling shows the same traits of excessive and exterior participation. He hears 26 or 30 masses and possesses a breviary that weighs (counting the filth encrusted on it) over 1,000 pounds. Ponocrates, in consultation with a doctor, establishes a new regime whereby Gargantua loses not an hour a day but spends all his time in activity healthful to mind, body, and soul. He exercises, eats with moderation, reads the Scriptures "*hautement et clerement, avec pronunciation competente à la matière,*" and frequents learned men. Memorization and recitation are important but, too, must be practiced "*clerement et eloquentement.*" The program does not seek to devise new methods but to use the old ones more judiciously and effectively. In substituting the reading of the Bible for the 30 masses, Rabelais made patent his continued Evangelical bent.

Pantagruel offers the spectacle of the war of the Dipsodes and the Amaurotes. *Gargantua* contains a war between Gargantua's father and Picrochole. Rabelais hated war. If he came back to the subject a number of times in his novel, it was to emphasize this sentiment and to contrast the psychology of war with the blessings of peace. War appears in *Gargantua* as an irrational and stupid act. When the honest citizens of Gargantua's land are attacked and ask the meaning for this war, the invaders can answer nothing more "*sinon qu'ilz leurs vouloient aprendre à manger de la fouace.*" War interferes with pursuits of much greater importance. Grangousier regretfully must recall his son from Paris and interrupt his studies to bring him to the aid of those people who are his subjects, "*car, ainsi comme debiles sont les armes au dehors si le conseil n'est en la maison, aussi vaine et l'estude et le conseil inutile qui en temps oportun par vertus n'est executé et à son effect reduict.*"

This belief that knowledge is useless if it cannot be called into action when needed returns the reader to Rabelais' accent on an active faith and indicates to what point war was an ethical rather than a political question for Rabelais in the early books. Picrochole's uprising ultimately pits the enlightened giants, who, when victorious, will treat the vanquished with love and charity against an evil man "*delaissé de Dieu.*" Good triumphs over evil, and Grangousier reacts toward the men of Picrochole with the understanding all fathers and kings show in Rabelais' novel toward their sons and subjects in imitation of God the Father's love for his creatures.

The closing chapters of *Gargantua* constitute some of the most elusive

Rabelais ever wrote. The Abbaye de Thélème episode has been interpreted as a bad joke, an ideal, a statement on free will, a spot consecrated to atheism! What is certain, because Rabelais tells us this himself, is that his abbey is "*au contraire de toutes aultres.*" It contains both men and women, no bells, no vows. It serves to protest against those demands of religious authority that Rabelais' own life proved he could not meet. Thélème suggests, in addition, that one should not have to comply with such regulations in order to lead an exemplary life. "*Toute leur vie estoit employée non par loix, statuz ou reigles, mais selon leur vouloir et franc arbitre,*" says Rabelais of the inhabitants of Thélème. Their only rule was "*FAY CE QUE VOULDRAS, parce que gens liberes, bien nez, bien instruictz, conversans en compaignies honnestes, ont par nature un instinct et aguillon, qui tousjours les poulse à faictz vertueux . . .*"

Such remarks have contributed much to the image of a "Renaissance" Rabelais. He has expressed, in the context of an anti-monastery, faith in man's innate goodness and in his ability to direct his own actions. But before we assume too much, it is important to note that each room in the abbey possesses a chapel and that the capacity for self-discipline is directly linked to a group of people "*bien nez, bien instruict.*" Religion has not disappeared, even if the usual monastic rules have. Thélème, moreover, is only for the few, the pure, the educated, the devout (see *Gargantua*, LIV). It has a distinct utopian air that is reinforced by the verb tenses Rabelais uses to speak of the abbey. Within chapter LII, where Gargantua announces that the abbey will be, the description already falls into the past tense, and the remaining chapters speak of it as having existed. Ideal and ephemeral, Thélème does touch on free will, however, and affirms its existence. Rabelais' position here foreshadows his opposition to the concept of predestination. Once again Rabelais shows that all opponents of the Sorbonne were not Protestants. More important, Thélème and *Gargantua* as a whole testify to the intimate bonds between Rabelais' novel and problems of the day, problems to which Rabelais offered basically Evangelical, even orthodox Catholic responses.

If Thélème is an obscure episode, the entire *Tiers Livre* can be termed even more obscure and difficult to interpret. Published many years after the first two volumes, the *Tiers Livre* exists in content no less than in time at a marked distance from *Pantagruel* and *Gargantua*. Entire passages, such as Panurge's praise of debts, the consultation of Hippothadée, Rondibilis, and Trouillogan, and the description of the Pantagruélion, remain to this day so hotly debated that they by rights cannot be discussed in brief if one wishes to do justice to the text. The book relates a quest. Panurge desires to know whether he should marry or not and if he should, whether he will be deceived by his wife. Pantagruel's attitude toward his friend's problem is expressed very simply: "*N'estez vous asceuré de vostre vouloir? Le poinct principal y gist: tout le reste est fortuit, et dependent des fatales dispositions du ciel.*" Panurge does not act as Pantagruel suggests, however. Since we lost sight of Panurge, he has become a bit of a philosopher, fond of disputes and rhetoric. When he and Pantagruel have recourse to diverse means of divination, Panurge systematically refutes Pantagruel's interpretation and recasts it to his pleasure.

From the beginning to the end of his novel, Rabelais speaks of God as all-powerful. Man must accept what his Creator has prepared for him—exactly what Pantagruel has told Panurge. Later in the volume when, in the presence of Gargantua, Panurge is listening to Trouillogan, a skeptic who refuses to make any firm commitment, the old King leaves, disgusted by what he has heard. These facts would suggest that Rabelais disapproved of Panurge's refusal to decide, which, in turn, causes the long series of consultations. However man's role is reduced in the determination of his destiny, he still possesses his will, and the abdication of one's responsibility to act is a failure to assume the role that God has assigned to him. Within such a framework of ideas, Panurge comes off very poorly, and yet he has his defense. What, indeed, is so complex about the *Tiers Livre* is Rabelais' elegant and extended program of consultations, not to mention the decision to make a voyage to the Dive Bouteille, the subject of the *Quart Livre*. So much just to censure Panurge? And does not Gargantua's disgust seem to apply to the equivocating of Trouillogan rather than to Panurge's questions?

It has been suggested that Panurge's refusal to accept what he hears or reads derives from a positive need to know, but as no one gives him a full and satisfactory answer based on experience, not professional jargon, Panurge decides to embark on a personal voyage of discovery. The two points of view are not necessarily incompatible. Even though Rabelais probably disapproved of Panurge's irresponsible attitude, he was quite capable of recognizing that this attitude could also be used to criticize authority. We must always be open to such complexities in Rabelais' work.

The question of will, the search for answers, these ultimately are old themes in Rabelais. Other ties bind the *Tiers Livre* to its predecessors, and one that has particular historical as well as literary interest is Rabelais' reaction to religious intolerance of the day. The last chapter of *Gargantua* contains a poem, an enigma whose final lines are singularly clear: "*Tel feut l'accord. O qu'est à reverer/ Cil qui en fin pourra perseverer!*" By 1546 religious persecution had reached new heights of barbarism. There are strong echoes of this mood in the *Tiers Livre*. Not only is the book dense to the point of being problematic (as if Rabelais genuinely feared to express himself except in a veiled language), but the tone is far from gay. The main characters have lost their heartiness. Pantagruel, though understanding, seems repeatedly at odds with Panurge. Gargantua's only appearance ends on a note of despair. In the same chapter Pantagruel announces that Bridoye, a famous judge, is in need of help. "*Je luy veulx de tout mon povoir estre aidant en aequité,*" says Pantagruel. "*Je sçay huy tant estre la malignité du monde aggravée que bon droict a besoing d'aide.*" Not a happy thought but one that must have often crossed the mind of François Rabelais, lover of peace and truth in a warring and ignorant society.

Maurice Scève (1501?–1560?)

In the twentieth century, when Paris remains the cultural center it has been in France for so many years, we may find it difficult to understand why an intellectual like Rabelais should have published in Lyons and chosen to work there at the Hôtel-Dieu. In truth, during the first third of the sixteenth century, Lyons was the richest and most brilliant city in France.

Behind Lyons' ascendancy lay both positive and negative facts. Lyons did not possess a Sorbonne and a Parlement, those conservative forces that made life so difficult for the humanists and reformers in Paris. In addition, Lyons' geographical position at the confluence of the Rhone and the Saone rivers and at the threshold to Italy made the city's commerce prosper until its merchant class attained great wealth. This position and wealth brought German and Italian printers to Lyons to cater to the needs and tastes of the bourgeoisie as well as the nobility. In the very earliest years of the century, the printers' successes (Wadsworth records as the best seller, *Auctores morales octo*) reflected the same continuity of prior religious and literary trends as one might note in Paris at the same moment. With the advent of the Italian Wars, the cultural climate received new stimuli. The French court came more and more to Lyons, giving rise to sumptuous entrées replete with poems, dancing, and so forth. The Italian population, already large in the printing and banking world of Lyons, grew with the arrival of exiles and others interested by France's designs on the peninsula. The Italians brought with them the cult of Petrarch, Ficino, and his commentaries on Plato which soon became the rage at Lyons.

In 1532 two translations in French of Boccaccio's *Fiammetta* appeared from the city's presses. Three years later, one of the same printers published *La Déplourable Fin de Flamecte*, an adaptation by Maurice Scève of Juan de Flores' *Breve tractado de Grimalte y Gradissa*. Only somewhat earlier (1533), this man had announced the discovery of the tomb of Petrarch's Laura! Nothing permits us to believe that Scève was right in his identification, but his "discovery" as well as his retitling of Flores' work notes the vogue of Italian literature and Scève's intimate connection with that vogue.

By the 1540s France was too far from a definitive victory in Italy to maintain a purely Italian policy. Francis I had long been negotiating with the German Protestants; Geneva and Calvin had entered the scene of European politics. All these phenomena hurt Lyons' position in the kingdom. The financial ruin that would sweep France under Henry II meant the end of many a Lyons bank. By the end of the Italian Wars (1559), Paris had replaced Lyons as the center of French intellectual life. Lyons ceded her position graciously, but not before her moment of glory had proved decisive in the propagation of Petrarchist and Neoplatonic literature or her Ecole de Lyon and especially Maurice Scève had formed the decisive link between Marot and the Pléiade.

The traditional term "Ecole de Lyon" is rather misleading. Louise Labé, Pernette du Guillet, Pontus de Tyard, Olivier de Magny, and Maurice Scève did not constitute a literary school. They knew and influenced one another. All wrote in the vernacular and prized Italian literature, but their association remained too casual to be given the term *école* that suggests a codification of principles with which each member complied. Moreover, serious divergence can be found among these poets as to form and philosophy. Pontus' works bear the imprint of Ficino more than any of the others. Scève's love verse was highly influenced by Petrarch, whereas Louise Labé wrote in a rather passionate vein. Louise used the sonnet form; Scève's great collection of love verse contains no sonnets, 449 dizains, and one huitain. Despite his adherence to the older forms (Scève's work includes only nine sonnets), this poet emerges from the Lyons group as its most remarkable writer.

He was not a prolific artist. In 1544 Scève published his great collection of love poems, entitled *Délie, object de plus haute vertu;* in 1547, the *Saulsaye, eglogue de la vie solitaire.* His only other important work is his *Microcosme,* published in 1562. The sharp decline in production and publication after 1548 testifies to the shift of interest and patronage to Paris and to the young set of the Pléiade. But in 1544, when Scève printed his *Délie,* Marot was destined to write no more, and the Pléiade had still published nothing. Scève did not fare well with the Pléiade, who set the tone for future centuries by stating in the *Deffence* that he had "*tumbé en obscurité.*" Their criticism is, at best, proof that they read his poetry; at worst, an indication of their youthful pride and desire to break with everything, even their masters.

In the main Maurice Scève is less obscure than difficult, but it is hard to reverse certain trends of thinking once they gain momentum. At the turn of the twentieth century, even the most reputable professors treated Scève as important (he was a link between Italian culture and the Pléiade), but obscure (incomprehensible and not worth reading). The first critical edition of the *Délie* (1916) reflected this mentality. Its editor, Eugène Parturier, endeavored to indicate for Scève's dizains as much source material as possible. The notes abound in references to Petrarch, Bembo, Sasso, Serafino, the same Italian poets who appear later among the early sources of Du Bellay and Ronsard. Parturier alluded to Scève's obscurity but had no intention of combatting the notion. He recognizes that this aspect of the *Délie* could be attributed to a long tradition present in works of both the Middle Ages and the Italian Renaissance and even added weight to the probability by citing the mystical formula $5 + (3^2 \times 7^2) + 3$ that Brunetière worked out to describe the arrangement of the poems with regard to the emblems inserted into the collection.[3]

The first important voice to react to this concept of Scève belonged to Valery Larbaud. In 1925 he wrote a short appreciation of Scève called *Notes sur Maurice Scève.* Valery Larbaud insisted that Scève's obscurity was exaggerated. A knowledge of the language and syntax of the period could unlock many a poem. Scève was hermetic rather than obscure, one of those superior artists "*qui nous font participer à cette existence d'une espèce surhumaine.*"

The concept of a hermetic Scève has lasted many years, but in the 1960s a general reevaluation of Scève took place, proving that the poet is neither particularly obscure nor hermetic but artistically original, even to the point of using Italian models more freely than Parturier's notes could ever suggest. Although Délie can be taken as the anagram of *l'idée* (the Platonic idea?), this is not a Neoplatonic work of the same inspiration as Pontus de Tyard's *Discours philosophiques.* While Scève introduced 50 emblems (pictures of various objects or people

---

[3] The arrangement of emblems and dizains is such that five dizains precede the first emblem, three follow the last. The emblems intervene, therefore, only with respect to the remaining 441 (9 x 49) dizains.

surrounded by a motto and an ornate border) into his collection and used most of the mottoes in the following dizain, *Délie* is not an emblem book, where picture and poetry are interdependent. The influence of Petrarch may be great, but Scève was capable of entwining his own themes about the traditional ones and of giving new depth to trite Petrarchist commonplaces. He is a master of his dizain form; his imagery shows that much attention has been given to the presentation and elaboration of certain themes. Since Scève used decasyllabic verse in his dizains, he was rather restricted in the amount of development his poem might have—more so than if he were writing a sonnet. The result: his poetry is extremely condensed, certainly a major source of Scève's "obscurity." Was he forced into such compression by the form he was using, or did he have a penchant for it? The latter possibility seems the more likely. Several of the dizains in *Délie* do not show any particular complexity. The most successful, however, make concerted use of images that are highly suggestive and placed within the dizain to maximize that suggestiveness. Scève also uses a very personal vocabulary and syntax such as adverbs in "-ment" and ablative absolutes that telescope his thought and reveal along with his imagery a decided interest in the evocative, as contrasted with the explanatory.

Such a tendency appears most vividly in the choice of the name Délie for the beloved. To think of it only as the anagram of *l'idée* betrays all the richness that Scève quite explicitly lavished upon this name. Délie is a name linked to Diana, thus to chastity and the moon. The former theme brings into play the traditional haughtiness of the Petrarchist lady, the second, the themes of absence and presence (as the moon waxes and wanes), light and darkness, which in turn evoke life and death. This final association is reinforced by Diana's further link with Hecate and through her to the underworld. Thus in dizain 22

> Comme Hecaté tu me feras errer
> Et vif, et mort cent ans parmy les Umbres:
> Comme Diane au Ciel me resserrer,
> D'où descendis en ces mortelz encombres:
> Comme regnante aux infernalles umbres
> Amoindriras, ou accroistras mes peines,
>   Mais comme Lune infuse dans mes veines
> Celle tu fus, es, et seras DELIE,
> Qu'Amour a joinct à mes pensées vaines
> Si fort, que Mort jamais ne l'en deslie.

Scève groups for one moment many of the principal ideas of his collection. Délie as Hecate symbolizes the love experience as darkness and suffering. As Diana, Olympian deity, she may raise him to the sky, but it is as an evocation of the moon that she defines her essence, which love has joined to his thoughts forever. Note how unspecific is the allusion to the moon. Only from its suggestive powers and the elaboration that this image receives in other dizains can Scève's precise meaning be derived. Even more important, while suffering and exaltation are stereotyped emotions in the Petrarchist context, Scève has both maintained and enhanced the tradition he chose to practice.

Here is yet another dizain, a poem of complaint,

> De ces haultz Montz jettant sur toy ma veue,
> Je voy les Cieulx avec moy larmoier:
> Des Bois umbreux je sens à l'impourveue,
> Comme les Bledz ma pensée undoier.
>   En tel espoir me fait ores ploier,
> Duquel bien tost elle seule me prive.
> Car, à tout bruyt croyant que lon arrive,
> J'apperçoy cler, que promesses me fuyent.
>   O fol desir, qui veult, par raison vive,
> Que foy habite, où les Ventz legers bruyent!

Hardly one of Scève's difficult poems, dizain 122 does reveal many of his technical subtleties and can serve as an excellent introduction to an analysis of the poems in the Délie.

The poem exposes a common theme of Petrarchist love poetry—disappointed and unfounded hope. Scève opens on a note of pathetic fallacy. From the heights where he looks down on Délie, he sees the sky weeping with him, and the rippling grain offers a perfect image of his thoughts as they waver. Now he hopes, now he sees too well that his desires seek the impossible. For an appreciation of the richness of the dizain it suffices to note how much more the poem is calculated to say than this summary would suggest. The positions of the poet ("haultz Montz" and "Bois umbreux") both accentuate his solitude and separation from Délie, whom Scève nonetheless succeeds in including with the simple (and concise) phrase "sur toy." Line 4 speaks of an "espoir" that is never defined. Yet the solitude, the weeping ("larmoier"), and the vacillating thoughts in this context of a love cycle have provided sufficient indications of the lover's unhappiness to give "espoir" a tacit meaning. The merely implicit ties between lines 1–4 and what follows is typical of the Délie. Prevented by his form from extensive detail, Scève sketches only the most pregnant elements. It is for the reader to provide the rest.

The poem's second phase (vv. 5–8), linked to the exposition by contrast of states (solitude, unhappiness, and hope), lingers over the fleeting qualities of rumors and promises (*"fuyent,"* *"bruyt"*) and therefore develops the movement already contained in *"undoier"* and accentuated by the adverbial phrase *"à l'impourveue"* ("without warning"). Similarly, in the final lines, while *"fol desir"* continues the realization contained in the poem's middle portion, Scève chose to close with yet another image. To desire that promises be true is to wish that *"foy habite, où les Ventz legers bruyent."* The image gently returns the reader to the mountains and the woods of the exposition. The world of the poem has come full circle, without, if one considers the constant accent on fluidity from verse 3's *"à l'impourveue"* through *"undoier,"* *"fuyent"* to *"bruyent"* in line 10, ever deviating from its central theme. If not especially dense, the poem does exhibit Scève's mastery of the dizain. The development is tight, yet not constrained; the vocabulary rich, yet exact. No aspect of the poem seems fortuitous or excessive. Finally, artistically excellent, the poem is also emotionally deep and penetrating. Throughout we are within the mind of the poet—his regrets, his hopes, his awareness—but in the three images of the sky, the grain, and the winds exterior and interior worlds come together. The movements and truths known to the mind of the lover have their counterparts, which accentuate the inner drama of love in a derisive (the winds) or sympathetic (the sky) form. The love theme thus gains in perspective. While the poem does not deviate from an analysis of the lover's thoughts, these thoughts mingle with the reality we all know. The lover's dilemma, seen swiftly in the form of natural phenomena, becomes immediate, comprehensible, moving. Scève could hardly have wished for more.

Petrarch, Italy, art, style, lyricism, these are the salient aspects of Scève's finest verse. All Scève is not affected by these factors. He was capable of trite verse and word games as much as Marot and the Rhétoriqueurs who influenced them both. Yet he could do so much more with poetry, and that added consciousness, that special sense of form and art which Scève possessed was ultimately his precious gift to the Pléiade.

3

𝕳enrp 𝕴𝕴

(1547-1559)

THE MAJOR EVENTS

Violence is a thread that runs throughout the reign of Henry II. This fact can be explained, in part, by difficulties and tensions that the King inherited from his father. On the other hand, with the passage of time, new problems took form, and old ones acquired an urgency that announced the Religious Wars. Behind the public violence of wars and persecution lay a more private variety, fanned by Henry's strong emotions. Love for Diane de Poitiers, hatred for Charles V, whose hostage he had been after the release of Francis I, resentment toward his own father, who had favored his eldest and youngest sons but never Henry were the most conspicuous of these private passions.

It was his sentiment toward Francis I that explains the violent turn of events with which Henry's rule opened. Francis I, on his death bed, hoped to obtain lasting promises from his successor with regard to the government then in power but in vain. The King dead, his mistress, the Duchess of Etampes, was banished; the Cardinal of Tournon lost his post as chancellor of the Order of St. Michael, a title that passed to a Guise, the Duke of Lorraine. Olivier was deprived of the royal seals; the finance minister fled. A friend of the Duchess was arrested, and her bitter enemy Montmorency returned triumphant from the exile to which she had sent him while Francis I was still alive. This gesture of revenge had been long nurtured by Francis' second son. When the Dauphin, also named Francis, died in 1536, the King immediately showered his youngest boy, Charles d'Orléans, with favor. Charles was also wooed by the Emperor and the Cardinal of Ferrara, whose negotiations with Francis I produced the treaty of Crépy (1544). Charles was to marry either a daughter of the Emperor who would give as a dowry

68

the Low Countries and the Franche-Comté or a daughter of the Emperor's brother, in which case Milan was to be his wife's dowry. From his father he was to be granted sovereignty over the duchies of Angoulême, Bourbon, Orléans, and Châtellerault. The Emperor's plan to split the royal brothers worked splendidly. Henry recognized at once the threat to his rights and publicly denounced the treaty. Fortunately for Henry, his brother died of the plague in 1545. However, these few facts show how precarious his position was prior to Francis' death and how justified were his recriminations against the previous reign.

His hatred for Charles V, likewise, found expression almost immediately. Choosing to forget that by the treaty of Cambray his father had renounced all suzerainty over Flanders (a fact that had made Charles V technically a vassal of the King of France), Henry II summoned Charles V to his coronation. The Emperor said that he would come, but at the head of an army of 50,000 men. Clearly France and the Empire were not to remain at peace for long. It was Henry's happy fate that the struggle would take place not only in Italy but in areas around France where conquest could mean territorial acquisition. It was his misfortune to find France involved in affairs not directly related to his quarrels with Charles V.

Before hostilities with the Emperor had come to a head, Scotland sought aid from Henry against England. As the English still held Calais and Boulogne, they were a thorn in Henry's side, but an entente could have come to pass had the proposed marriage between Edward VI of England and Mary Queen of Scots, a Frenchwoman, been effected. The Queen Mother of Scotland, Mary of Lorraine, a sister of the Guises, seeing that England hoped to unite Scotland and England, not only sought aid from Henry II but proposed that her daughter become the wife of the French Dauphin, not the King of England. The Guises had their way. A conflict ensued that brought no one great victories. Henry laid seige to Boulogne, which he was ceded to bring the "war" to a close (1550).

Charles V did not take sides in the skirmish between England and France in the hope—so well realized—that it would keep his enemies preoccupied while he attended to domestic problems. Of these he had many but principally the rebellious nature of the German nobles and the religious question posed by the Lutherans. The first he seemed on the verge of settling once and for all. The second, left hanging because Protestants and Catholics still could not agree on the place and nature of the Council that was supposed to end their differences, Charles tried to alleviate with the Interim of Augsburg (May, 1548). Drawing upon both Catholic and Protestant tenets, the document presented a temporary declaration of faith which was to remain in effect until the Council had done its work. It in fact infuriated both Protestants and Catholics in Germany who saw Charles's power to dictate to them growing by leaps and bounds. William, Count of Nassau, rushed to Fontainebleau to lay before Henry II the grievances of the German princes. He also suggested that Henry might occupy certain Free Towns of the Empire that were close to the French border and on which Charles V had evident designs. The idea appealed to the French King, to the Guises, but not to Montmorency. Again the Guises had their way.

Once free of the English question, Henry II entered into serious negotiations with Maurice of Saxony and some Lutheran princes. In 1552 a treaty was signed at Chambord. Henry promised aid to the reformed princes in return for the Free Towns of Metz, Toul, and Verdun. The treaty was signed in January. By February he was ready to set forth. Such haste betrayed his true intent: to push far beyond the three Free Towns and to hold, not protect, these areas. Indeed, when Metz, Toul, and Verdun had been reached and occupied, Henry II's march did not stop. His persistence alarmed all Germans, including his allies, and after Strasbourg refused to welcome the French, Henry II was obliged to fall back to Verdun.

Charles placated his German nobles, who were growing more hostile to Henry, by granting certain of their demands, including a revocation of the Interim of Augsburg. Eighty thousand Imperial troops marched upon Metz in September to besiege it and free the town of the French. François de Guise prepared a heroic and successful defense. As winter approached, disease ravaged the Imperial army to such an extent that Charles V raised the siege and retreated. When Guise ventured forth from the fortifications, he found dead and dying men by the thousands. He told his sovereign that Charles V took away with him only twelve thousand men of his original army—an exaggeration no doubt, but Metz did end Charles's campaign in these regions. Henry II kept the Free Towns. Guise won a reputation which a number of defeats that Montmorency was about to suffer only enhanced.

Between the retreat from Metz (December, 1552) and the abdication of Charles V (October, 1555), two events of note took place. Charles married his son Philip to Mary Tudor, who was now Queen of England after the death of Edward VI, and managed the Peace of Augsburg, which granted freedom of worship to the Lutheran princes. England was now the ally of the Empire; the religious question had been solved, however unsatisfactorily. Charles had put his house in order, and ill, tired, haggard, he divided his possessions between his brother Ferdinand (who received the Crown of Holy Roman Emperor) and his son Philip (who received Spain, Milan, Naples, and the Netherlands). "Fortune is a woman," said Charles V, "she does not like old men." He went to a monastery in Spain and died within two years. His is a sad story. He owned so much, wielded so much authority, and yet found himself so often checked that he could never destroy his French enemy nor keep peace at home. The problem was largely one of tactics (something Charles V may well have come to understand). His aims were fully out of line with the temper of his subjects. He could act only after subjugating the diverse groups in his kingdom and subordinating their interests to his own. He could never favor (as Francis I did) the independent designs of the Italians, the Germans, and the Lutherans. He was fighting a losing battle.

The abdication brought overt joy to France. Henry II, lacking the funds to continue hostilities, concluded the Truce of Vaucelles (February, 1556) that was to preserve peace for five years. It lasted less than one. Before 1556 had ended, François de Guise was leading an army into Italy. This new attempt at a conquest of Italy made even less sense than preceding ones. The acquisition of Boulogne and the Free Towns required administrative action and consolidation within the kingdom. Montmorency saw all this, but the Guises wanted war.

For reasons as numerous as the Italian exiles—the fuorusciti—who flocked to France, as numerous as the livres owed by the kings of France to Italian bankers who had financed the folly begun in 1494, Henry II was tied to Italy. He had an Italian wife. The court welcomed in droves such adventurers as Pietro Strozzi, adored by Catherine de Medici. Henry II married his illegitimate daughter Diane to a Farnese. Anne d'Este, herself the granddaughter of a king of France, was married to a Guise. Virtually all these groups wanted war: the Strozzi and the Guises to gain honor and power, the fuorusciti, to recapture their lost position in Italy, the bankers, to recoup the fortunes already loaned. The voice of moderation was hard to hear over so great a tumult. After all, the Emperor was still a power in Italy and had to be dealt with there, too. As a result, during the years of Henry's reign we find France posing as the "protector" now of the Farnese, now of the Siennese in order to upset the balance of power. Against such a background of commitment, passion, even tradition, Henry II's acts are more understandable, if still ill-advised.

Once in Italy, the Duke of Guise did not cover himself with glory. His destination was the Kingdom of Naples—that old chimera to which both the Guises and Henry II could lay claim by virtue of their Angevine ancestors. However, the Pope, fearing Spanish retaliation for the French move, detained the Duke in Rome a full month. When Guise finally reached the Kingdom of Naples, he progressed little and fought only defensive skirmishes. Suddenly he was recalled to France. The King had suffered a stinging defeat; France was in panic.

Philip II had proven Henry's match. The march on Naples was not only a breach of the Truce of Vaucelles, it was also an attack on Spanish territory. Philip secured aid from his English wife and moved rapidly. His army, commanded by the brilliant general Emmanuel-Philibert of Savoy, whose country remained in French control, invaded France from the Low Countries. He attacked the village of Saint-Quentin, defended by Coligny. Montmorency arrived to help his nephew, and the two armies engaged in a battle that proved as disastrous for the French as Pavia. Thousands died, and the principal personages, including Montmorency, were taken prisoner. Why Emmanuel-Philibert did not follow up this victory with the sack of Paris can only be explained by his lack of money and food for his troops. In addition, Coligny resisted the siege of Saint-Quentin for some weeks more. When the Spanish finally overcame the town, the massacre and destruction were unspeakable.

Guise arrived to find that his Italian adventure had been forgotten and he was the man of the hour, the hero of Metz who alone could save France. But how? He decided to do the unexpected: seize Calais, in English hands since 1347. The attack succeeded. Saint-Quentin, too, disappeared from memory. The French chose to remember only Calais and Metz. The following year (1558) saw little action on both sides, and what transpired amounted to a draw. By 1559 Philip and Henry were ready for peace. Their desires produced the Treaty of Cateau-Cambrésis, signed April 3, 1559. Its clauses were many, but most important among them was the promise by France to renounce forever all rights to Naples and Milan. The Italian campaign had at last ended. In the same treaty, France recognized Emmanuel-Philibert's rights over Savoy. To seal the new entente, two marriages were planned, one between Henry II's sister Marguerite and Emmanuel-Philibert and the other between Philip II (Mary Tudor had now died) and Henry II's eldest daughter Elizabeth. Ironically, it was the celebration of these happy events that led to the final moment of violence in Henry II's reign and to the cause of his death. While he was jousting, a broken lance opened his visor and pierced his brain. He died nine days later. The royal weddings took place in the most solemn of atmospheres, and Catherine de Medici was prostrate with grief.

THE DOMESTIC SCENE

The Treaty of Cateau-Cambrésis did not please all of France. It did not even please all who represented Henry II at the negotiations. Montmorency was its main architect, while the Guises smarted, convinced that the war need not be over. We have encountered this pair before and with the same divergent opinions. The parallel is not an accident. The violence of warring armies in Henry II's reign was well matched by the bitter clash of the Montmorency family and the Guise clan. Both rich and powerful, they possessed quite different temperaments and, unfortunately for France, very different ambitions. Montmorency was cold and abrupt, where the Guises were wily and charming. A family of dukes and cardinals, the Guises used their charm to achieve remarkable matches, such as the marriage of Mary of Lorraine with James V of Scotland and of Mary Stuart with the Dauphin of France. They did not stop there. They were related to Diane de Poitiers and the d'Estes. Fanatically Catholic, the Guises were also fanatically egotistical. It is not entirely clear whether the Duke of Guise meant to conquer Naples for France or for the Guises. Their ambitions, respecting no bounds, made them the constant voice for war.

The ambitions of the Montmorency were quite different. The family had known years of service to the Crown and tended to act in accordance with the king's best interest. The Treaty of Cateau-Cambrésis remains a monument to their good sense. It is true that Montmorency, in the light of history, committed many errors while commander of the French army; it is also true that his decisions were prompted by a prudence and loyalty that the Guises never knew. Henry II cut a poor figure between these rivals, but at least he was well of age to reign when his father died. In 1559 the new King, Francis II, was fifteen, his brothers Charles, nine and Henry, eight. "Woe to thee, O land, when thy king is a child," says Ecclesiastes. France was soon to know the full meaning of these words. Italy, Philip II, and Henry's presence had kept the Montmorency family and the Guises involved in problems of national importance. The ascension of an adolescent to the throne, coupled with the cessation of the Italian Wars, made it possible for the personal ambitions of the Guises to come to the fore and to use France's problems to their own advantage. The main difficulty now facing France and all western Europe was that of the Protestant religion. On this point, too, by a queer twist of fate, the two families were to find themselves firmly opposed. The Guises were Catholic; D'Andelot and Coligny, Montmorency's nephews, embraced the Protestant cause. To their divided loyalties corresponded a divided France.

An added dimension of violence in Henry II's story is that of constant, terrifying religious persecution. Incapable of his father's vision, Henry was a bigot. He led an unintellectual life and had caught none of the spirit of innovation to which Francis I contributed, whatever his precise motivation may have been. His mind could grasp only that Lutheranism was a heresy. In 1547 he created a special court in Paris for the prosecution of heretics. It was baptized the *Chambre ardente* for reasons that are only too obvious. In 1551 he published the Edict of Châteaubriant. It provided among its articles that the penalty for holding Lutheran beliefs was death, that informers would get one-third of the goods of those on whom they informed, and that every three months special sessions of the courts be held to test the faith of the magistrates. These measures reveal in all its horror the narrowness of Henry's mind and the disastrous means he adopted to deal with the religious problem. The more he worked to stamp out Lutheranism, the more it spread, even to the princes of the blood, for Montmorency's nephews were soon joined by the younger branch of the royal house. The King and Queen of Navarre (Jeanne d'Albret and Antoine de Bourbon) and Antoine's brother, the Prince de Condé, all embraced the new heresy. It grew, it multiplied, and, to make matters worse, it became an organized force.

However widespread the Reform had been under Francis I, it remained a disjointed movement without a clear doctrine, without established churches, without a spiritual leader to inspire and enflame the hearts of the persecuted. Lefèvre was a scholar; Luther did not concern himself with France. During the reign of Henry II, this state of affairs changed rapidly and, in many ways, because of one man alone, Jean Calvin, who gave to the French Protestants those essential elements of leadership, organization, and doctrine.

Calvin was born in France at Noyon in 1509. Disaster haunted the Calvin family during Jean's young years. Both his father and brothers were excommunicated, disgraced, and refused a Christian burial upon their deaths. Jean studied in Paris and Orléans. He took up law but later abandoned this discipline for letters. He impoverished himself to publish in 1532 a commentary of Seneca's *De Clementia*. Paris brought him into contact with several reformers whose ideas could not help appealing to one who had seen his family destroyed by the Church. With the *Affaire des Placards*, Calvin found his friends suspect and hunted down by the authorities. He, too, fled. At Noyon he was arrested but later released. Calvin then travelled to Basel, where he published in 1536 his *Institutes*. The same year, attracted by the fervent reformer Guillaume Farel, he went to Geneva. This city, now independent of

Savoy and entirely sympathetic to the Reform, was the perfect haven for young Calvin. His rigid views did not please all Genevans however, and he was obliged to leave the city between 1538 and 1541. When he returned, it was in triumph, and Calvin ruled Geneva from that time until his death in 1564.

The world he created at Geneva represented a complete theocracy. Church and state fused to a point where citizen and church-member could no longer be effectively distinguished. The basis of government was the Word of God, and the function of government became tantamount to the enforcement and preservation of virtue. To do this work, Calvin created an elaborate organization headed by a Consistory of twelve elders and the pastors of Geneva. Through the *Institutes,* he worked to provide the faithful with a clear doctrine. The first edition, published in Latin and containing only 514 pages, was in fact only the basis for an extensive effort of revision and translation that culminated in the Latin edition of 1559 and the French translation of 1560. Though Calvin meant his French version (first published in 1541) to instruct those who could not read Latin, he affected his readers' style as well as their faith. His lucid, yet elegant, prose became a model greatly imitated by French writers in the late sixteenth and seventeenth centuries. Finally, Calvin used his position in Geneva to train men to go forth and preach the doctrine contained in the *Institutes.* By 1557 the Geneva Company was sending ministers to France on a regular basis. For those communities seeking advice and solace, Calvin maintained an enormous correspondence. A Frenchman himself, Calvin was destined to create an emotional nexus with the Protestants of France that could never have been achieved by Luther or even Zwingli. No less a part of his success was his insistence on discipline and order.

The Geneva of Calvin's time allowed no festivals, no luxuries, and no heresies. Like his Catholic opponents, Calvin was completely intolerant and went so far as to burn at the stake one Michael Servetus (1553), whose ideas he considered suspect. The men of the sixteenth century were divided not by the question of whether religious tolerance should be implemented or not but of which sect possessed the true word of God. Ministers destined to be sent out of Geneva received, therefore, a strict training. Their views were carefully questioned; their ability to speak and interpret the Scriptures developed with skill. Above all, Calvin instilled in his followers a sense of organization. As early as 1555, the French Protestants were being grouped into synods.

Calvin's organization, as it was applied to France, entailed a strict hierarchy beginning at the lowest level with the Consistory. It was responsible for governing the local church. Several churches were grouped together to form a Colloquy. It oversaw the business of the larger district formed by their churches. The Colloquies were themselves watched over by a Provincial Synod responsible to the National Synod. Simple and solid, Calvin's system had none of the complexities that crippled the Catholic Church whenever it sought to act at the national, provincial, and local level. It was also strict, even militaristic, in its effort to maintain discipline. The adjective "militaristic" is used expressly here. While Calvin's principal intentions concerned the faith, the system he devised bound the Protestant churches together in such a way as to make swift communication and mobilization of forces more than a possibility.

Lists of ministers sent out by Geneva show that the Protestants were particularly strong in Guyenne (except for the city of Bordeaux), Gascony, Navarre, Normandy, Dauphiné, and Languedoc. The North and East, however, remained firmly Catholic. The divisions reflect directly the dispositions of their rulers. As we have seen, the King and Queen of Navarre had gone over to the new religion; so had Coligny, who was governor of Normandy. Since the Guises controlled Lorraine, the East was effectively closed to the Calvinists. Between 1555 and 1557, churches were formed in the following places: Meaux, Poitiers, Angers, Iles de Saintonge, Agen, Bourges, Issoudun, Aubigny, Blois, Tours, Lyons, Orléans, and Rouen.

Why this upsurge? Calvin can provide us with only part of the answer. The remaining part concerns a growing dissatisfaction of large segments of the French population with their lot.

The professional and merchant classes had been the first to respond to the Reform movement. The teachers and the lawyers, if curious or critical about their work, were long aware of the need for a reexamination of established traditions. The merchants watched with disgust as the Italian campaigns wreaked havoc with their trade and consumed their profits through taxes. As the years advanced, other groups, no less significant, joined the movement.

When Francis I succeeded in concluding a Concordat with the Pope and in formally increasing his power over the French church, he also increased the problems of that church. Francis I quite blatantly abused the rights he received to fill the higher offices of the clergy as he saw fit. Abbeys and bishoprics were given in return for favors and often to men who had no means or intention of fulfilling their duties. Besides augmenting the scandals to which reformers could point an angry finger, the Concordat effectively split the clergy into two groups, the privileged high clergy and the humble priest and friar on whom fell the major responsibilities of their calling but none of the perquisites their superiors enjoyed. To make the situation even more dismal, the few important prelates who dared to criticize the state of affairs were immediately linked to the Reform, and the attitude adopted by the Faculty of Theology with regard to the Reform rivaled that of Henry II in its bigotry and lack of understanding of the issues involved. The Faculty thundered against the heresy in good scholastic form. It debated and defined but made no significant effort whatsoever to fight inspiration with inspiration. Logic and dogma were incessantly employed to decry a religion that was spreading rapidly because it placed love, simplicity, and purity above that very logic and dogma.

As a result, it is hardly surprising to discover that throughout the reign of Henry II members of the Church, too, became involved in the propagation of the Reform. Certain Jacobins and Cordeliers in Paris were suspect as early as 1549. Augustinians in Bourges, Rouen, Chartres, Toulouse, and Bordeaux reacted by forming secret groups and in some cases, by preaching Protestant ideas openly. Between 1558 and 1559 priests were among the most efficacious disseminators of Protestantism in the area around Orléans.

Henry II's rule brought about similar developments in the world of the nobility. Before 1547 French nobles had hardly been affected by Protestantism; when Henry II died, the nobility had become a vital aspect of its inroads into France. Their difficulties were primarily financial. To finance his numerous campaigns, Henry II had had to renew loans from the Italian bankers. The nobility, along with many other Frenchmen having money to invest, poured fortunes into this scheme. By 1557–1558 inflation was rampant, and the country was bankrupt. Many lesser nobles found themselves ruined, with virtually no recourse at hand. A more effective government might have been able to act in the crisis. As it was, the Crown had long indulged in selling state offices to procure additional funds. Removing any incompetent or inefficient officer meant that he had to be reimbursed for the sum he originally paid. Thus, in a state of financial crisis, the government was completely immobilized and incapable in the extreme to deal even with its own internal problems.

In this situation the Peace of Cateau-Cambrésis came as a final blow. War, the time-honored career for younger sons of the nobility, ceased to be a possibility. The whole class was idled and given time to seethe at the thought of its losses and difficulties. Sedition was in the air, and Calvin knew how beneficial the nobility could be to his cause. In fact, his missionary pastors had two recognized aims—to maintain secrecy and to win over the French nobility.

In retrospect, the greatest violence of Henry II's reign was a silent one, a tacit anger that would not find expression for some years to come yet, once unbridled, eclipsed in passion and ferocity anything that could be encountered before 1559. The tensions existed on both the Protestant and the Catholic side. They mounted yearly as the inevitable admixture of politics and religion now stimulated, now frustrated all attempts to bring the dissident theologians into agreement and heal the split. Where Francis I had failed, Charles V maintained hopes of succeeding. The instrument of concord was still to be a Council, and Charles pursued this goal with insistence.

The Emperor fondly hoped to make himself the master of Germany. The Protestant revolt was a continual threat to such dominance. Therefore, when Pope Paul III adjourned *sine die* the Council he had originally called for in June, 1536, Charles V convoked a meeting of theologians at Worms and Regensburg. The move had its effect. Rome, fearful that Charles would do its work and to Charles's satisfaction, announced a Council in May, 1542, and agreed that it should meet in Imperial territory. Unfortunately, war between France and the Empire caused further delay. The Council of Trent effectively began on December 13, 1545.

From their varying attitudes toward the Council, it is clear that Rome and Charles V expected rather different results. As time went by and a Council became so difficult to arrange, Charles seemed to lose any conviction that a Council would cure all the religious ills of the time. He did envisage it as an important step toward reforming the more blatant abuses of the Church, however. As a result, after the Council of Trent first convened in May, 1545 (only to adjourn for lack of attendance), Charles's wish that the Council begin its work not with questions of dogma but of reform caused further delay as the Pope had other ideas. The Council's function, as he saw it, was to condemn the Protestant heresy once and for all and to reaffirm the traditional beliefs of St. Thomas and the Councils of Constance and Basel. At the December session, the Spanish prelates, joined by a few Italians, upheld the Emperor against Rome. A compromise ensued. The two problems of dogma and reform would be discussed at the same time. It was a futile arrangement. All the proclamations of the Council dealt with dogma— original sin, the Holy Scripture and tradition, the sacraments—and effected a reaffirmation that entombed forever (as Charles had foreseen) the hope of a reconciliation with the Protestants. In June, 1547 the Council adjourned with the questions of reform untouched. Charles demanded that the Council reconvene. The Pope refused. Then, Charles obtained his greatest victory against the Schmalkaldic (Protestant) League. He proclaimed the Interim of Augsburg to impose some order on the scene until the Council reconvened. Pope Paul, however, remained adamant to his death.

His successor, Julius III, called the second session of the Council of Trent which met on May 1, 1551. For the first time Protestant deputies were present. They soon realized that their presence was useless; the first session's work had already settled those issues they wished to debate. The sessions dragged on until, suddenly, in March, 1552, the Elector of Saxony, hitherto an ally of Charles V, revolted against him and marched on Innsbruck. The Emperor fled and the Council, too, after having declared itself on the touchy subject of transubstantiation on which the traditional Catholic view was upheld.

Charles's situation grew tense. The Elector of Saxony reinstituted the Schmalkaldic League and made overtures to Henry II. It was at this point that Henry conceived of seizing Imperial territory, and Charles made some concessions to the reformers by revoking the Interim and disavowing the work of the Council. On October 3, 1555, the Peace of Augsburg brought formal recognition to the German Protestants. The Council had not only failed to bring the two sides together but had effaced the grounds for accord. Now that the German Protestants were politically recognized, the Council ceased to have any positive function for Charles V. Protestant gains were matched by Catholic gains. With the death of Edward VI of England (1553), the Catholic Mary Tudor ascended the throne. It was a feeble equilibrium, however, and the very idea of an equilibrium emphasizes the collapse of the Imperial policy to dominate all Germany and of the papal hopes to see the new heresy eradicated.

The bull convening the next session of the Council of Trent was issued on November 29, 1560. The Council met on January 18, 1562. During the lapse of time between the Peace of Augsburg and the bull of 1560 innumerable forces conspired to destroy the existing equilibrium. The Protestants made rapid strides in France. Even Spain knew increasing discontent. Suddenly Mary Tudor was dead (1558) and her sister Elizabeth, queen. Elizabeth's religious policies remained in doubt for some time, but for that very fact the Church could only feel it had lost a valiant if vicious ally in her predecessor. Henry II's death was no less unexpected, and if the powerful Charles V had been unable to repress the Protestant forces within his domains, how was an adolescent King to deal with these heretics whose number now included some of the most powerful of the kingdom of France? Conflict loomed on the horizon, an old conflict arrested by truces and treaties that could only exacerbate the absolute goal of either side: to prevail.

THE ARTS

History has a peculiar penchant for political balance in these years (France versus the Empire, the Montmorency family versus the Guises). So, too, in the dimension of social and cultural development a distinct balance can be observed. The events just described have the grimness of approaching catastrophe. Henry II was not the man or king his father had been. Yet his reign saw some of the greatest accomplishments of French (as distinguished from Italian) artists and the emergence of the Pléiade, that band of writers who laid the foundations of modern French poetry. Whatever might be about to befall the nation, the "cultural revolution" effected by Francis I, as well as the influx of Italian literature, already visible in the Ecole de Lyon, had taken root.

The important names in architecture during the reign of Henry II are Philibert Delorme, Pierre Lescot, and Jean Bullant, all Frenchmen. Delorme and Bullant both made trips to Italy and studied classical styles which they used in reaction against the Italianate style of the Loire châteaux. The transition to classical forms was gradual. Traces appeared as early as 1528 and 1530 in the great château of Chantilly, the château of Madrid, built near Paris, and, of course, St. Michael's at Dijon. But it remained for Delorme and Bullant in particular to produce a distinctly French classical architecture. They were aided by two texts dealing with the architecture of antiquity: Sebastiano Serlio's *Regole generali di architettura*, of which books 1, 2, and 5 were translated by Jean Martin in 1545–1547, and Vitruvius' *Architecture*, rendered into French in 1547 by the same translator as *Architecture, ou Art de bien bastir*.

Diane de Poitiers greatly appreciated Delorme, and with the coming to power of her lover, she immediately commissioned the architect to build for her a château at Anet. Above its main gate was placed Cellini's bronze nymph. The conscious use of correct classical orders and symmetry announced the new style and recalls certain parts of the Louvre, still extant, which Lescot began reconstructing in 1546. There are also significant differences between the two buildings. Lescot's Square Court of the Louvre is a busy, highly decorative structure. He has used classical material but without breaking away from the ornamentation of earlier French architecture in this century. Horizontal lines vie with the vertical thrust. Each story has a different form of fenestration. The second-story windows are completed by alternating round and pointed pediments. "The effect," as Blunt says, "is one of ornamental beauty rather than of monumentality." The portions of Anet remaining today demonstrate just such monumentality. Through Delorme's use of columns for structure, not decoration, and simple, unadorned mass, the entrance gate and avant-corps become imposing in a way Lescot could not achieve.

Jean Bullant began his career after Lescot and Delorme. In the middle fifties he constructed the north wing of Montmorency's château at Ecouen and, in 1560, designed the châtelet of Chantilly. Charming and unpretentious, the châtelet of Chantilly has often been singled out by French historians of architecture as one of the masterpieces of the French Renaissance and an impressive example of the adaptation by the French of those styles and techniques imported from Italy.

The building consists of two stories with a pavilion at either end. Though the pavilions are higher, they contain only two stories at the same level as those of the connecting structure. This fact is not easily recognized since Bullant arranged the elements of the façade to deceive the eye. The pilasters and columns end midway between the stories, and the windows of the upper story break the entablature so that the façade acquires a singular variety of lines and areas. With such architectural trickery, Bullant reveals the particular quality of the French classical style. It is simpler, more architectonic than the style of Azay-le-Rideau or Blois and yet eschews the severity of Italian architecture of the same period. As with so much Italian culture, the classical mode of architecture was only partially understood. The passage of time brought about a deeper commitment to classical forms, but it was a limited classicism and wedded to such busyness and decoration as the French knew from the Gothic and visibly would not do without.

Regarding indigenous artists of the period, none stands out so prominently as the sculptor Jean Goujon. In his early years, the influence of the Italians at court marked his major productions. With his great piece —the "Fountain of the Innocents" (1547–1549)—it became clear that Goujon had found new sources, classical ones. The numerous nymphs of this work have little in common with some of the violent, melodramatic poses of the Il Rosso paintings, so prominent in Goujon's first efforts. Their prototypes are rather the Greek and Roman forms which Il Primaticcio introduced into France after his Italian trip. Goujon's figures stand in traditional, even academic poses. They wear gracefully draped gowns. The classical influence on Goujon appeared in full bloom with his "Tribune des Cariatides," commissioned on September 5, 1550, for a room in the Louvre. Four female figures are used as columns to support a gallery which extends out over an entrance door.

Armless, elegantly draped, these caryatids were directly inspired by those of the Erechtheum which Goujon probably knew from a plaster cast made by Lescot.

There is great beauty in Goujon's art, a fine sense of line and form, a genuine promise. Unfortunately for him and for France, the Massacre of Vassy (1562) forced him to flee his native land, for Goujon was Protestant. He died in Bologna, a symbol of the brilliant rise and rapid decline of French Renaissance art. Il Primaticcio, Delorme, Lescot, and Bullant all lived well beyond the Massacre of Vassy. They stayed in France, but the chaos and the financial drain curtailed immeasurably what had been during the time of Henry II a spectacular burst of talent.

PROSE AND POETRY

Literature fared better, although the years 1547–1559 produced a group of mixed offerings. In the case of those writers, like Marguerite de Navarre and Rabelais, who had known the enthusiasm of the thirties, the *Chambre ardente*, and Henry II's general policy of repression gave life a somber cast.

L'Heptaméron

Marguerite's final years brought her little joy. Her frivolous husband did his best to arrange a marriage between their daughter Jeanne d'Albret and the Infant of Spain in order to bring Spanish Navarre back into his kingdom. The French Crown naturally disapproved of such a union, and Marguerite found herself torn between the interests of her husband and her love for her brother Francis I. Then, Francis I died. The new King treated his aunt with cold indifference. He imposed upon Jeanne d'Albret a marriage with Antoine de Bourbon against the wishes of Marguerite, who, already grieved by the loss of her brother, declined in strength until, less than three years after the passing of Francis I, she herself was dead.

Besides a series of works lamenting the demise of her brother and her own earthly state, Marguerite produced in her final years her major prose work, the *Heptaméron*. This collection of 72 contes has a complicated history. It was never published during Marguerite's lifetime. When the Queen died, she left behind her a manuscript, untitled and containing an undetermined number of stories. In 1558 a collection called *Histoires des Amans fortunez* was printed. It contained Marguerite's stories, but in no order whatsoever, without a prologue, and without certain *contes* included in all modern editions. Marguerite's daughter, horrified by the mutilated text, authorized Claude Gruget to publish her mother's work. The volume appeared in 1559. Gruget entitled it the *Heptaméron* and reinstituted Marguerite's order and prologue. An editor's preface stated that he had printed all the stories that could be recovered. Did Marguerite write more than Gruget printed? We may never know the final answer.

The question of dates is equally unsettled. Some have thought that Marguerite worked on her stories throughout her lifetime. The numerous historical allusions to be found in the collection suggest, on the contrary, that she composed few nouvelles before 1540. It is true that as early as 1531 she had Antoine Le Maçon read her stories from the *Decameron*, but Le Maçon's translation was not ready until 1545, and again using the historical allusions, we find that most of the nouvelles can be situated between 1542 and 1546. The prologue definitely dates from 1546. These facts would seem to represent the period of Marguerite's most intense work. A few nouvelles were written as late as 1548, a date which intimates that the collection was unfinished because of Marguerite's death. There is no certainty of this fact, however. What does seem certain is that the *Heptaméron* was produced in Marguerite's maturity and postdates, for example, her "Miroir de l'âme pécheresse."

The framework of the *Heptaméron* is quite reminiscent of the *Decameron*. A group of people is isolated by the weather and decides to tell stories to pass the time. Each day has a theme, and each storyteller (*"devisant"*), upon finishing a tale, chooses his successor. What Marguerite adds to Boccaccio's framework is a discussion after each tale. All the *devisants* take part and reflect upon the tale's moral, the comportment of its characters, and so forth. This is not Marguerite's only personal touch. While the *Heptaméron* makes one think immediately of Boccaccio, exhaustive comparisons between the tales of the *Heptaméron* and Italian *conteurs* of the day, such as Bandello or even Boccaccio, reveal that Marguerite in fact borrowed little or nothing from them for the substance of her work. Her debt to them is most evident in the tone of her discussions. Her *devisants* love to argue and to debate in that refined and witty style of the *bel parlare* to be found in Castiglione's *Il Cortegiano*, for example.

The content of Marguerite's 72 nouvelles is, admittedly, a "mixed bag." She is not adverse to including certain droll stories that in word and description seem rather earthy for a queen. This fact merely points up the differences in social conventions in the sixteenth century. France had not yet known the *Précieuses* or Malherbe. It did know its medieval literature, however, and especially the *Roman de la Rose*, works in which a combination of elegant and bawdy styles was long established. Where Marguerite departed from this tradition was in giving her tales a moral and artistic content. Previously, contes had been meant to make people laugh, not think, and to insure that the stories would succeed, the authors reduced all to the preparation of the dénouement. While Marguerite's more involved nouvelles maintain the stereotypes of courtly literature, she often did attempt to study her characters as well as to present them, and if the moral content of the tale is not directly brought out in the telling, it appears and is discussed during the commentary.

The *Heptaméron* is a work of maturity, originality, and experience. Many times the *devisants* remark that the people involved in their stories are real and known to the others. These people often represent Marguerite's own brother and daughter just as the *devisants*, Dame Oisille and Hircan, can be positively identified as Louise de Savoie and Henri d'Albret, Marguerite's mother and husband. The author even portrayed herself as Parlamente and gave to this character the ideal and the religious convictions that she had expressed in her poetry.

Parlamente's ideal is called "*la parfaicte amour.*" It combines Marguerite's mystical longing for a spiritual reunion with God with the Neoplatonic theories of love brought into vogue by Marsilio Ficino. Parlamente exposes her ideal at the end of the nineteenth nouvelle: "*Encores ay-je une opinion, . . . que jamais homme n'aymera parfaictement Dieu, qu'il n'ait parfaictement aymé quelque creature en ce monde.*" Perfect love is a progression. It begins with the attraction for an earthly being. The soul, longing for divine beauty and perfection, searches first in the being's exterior beauty, but if pure in its intent, it will soon realize that the perfection it is seeking cannot be found in worldly objects, but rather in their Creator. Then the soul passes beyond the exterior beauty to a contemplation of that loveliness which is spiritual in nature and, in loving God in his creatures, attains communion with the divine.

This affirmation, in yet another context, of the pure and simple faith that one finds throughout the Evangelist literature of the day, can also be approached as a document in the *Querelle des Femmes*. Parlamente's ideal is not only presented, it is discussed. Parlamente receives support from Oisille and Dagousin in particular; Hircan and Geburon cast grave doubts on the desirability or even the possibility of such a love. The tales center on the condemnation of woman as a faithless creature (stories told by Hircan and Geburon) or on praise of woman as an honest soul, pursued by men who think only of dishonoring her. Parlamente possesses—as did her society, perhaps—a keen awareness of the demise of chivalry. "*Le temps est passé,*" she says, "*que les hommes oblient leurs vies pour les dames.*" Her new ideal of "*parfaicte amour*" with its accent on spirituality and adoration of inner beauty makes an obvious effort to fill the gap. But if "*la parfaicte amour*" can be justified in terms of both religious and social phenomena of the day, it remains a particularly somber ideal.

The perfect lovers of the *Heptaméron* are more than religious and pure, they are intensely unhappy, beset by social and familial problems. The protagonist in story 9 belongs to a social rank inferior to that of the lady he desires. In number 19, he is judged too poor to marry his beloved. In number 21, he is an illegitimate child, poor and ugly. The girl he loves, Rolandine, is regarded with indifference by her avaricious father, who seeks to avoid paying a dowry. In every case, the suffering of these lovers leads to actual death or a retreat from society to a religious order. The situation, so in keeping with certain sentiments of the "Miroir de l'âme pécheresse," has little to offer those who love life. And with the exception of Dagousin, the men of the *Heptaméron* love life (and love). Their reaction to "*la parfaicte amour*" is, then, more than a staid debate on woman's vice and virtues. It is a discussion of one's philosophy of life. Only in the light of this diversity of opinion and the realization that Parlamente's ideal is but a small part of the *Heptaméron* does the work's greatness emerge.

There are two Marguerites present in this collection of tales: Marguerite in the guise of Parlamente and Marguerite, the author of the entire work and the creator of each character as well as the commentaries following each story. In Parlamente we see the Evangelist, the reformer, the wronged wife, the tired queen, who has grown to know the foibles of earthly life and who longs for that existence which transcends all terrestrial imperfections. It is a firmly anti-Renaissance mentality, and certain of the *devisants* are quick to note that life is perhaps worth living, that perfection is not within human grasp, that physical love need not be repugnant, nor all women good and all men treacherous.

Ultimately, this dissident voice is Marguerite's, too. It represents a position not necessarily hostile to Parlamente's, but broader, skeptical even, and capable of embracing a greater range of human experience. "*Une femme de bien,*" says Hircan to his wife Parlamente, "*ne doibt jamais juger ung autre de ce qu'elle ne vouldroit faire.*" He (and Marguerite) sense Parlamente's intransigent attitudes, her holier-than-thou approach to moral problems. "*La parfaicte amour*" may be fine for her, but this does not mean that she can speak for all women.

Indeed, throughout the *Heptaméron* the surest form of rebuttal is recourse to relativity. When Hircan sarcastically criticizes Dagousin for speaking harshly against women who have affairs with priests since, according to Hircan, many women find great pleasure in sinning with men who can absolve them, Dame Oisille retorts, "*Vous parlez de celles qui n'ont poinct congnoissance de Dieu . . .*" These are isolated examples. The whole collection can be said to revolve about the eventual criticism of all sweeping judgments, since from its inception the *devisants* promise to relate only true stories. Perhaps Marguerite thought that her tales would be more interesting if the principals could be recognized. What is certain is that this simple criterion becomes an effective weapon against all those who would present a dogmatic, an absolute interpretation of human behavior.

For those who relate how woman is unfaithful, there is always the story of the reverse or of how man can and does share this frailty. In addition, by selecting for her little group a wide spectrum of views, she insured that differences would arise, and to crown her inquiry into human behavior, she created after each nouvelle a debate, a battleground for ideas. In this way, Marguerite goes beyond the polite chatter of the *bel parlare*. As French literature before her had done and as it will do for many more centuries, through a discussion of love and of people in love Marguerite endeavored to bring to light the wisdom of her long life. Her spiritual side held fast to its absolutes, but another facet of her character demanded that such absolutes be questioned and analyzed. Her religious nature insisted with the Middle Ages that Truth was one and the afterlife, the only life, but her worldly self knew that truth could be plural, that human beings were not all alike and did not all share her prejudices and her absolutes.

Thus, in the works of both Marguerite and Rabelais, beneath the medieval forms and expression, the religious involvement, and theological propaganda, appears a protest against bigotry. Where Rabelais used satire, Marguerite uses discussion and debate, but the results are comparable: if there could be no doubt about the devotion owed God, there could be much doubt about most pronouncements of the human mind. Within the earthly sphere there was much to question and to reexamine. Authority was becoming harder and harder to define.

This intellectual unrest is of undoubted importance; yet it can also be overemphasized. The literature of the reformers has not afforded us any examples of a renaissance as defined by Panofsky. What is central in Marguerite's collection of stories does not derive from the *Decameron*, and, however unconventional Rabelais may have been, the basic characteristics of his work with its mixture of styles and tones make apparent a strong medieval influence. These Evangelists forgot less easily than we are wont to do that their principal aims were spiritual, not literary. By the same token, the anger, the fervor of these reformers opened new paths of thought and established an intellectual climate which was crucial to France's future literary history.

Rabelais

The *Quart Livre*, published in its entirety in 1552, adheres closely to the *Tiers Livre* in that it offers the voyage toward the Dive Bouteille announced before the *Tiers Livre* ends. As the author describes the preparations for the voyage, he notes, "*Le nombre de navires feut tel que vous ay exposé on tiers livre,*" and the boats carry in abundance Pantagruélion, that remarkable substance to which Rabelais devoted the final chapters of his preceding volume. Yet once the voyage begins, we pass from the unity of the *Tiers Livre*, furnished by Panurge's persistent desire to know whether he should marry or not, to the variety of the *Quart Livre*: the account of the many different adventures and lands these travellers experience.

To this distinction in structure corresponds a shift in perspective. After Panurge's original request, "*dictez m'en vostre advis,*" Pantagruel had answered, "*une foys en avez jecté le dez, et ainsi l'avez decreté et prins en ferme deliberation, plus parler n'en fault, reste seulement la mettre à execution.*" Little transpires within the volume to suggest that the variety of consultations would cause Pantagruel to change his advice. The Prologue to the *Quart Livre* offers Rabelais' final definition of Pantagruélisme: "*c'est certaine gayeté d'esprit conficte en mespris des choses fortuites.*" Where Rabelais once spoke rather positively—decide and act—he now accentuates an attitude, an attitude that we must adopt in the face of fortuitous events. This shift in emphasis pervades the paragraphs that follow.

Rabelais insists on the importance of health, "*Sans santé n'est la vie.*" The author is sure that God will hear our prayers for health as it is a "*mediocre*" (modest) demand. "*Mediocrité a esté par les saiges anciens dicte aurée, c'est à dire precieuse, de tous louée, en tous endroictz agréable.*" Can it be here the same man who created the giants of *Pantagruel* and their habits and their appetites? The answer is yes, but the time of the giants' ideals is past, and it is best now to preserve a "*certaine gayeté d'esprit,*" a more modest hope with which to meet the ills and injustices of the world.

Just such a meeting will account for several of the most important episodes in the *Quart Livre*. The voyagers soon come to the country of the Papefigues (those who have mocked the pope). This land they find was once rich and free. Now it is ruined and desolate. At the court of Gaster (stomach), Pantagruel sees two groups of men "*les quelz il eut en grande abhomination,*" very strong sentiments for the understanding giant who so patiently listened to the impossible Panurge throughout the *Tiers Livre* without once expressing anger. The feelings of Pantagruel show how far we have come in our contact with those "*choses fortuites*" that try our souls. The men in question are the Engastrimythes (ventriloquists) and the Gastrolates (adorers of the stomach). Rabelais' description of both is bitter. The Engastrimythes are prophets who fool the simple people. The others, distinguished by their multiple disguises, have made Gaster their idol and substantiate St. Paul's observation that many enemies of the Cross have made the belly their God. Charity, Truth, persecution—the *Quart Livre* has many of the familiar themes, but where once one read the chiding of the reformer, one finds now only facts, cruel facts, too real to be transformed into the laugh-provoking spectacles of *Pantagruel* and *Gargantua*. Telling is the episode in which Pantagruel discusses the death of Pan and relates it to the deaths of Guillaume Du Bellay and Christ: "*Pantagruel, ce propous finy, resta en silence et profonde contemplation. Peu de temps après, nous veismes les larmes decouller de ses oeilz grosses comme oeufz de austruche.*"

For many decades, it has seemed likely that part, if not all, of the *Cinquième Livre* is not of Rabelais' hand. Conclusive proof of its authenticity or the opposite has not been forthcoming, however. Many scholars accept the episode of the "Isle Sonnante" as genuine and hypothesize that a Protestant made this and perhaps other pages left by Rabelais at his death the basis of what we know as the *Cinquième Livre*. What is interesting in the present context is the hesitation by scholars to attribute this last volume to Rabelais because of the violence and bitterness of its satire. Perhaps the book properly belongs to another person, but if it does not, the final step from regret to bitterness is not so hard to imagine.

La Deffence et Illustration de la Langue Françoyse

Marguerite and Rabelais had watched the promises of the 1530s destroyed by the smoke of the stake. The reform they envisaged was not to be. As a result, the *Heptaméron* reveals an ideal constituted of a flight from life; the fourth and fifth volumes of Rabelais' novel speak with depression or bitterness of those forces more amiably discussed in his earlier works. Fortunately, their disappointment, nourished by their early hopes, died with them and in rapid succession. The generation of the 1490s disappeared within a decade, Marot in 1544, Marguerite in 1549, and Rabelais around 1553.

Their place in French letters was taken by a group of young poets and writers who more than compensated for the discouragement of their elders. They continued the spirit of review, but with a positive orientation. The small "brigade" of poets who rallied about Jean Daurat at the Collège de Coqueret decided to recast French poetry and raise it to new heights. Great minds such as Jean Bodin and Michel de Montaigne embarked on a reexamination of authority and education that would lead to cultural and intellectual innovations of the greatest magnitude.

Francis I had failed his sister and her generation, but he ultimately succeeded with the brigade. The splendor of Fontainebleau, the influx of Italian artists and nobility (either exiles or allies), the impulse given scholarship by the creation of the *lecteurs royaux*, all these elements contributed to the establishment of a new culture such as Marot and Marguerite had not known in their youth. The veneer was very thin to be sure. As the *Heptaméron* and certain conversations of Catherine de Medici show, the court maintained much of its crude and swaggering ways. But Francis I did introduce something novel, and that something remained and grew.

It made itself felt in many different ways. In attempting to rival the Italian courts and, more precisely, in succeeding in rivaling them, he gave his country a decided pride, a sense of being that his defeat at Pavia could only solidify. Francis' reign also meant changes in the world of education. While most students still debated endless points of logic, a few were reaping the rewards of those efforts by the humanists to provide the best texts of Latin and Greek authors as well as ample means to learn the Greek language. The Collège de Coqueret provided just such an education. The fare consisted of a firm introduction to the classical languages, especially Latin, and intense study of classical literatures. Translation and memorization must have been stressed, as was industry. It is said that Daurat's students (Ronsard, Du Bellay, and Baïf) worked well into the night as long as the candles lasted, waking one another before retiring, so that the chair was always occupied (and warm). Such legends are most likely apocryphal, but the erudition revealed by the poetry of the brigade affords concrete evidence of exhaustive study. In the first work published by the Pléiade (as the group of poets has come to be called), both patriotism and love of classical letters combined to form a loud protest against their literary heritage. That work was the *Deffence et Illustration de la Langue Françoyse* (1549).

This manifesto did not spring spontaneously from the group. It was written hastily by Du Bellay as an angry answer to a volume published in 1548 by Thomas Sébillet entitled *Art Poétique François*. The group's anger derived less perhaps from the fact that they disagreed with Sébillet on many points than from the fact that he proposed certain ideas dear to the young poets who suddenly found that they had not published first! A humanist of distinction, Sébillet, too, greatly admired the Greek and Latin poets, whom he called *"les Cynes, des ailes desquelz se tirent les plumes dont on escrit proprement."* In his discussion of genres, he devoted a chapter to the sonnet, where Petrarch is recognized as *"le prince des Poetes Italie[n]s."* At the same time, Sébillet discussed the rondeau, the lai, the ballade and took most of his examples for his reader-apprentice's edification from the works of Marot. His ties to the past were no less apparent when he attempted to define the more unfamiliar genres. The sonnet, we are told, *"n'est autre chose que le parfait epigramme de l'Italien."* For Sébillet, *"la chanson approche de tant pres l'Ode, q[ue] de ton & de son se resemblent quasi de tous poins,"* and *"si le François s'estoit renge a ce que la fin de la Moralite fut touiours triste & doloreuse, la Moralite seroit Tragedie."* The brigade could not accept these ideas and hurried to say so.

The principal ideas of the *Deffence* can be found in its title. The volume is divided into two books. The first "defends" French against those who would prefer Latin; the second enumerates the many ways the French can render their language and literature "illustrious."

Du Bellay began his manifesto by declaring that since all languages have the same origin, they should all be valued alike. Unfortunately, French had not been favored by history. The proud and ambitious Romans imposed their culture upon that of the ancient Gauls and retarded the progress of the Gauls' native tongue. In addition, noted Du Bellay, we must recognize *"l'ignorance de notz majeurs."* "Majeurs" means ancestors, and the poet was referring specifically to the negligence of previous generations of Frenchmen *"qui ont laissé [leur] Langue si pauvre et nue, qu'elle a besoing des ornementz & . . . des plumes d'autruy."* Such remarks serve to prepare the specific program for embellishment that is outlined in the Second Book, but Du Bellay first completed his "defense."

He had demonstrated that if French may be considered inferior to the great classical tongues, the fault lay not in any congenital failing but in its history and the neglect that earlier centuries showed this language. He now insisted that French could not be elevated by translation. Every language possesses something that belongs to it alone. The perfecting of French could come only with work upon that language— a direct slap at the humanists who were more eager to develop their knowledge of Latin and Greek than to improve their own language. The Romans enriched their language by imitating Greek; the French could now do likewise, using both Greek and Latin. What the author understood by imitation here is not perfectly clear. He certainly was not referring to translation. Imitation is a difficult thing if one tries to "*bien suyvre les vertuz d'un bon aucteur, & quasi comme se transformer en luy.*" What Du Bellay meant by these "*vertuz*" (a phrase, a *topos,* an image?) and whether any conflict could arise between the use of another poet and one's effort to attain some personal expression are points that the *Deffence* leaves untouched. The early works of the brigade suggest that the young poets at Coqueret may not even have considered these questions. The *Deffence* records their enthusiasm, not their experience.

Chamard, in discussing the assumptions of this manifesto, emphasizes a contradiction between the nationalism that is manifest in the desire to improve French language and the humanism of the poets, who turn to antiquity as the model of perfection. The contradiction can be quickly resolved if we note that all of Du Bellay's remarks have a common aim: to elevate French letters. The past had not been kind to French; the language was definitely deficient with respect to classical languages and literature. One had to be realistic and use the superior to improve the inferior.

The *Deffence,* if not particularly complicated, is rich in implications concerning the development of a new aesthetic. Its general attitudes reflect the reevaluation taking place in France at this time in all the various art forms. The call to imitate antiquity can also be found in treatises on architecture by Bullant and Philibert Delorme. What strikes in the *Deffence* is a new awareness with respect to the very nature of poetry and language. When Du Bellay insisted that the French had to add "*des ornementz*" to their language, it is easy to think of a decorative language that would correspond to the ornamentation of the early château architecture. In truth, the number of words not present in French at this time is amazing. *Concret, primitif, nébuleux, attraction, concept, critère,* for example, familiar words we take for granted, had not yet come into the French language. Among the neologisms and the mythological trappings the brigade introduced into their poetry can be found much erudition and superficial embellishment, to be sure.

But they also fixed on *patrie* and proved that the many hours of translation and composition spent under Daurat had inculcated into each a sense of language that made the works of Marot and his school appear painfully crude, simple, unpoetic. To place Marot and the ancients on the same level as Sébillet did in his *Art poétique* was not only wrong, it was inconceivable.

The aesthetic of the *Deffence* takes further shape in Du Bellay's Second Book. Here, in addition to insisting on the creation of new French words from Latin and Greek and increased use of technical words and archaisms to enrich the French language, the brigade listed the acceptable genres to be used and the models for each. The medieval genres—the lai, the ballade, the rondeau—are swiftly dismissed as "episseries." In their place, the brigade offered the elegy as practiced by Tibullus, Propertius, and Ovid, the Italian sonnet of Petrarch, the ode (but it was not to be confused as Sébillet had done with the chanson, a medieval genre). They hoped also that the *moralités* and farces would be replaced by classical tragedy and comedy and that a French poet would dare to rival Homer and Virgil in the composition of an epic.

Du Bellay offered no reasons to explain this preference for classical and Italian genres; yet fundamental (and revealing) differences do exist. The *formes fixes*[1] of the Middle Ages could be extended to remarkable lengths for the number of rhymes used per poem. Villon's ballades contain three stanzas of either eight lines or ten lines plus the envoi. In the former case the ballade can attain a length of 28 lines for three rhymes; in the latter case, the poems contain 35 lines to only four rhymes. Marot's rondeaux have 15 lines, two of which are the refrain so that each poem has 13 lines but two rhymes! Naturally, any rhyme scheme of this nature created enormous technical difficulties. But the Rhétoriqueurs thrived on these difficulties, and the idea of poetry as a second rhetoric hardly contradicted such practices.

Of the genres upheld by the *Deffence*, not one presented the complexities of the medieval *formes fixes*. The elegies were written in rhymed couplets; the shorter odes, as practiced by Ronsard, for example, were usually divided into stanzas of six, seven, or eight lines. There were three or four rhymes per stanza and the series of rhymes in each stanza was entirely independent. The one *forme fixe* among their choices, the sonnet, could not have been more different from the ballade or the rondeau. Unlike these forms, it had no refrain. It was

---

[1] The term *forme fixe* designates a poem that possesses a fixed rhyme scheme and strophic structure.

not obliged to return to its main theme but, like the elegy, could enjoy a free development of its subject. The poet's control over his material in the sonnet was further enhanced by the fact that for a mere 14 lines he had a minimum of four rhymes, and most poets came to prefer five. This is not to say that the sonnet was a simple genre. It was rather a genre whose complexities differed significantly from those of the ballade, the chanson, or the rondeau. Rhyme was no longer an overriding preoccupation. Cleverness with respect to the preparation and use of the refrain also receded from the picture. The poet was now faced with the problem of exposing and developing a theme within a very limited span of verse. Without a refrain, the sonnet could evolve as a narrative, as a drama.

In condemning *moralités* and farces, Du Bellay expressed the desire to see theatre return to its "*ancienne dignité.*" Dignity might well suffice to summarize the issues involved in the Sébillet–Du Bellay clash. The brigade, so conversant with the richness of expression to be found in classic poetry, could no longer believe that the language they inherited equalled a dignified poetic style. They seem to have doubted as well that serious verse could be created within the *formes fixes* so dominated by technical considerations. They wanted depth. They wanted a new conception both of poetry and of poet.

The épître, Du Bellay said, was not a genre likely to enrich French "*pource qu'elles sont voluntiers de choses familieres & domestiques.*" They were worthwhile only when patterned after the elegy as Ovid used it. Similarly, the *Deffence* distinguished carefully between the ode and the chanson since the ode *must* shun the common. In every verse of the ode erudition had to appear, and fit subjects were "*la louange des Dieux et des hommes vertueux, discours fatal des choses mondaines,*" etc. The brigade had taken Horace's "*Odi vulgus*" to heart. Dignity, seriousness, and beauty were linked to erudition and to all that is elevated in contrast with the commonplace. The poet, too, acquired a definite complexity. The entire third chapter of the *Deffence's* Second Book was devoted to emphasizing "*Que le naturel n'est suffisant à celuy qui en Poësie veult faire oeuvre digne de l'immortalité.*" To be born a poet was not enough. The true poet developed a craft; he had a doctrine and erudition.

The efforts of Du Bellay and his companions to raise both poetry and poet to a new level of seriousness did not stop with the *Deffence.* Innumerable works by the Pléiade portrayed the poet as the minion of the gods, divinely inspired, transmitting divine knowledge. Their social position contributed to their enthusiasm. Forever dependent on patrons for their subsistence, they reacted by insisting on their uniqueness. At the same time, it can be argued that these remarks were part of a long campaign to redefine the entire process of poetic creation. It was not inspiration alone. It was not technique alone. It was not a skillful juggling of rhymes. They attempted to speak of *invention* and *imagination* but were confounded by the limitations of their vocabulary. *Imagination* (and fiction) had pejorative overtones and called to mind wild or deceitful imagining. *Invention*, possessing a strongly rational connotation (from the Latin *invenio*—to discover), could be a more positive word to use but, by the same token, did not convey anything of an intuitive process. When the term indicated a more creative process, it, too, denoted a deceitful action. *Fureur*, often used to describe the state of the inspired poet, was too close in meaning to madness to allow for that mixture of inspiration and discipline upon which Du Bellay insists. Their project was in many ways doomed before it began, and it is perhaps dangerous to say that the brigade ever devised a coherent doctrine or a satisfactory definition of the poetic experience. That they sincerely tried proves how far poetry had come from being merely the second rhetoric, how much poetry had come to mean for the brigade an intensely personal experience.

Ronsard (1524–1585)

Those who know Pierre de Ronsard already as the author of sonnets and short, *carpe diem* odes may be surprised to learn that the poet's initial work contained no sonnets and was published in 1550, two years before the *Amours*. It was *Les Quatre Premiers Livres des Odes*, to be followed in 1552 by the *Cinquième Livre des Odes*. In addition, Ronsard's principal inspiration was not Horace, who furnished the poet with the more famous of his odes, but Pindar. The 1550 edition of the *Odes* did contain some of Ronsard's most direct borrowings from Horace, the "Fontaine Bellerie" poems and "Plus dur que fer j'ai fini mon ouvrage" (from "Exegi monumentum"), but whereas the more personal tone of Horace, singing of nature and his ability to immortalize with his poetry, corresponds to the traditional image of Ronsard, the poet in his beginning devoted considerably greater time and effort to his Pindaric odes.

The choice of form and of model reflect portions of Du Bellay's program. "*Chante moy ces odes incongnues encor' de la Muse Francoyse,*" said the *Deffence*. Their worthy subject was praise of the gods and virtuous men, the very matter of the Pindaric odes. Since the extent of Ronsard's knowledge of Greek has never been firmly established and given that Pindar's encomiastic outpourings are difficult to understand even today, it is possible to wonder how much of Pindar, then the victim of corrupt and incomplete texts, Ronsard read firsthand and appreciated. The question may be immaterial. The long Pindaric odes, unfolding by triades of strophe, antistrophe, and epode, in which the poet lavished Olympic heroes and others with praise, decidedly appealed to the imagination of Ronsard. Long, often complex, the Pindaric ode was a monument to poetic *fureur* and a challenge to the band that wished to repudiate the medieval *"episseries"* in favor of classical forms. There alone may have been sufficient inspiration for Ronsard to undertake the form of the Pindaric ode. He was a beginner. The virtuosity required to imitate Pindar could be a useful springboard to fame. In addition, since praise of famous people was the subject of the form, how better to commence one's career than by exalting the French royal family!

Reread today, the Pindaric odes of 1550 leave much to be desired. Bombast and nonsense appear too often to allow for even qualified admiration. When Ronsard says of Marguerite de Valois, sister of Henry II,

> *Par un miracle nouveau*
> *Pallas du bout de sa lance*
> *Ouvrit un peu le cerveau*
> *De François seigneur de France.*
> *Adonques Vierge nouvelle*
> *Tu sortis de sa cervelle,*

or attempts in the same poem to praise her patronage of the arts,

> *Tes mains s'armerent alors*
> *De l'horreur de deus grands haches:*
> *Tes braz, tes flancs, & ton cors,*
> *Sous un double fer tu caches:*
> *Une menassante creste*
> *Branloit au hault de ta teste*
> *Joant sur la face horrible*
> *D'une Meduse terrible:*
> *Ainsi tu alas trouver*
> *Le vilain monstre Ignorance,*
> *Qui souloit toute la France*
> *Desous son ventre couver,*

our reaction is probably not that intended by Ronsard. Perhaps our own imagination is at fault for not being able to forget sufficiently the reality of Marguerite in order to enter comfortably into the poet's allegory, but then the excessive quality of such passages does not facilitate our task. Continued use of erudition and mythology throughout undermines further the potential success of the poetry for a modern reader. Significantly enough, the most interesting, if not the most successful, of the Pindaric odes is the "Ode à Michel de l'Hospital" which has little to do with the royal family and their praise.

Published in the *Cinquième Livre* and intended to flatter Michel de l'Hospital, the poem is also a commentary on the state of French letters much in the vein of Gargantua's letter from *Pantagruel*. The poem relates the birth of the Muses and how, after the defeat of the Giants, they ask their father Jupiter for permission to reign over poets, prophets, and deviners. Permission is granted, and all is well until the fall of the Roman Empire. Ignorance overcomes the world, and the Muses retire. But Destiny announces to them that a Michel de l'Hospital will be born to disperse Ignorance, and in the last stanza of the ode he shares with Marguerite de Valois the credit for creating a new atmosphere, one in which the Muses can return to earth. Needless to say, the brigade is also a part of this atmosphere and the cry of a Renaissance, stilled in later works of Rabelais, is heard again.

After Pindar came Petrarch. With the *Amours* of 1552-1553, Ronsard consciously added another element to the Renaissance described in the ode to Michel de l'Hospital. A number of coarse sonnets (to be excluded from subsequent editions) suggests that all is not Petrarchist in the collection, but even the most cursory perusal of the *Amours* would reveal that the remaining works have been formed in the Italian mold. In vocabulary, attitudes, sources, descriptions, these poems ape the many tired clichés of Petrarch's *epigoni*. The imitation is not slavish if by the term we mean that Ronsard resorted to transcribing his sources; few, if any sonnets in the *Amours*, have sources embracing the whole poem. The imitation was slavish in that the bits and pieces of Petrarchist conceits comprising Ronsard's sonnets demonstrate inordinate fidelity to another's vision of love. Just as Pindar cast a long shadow over the Horatian themes of Ronsard's odes, so Petrarchist attitudes engulfed the lighter, more sensual overtones with which we are accustomed to associate the prince of poets.

Both facts testify to the brigade's commitment to the *Deffence* and to the creation of the literature for which it called (versus, perhaps, the expression of more intimate, less programmatic themes). Was a moment to come when the group would reorient its efforts and acknowledge that the program had become a difficult if not, in part, undesirable pursuit?

Ronsard's *Continuation des Amours* (1555) and *Nouvelle Continuation des Amours* (1556) intimate that, for one poet at least, by the middle fifties such a moment had come. Much of the text is indistinguishable from the earlier *Amours*, but signs can be found that point to new techniques and new attitudes. The *Continuation* of 1555 follows the same format Ronsard used in the *Amours* of 1552: sonnets followed by non-sonnet forms. The latter are more numerous, however; more revealing, some derive from traditions other than the Petrarchist. The *esprit gaulois* "Gayetés," and the voice of Anacreon create quite a departure from the dominant tone of 1552–1553. When composing the *Nouvelle Continuation,* Ronsard decided to do away completely with any distinction between the sonnet and other genres included in the cycle and added to the collection such complete departures from love verse as the odes, "Bel Aubepin" or "Quand je dors, je ne sens rien." These pieces and the famous "Mignonne, levez-vous" (1555) are among the works often referred to as examples of Ronsard's "*stille bas*." The poet used this expression himself within the cycles to distinguish them in execution from his earlier Petrarchist verse. "*Thiard,*" he notes in the opening poem of the *Continuation,* "*chacun disoit à mon commencement/ Que j'estoi trop obscur au simple populaire.*" Now he was aware that everyone said he had strayed too far in the opposite direction: "*Et que je me dements parlant trop bassement.*" It is easy to exaggerate the transformation of styles and to overlook the obvious meaning of *Continuation* and *Nouvelle Continuation,* titles that relate the new poetry to the old, rather than the opposite. On the other hand, Ronsard had begun to give serious thought to varying his styles. There may have been both personal and literary reasons behind Ronsard's experiments.

Wishing a renaissance or a break with the past could not make it so, at least not without considerable effort. Always sensitive to criticism, Ronsard might well have wondered if the reception of his first *Amours* did not reveal the limits of exhuming a literary past for a public less versed in that past than the artist. Did he have second thoughts himself about the Pindaric odes? The last major addition to the *Odes* occurred in 1555, before the publication of the *Continuation.* How easily could Ronsard, in composing the Horatian odes of 1550, enter into the style and world of his source? Studies on the "Fontaine Bellerie" odes show that more elements in these poems possess a French (and perhaps medieval!) origin than is usually supposed. The pastoral context, the simple adjectives, the ornamental aspect of the sacrifice, none of this derives from Horace's "Fons Bandusia," whereas, as we have seen, the pastoral scene with its "*pré verdelet*" abounds in the Rhétoriqueurs' poetry, derived in turn from the *Roman de la Rose*. Clearly the problem of how to render the great in French had unforeseen complications; so, too, the problem of how and when to be oneself. The final work of the *Nouvelle Continuation des Amours* is a long poem entitled "A son Livre." It is a petulant piece in which Ronsard insists that Petrarch's *"authorité"* will not dictate his actions. The immediate context concerns the question of fidelity. Petrarch was faithful to a single woman. Ronsard began by singing Cassandre; now in the *Continuations* he writes of a Marie. Despite this accent on fidelity, poetry always lurks in the background. When justifying his change of lady through Cassandre's disdain, Ronsard notes that if Petrarch did not enjoy his Laura, he deceived both his youth and his Muse. This linking of poetry and the demands of nature against the model of Petrarch's poetry broadens the base of Ronsard's criticism and reveals a tension that could have inspired Ronsard to rethink his commitment to Petrarchist verse and usher in the *stille bas* so significant in the development not only of Ronsard but of his gifted friend Joachim Du Bellay.

Du Bellay (1525–1560)

With the *Deffence*, Du Bellay published *Cinquante sonnetz à la louange de l'Olive*, usually referred to as *L'Olive*. The poems were intended, like the *Délie*, to form a *canzoniere* in imitation of Petrarch's songs to Laura. Du Bellay used the sonnet, not the dizain, however, and a sonnet very Italian in origin, that is, divided into an octave and a sestet with variation in the rhyme pattern of the sestet. Italianate in conception and form, *L'Olive* proves to be so in substance as well. Scholars have shown that of the 115 sonnets appearing in *L'Olive augmentée* of 1550, at least half are composed of material taken from the works of Italian poets. Petrarch and Ariosto head the list of individual sources. By no means negligible, however, is Du Bellay's debt to such minor Italian writers as Sansovino and Mozzarello, whose poems had been collected by the Venetian printer Gabriel Giolito and made known to the brigade in his anthologies.

The use Du Bellay made of his sources ranges from blatant translation to reminiscences of Petrarchist commonplaces with an intermediate technique whereby Du Bellay recast the general lines of the Italian poem but preserved its main ideas and images. Such extensive use of literary material inevitably poses the question of Du Bellay's sincerity in suggesting that he was writing of an experienced, biographical event. The question arises for each of the brigade's loves (Baïf's Méline, Ronsard's Cassandre, Marie, or Hélène, for example). While attempts to identify the lady in question have met with varying degrees of success (Marie, like Olive, is still a mystery; Cassandre and Hélène can be more positively identified), the literary quality of the cycle must predominate in our appreciation of the poet's intent. It is possible that Du Bellay wished to sing a personal love, but in the last analysis, the works both he and Ronsard composed derive from Petrarch and his imitators.

The modern mind may find these facts difficult to reconcile, but only because we have passed through the Romantic movement which gave the popular imagination to understand that poetry was the fruit of emotion and biography rather than work and imitation. The poet of the sixteenth century was a craftsman, highly aware of his models and the forms at his disposal. Du Bellay spoke openly of his borrowings from the Italians when he wrote a preface to the 1549 edition of *L'Olive*. They furnish the best models for the subject he is treating, he says and by adding "*Et si les anciens Romains, pour l'enrichissement de leur langue, n'ont fait le semblable en l'imitation des Grecz, je suis content n'avoir point d'excuse,*" he reveals to what degree *L'Olive* was destined in his mind to comprise the first concrete example of the program for which his manifesto called.

Convinced in 1549 that the Italians were the masters of love poetry, Du Bellay placed his talent and his inspiration in their hands. The range of emotions and subjects scarcely ever goes beyond the established lines: the woman is praised and adored as exemplifying perfection; the poet is described as unhappy, yet more than willing to accept such woe for so perfect a lady. Since these themes had long been set down and elaborated, the Petrarchist poet did not create so much as rephrase. A typical example of this procedure is Du Bellay's sonnet "Rendez à l'or cete couleur, qui dore," composed for *L'Olive*.

The poem praises the lady by telling her to return certain of her traits, physical and moral, to the person or phenomenon with which that trait's perfection is associated.

Rendez à l'or cete couleur, qui dore
Ces blonds cheveux, rendez mil' autres choses:
A l'orient tant de perles encloses,
Et au Soleil ces beaux yeulx, que j'adore.
Rendez ces mains au blanc yvoire encore,
Ce seing au marbre & ces levres aux roses,
Ces doulx soupirs aux fleurettes decloses,
Et ce beau teint à la vermeille Aurore.
Rendez aussi à l'Amour tous ses traictz,
Et à Venus ses graces & attraictz:
Rendez aux cieulx leur celeste harmonie.

Rendez encor' ce doulx nom à son arbre,
Ou aux rochers rendez ce coeur de marbre,
Et aux lions cet' humble felonnie.

In reading Giolito's anthology, Du Bellay came upon two different poems, one by Bernardino Tomintano, one anonymous, but both constructed solely around this complimentary device. Each uses a slightly different list, however, and Du Bellay's poem becomes a curious mixture of the two. In expression and structure the French poem is closer to the anonymous sonnet, which also begins each quatrain and one of the tercets with "return." But Tomintano asked his lady "la celeste harmonia rendete al cielo" and "a Cipri bella il bel suave riso." Du Bellay seized upon their poetic qualities to write lines 11 and 10 respectively of his sonnet. Did such a technique produce in the eyes of the brigade an original work? The second preface to L'Olive would suggest so. Accused of pillaging his sources, Du Bellay claimed that his poems contained "plus de naturelle invention que d'artificielle ou supersticieuse immitation." Few remarks by the brigade point up more succinctly the distance which separates their ideas from the modern conception of originality.

At the same time, all of the poetry in L'Olive is not so derivative as "Rendez à l'or cete couleur, qui dore." Anthologies love to quote "Si nostre vie est moins qu'une journée," where Du Bellay described in patently Neoplatonic terms the return of the soul to the highest sphere. This poem, too, had its source in Giolito but Du Bellay, to accentuate the rewards of the liberated soul, begins their enumeration each time with the word "la" ("there"). This technique continues throughout the first tercet and the first line of the second, whereas the Italian poem used such repetition only in the last tercet. Du Bellay has more effectively separated quatrains and tercets, as well as heightened the qualities of the afterlife as contrasted with our earthly existence.

No less popular among the poems of L'Olive is this sonnet:

Deja la nuit en son parc amassoit
Un grand troupeau d'etoiles vagabondes,
Et pour entrer aux cavernes profondes
Fuyant le jour, ses noirs chevaulx chassoit:
Deja le ciel aux Indes rougissoit,
Et l'Aulbe encor' de ses tresses tant blondes
Faisant gresler mile perlettes rondes,
De ses thesors les prez enrichissoit:
Quand d'occident, comme une etoile vive,
Je vy sortir dessus ta verde rive,
O fleuve mien! une Nymphe en rient.

Alors voyant cete nouvelle Aurore,
Le jour honteux d'un double teint colore
Et l'Angevin & l'Indique orient.

It, too, had an Italian source which in a free translation would run:

The sea was still; the woods and meadows were revealing their beauties —flowers and branches—to the sky; and the night was departing, rending the veil and spurring on its dark and winged horses. The dawn was shaking from its gilded tresses pearls of a bright, transparent frost and already that God born at Delos was making to turn rays from the richly embaumed Aeolian shores, when behold from the West a more lovely Sun rose to rival him, making the day serene and the Eastern form grow pale. Most swift rays, eternal and unique, by your leave, my fair adorned face seemed now more bright and beautiful than you.

In addition to the general theme, the Italian work has supplied Du Bellay with his most precious details, the *"tresses tant blondes"* of the dawn and the *"perlettes rondes."* The opening quatrain, the more rich and beautiful, owes little to the Italian, however, save the horses. The setting, the movement, the images, all come from Du Bellay. Nothing in the Italian can compare with the precise, yet unobtrusive structure of *"Deja . . . Deja . . . Quand . . . Alors,"* or the force of the adjective *"vagabondes"* in the first quatrain. Here Du Bellay could definitely take pride in his work and insist that all imitation in *L'Olive* was not servile. Furthermore, the qualities that Du Bellay displayed in the sonnet (a concern for structure, words, and imagery) announce the poet's great works to come: *Les Antiquitez de Rome* and *Les Regrets.*

The years that separate *L'Olive* from the works just mentioned were not kind to Du Bellay. An illness left him partially deaf. Weak and tired, he went back on his condemnation of translators in the *Deffence* and completed a translation of the fourth book of the *Aeneid* into decasyllabic verse. His own poetry of the period, whether religious or amorous, reveals a deep melancholy strain in the poet, broken only by his famous "A une Dame" (1553), a pitiless satire of Petrarchist poetry. The same year Du Bellay's relative, the Cardinal Du Bellay, planned a trip to Rome and asked the poet to accompany him. The trip across the Alps brought on a near-fatal fever, but such was a small price to exchange his melancholy state for an opportunity to visit the capital of what had been the Roman empire and culture. The trip, in brief, was to be a humanist's delight.

Du Bellay remained in Rome from 1553 to 1557, more than enough time for his humanist enthusiasm to confront the realities of the city. *Les Antiquitez de Rome* and *Les Regrets* comprise the journal of his reactions and a perfecting of those tones of sadness and satire he had practiced before leaving France. All the poetry contained in these volumes is in the sonnet form, but Du Bellay no longer treats of love. This use of the sonnet to express a new emotion constitutes one of Du Bellay's most impressive innovations. He was doubtlessly influenced by a variety of factors. Ronsard was prince of poets and king of the love sonnet. Though away from France, Du Bellay could not have wanted to lose a reputation already acquired. What better means to impress his public than to transform the sonnet into a vehicle for those sentiments, both tender and bitter, which Rome brought out in him.

Both *Les Antiquitez* and *Les Regrets* were published in France in 1558. The incompleteness of *Les Antiquitez*, (a first book for which no second one was ever written), the use of both decasyllabic verse and the alexandrine (*Les Regrets* sonnets are all in alexandrines) and Du Bellay's extensive borrowings lead Chamard to believe that *Les Antiquitez* were written, in part at least, before *Les Regrets* and form a bridge between the mannered style of *L'Olive* and the personal frankness of *Les Regrets*.

In the introductory sonnet of *Les Antiquitez*, Du Bellay addresses the "*Divins Esprits*" of ancient Rome and invokes their "*antique fureur*" to help him sing their glory. That glory and the seven hills of Rome are Du Bellay's subject. It is a double subject, embracing, on the one hand, the physical grandeur and the cultural achievements of the past and, on the other, the material and spiritual ruin of the city that Du Bellay discovered. A famous guidebook of the day, Lucio Fauno's *De antiquitatibus urbis Romae*, published in 1549, may have given the poet the inspiration for his title. At the same time it pointed out to him the meagre remnants of Roman civilization. Unattended and unappreciated, the ruins were themselves in a state of decay and provoked in the sensitive mind of Du Bellay a stark awareness of the mortal state of all things—the metaphysical reality that lurks behind all the verse of *Les Antiquitez*, although its most forceful expression can be found in the final group of sonnets, entitled "Songe." In sleep a demon appears to the poet and orders him to contemplate the heavens. A series of visions follows in which magnificence, force, beauty, and the like live and die before his eyes, proving, as the demon had announced, that "*tout n'est que vanité.*"

To render the decay of the Roman empire, Du Bellay borrowed principally from Horace, Virgil, and Lucan, while adding more and more signs of his own developing art. The following sonnet

Nouveau venu, qui cherches Rome en Rome
Et rien de Rome en Rome n'apperçois,
Ces vieux palais, ces vieux arcz que tu vois,
Et ces vieux murs, c'est ce que Rome on nomme.
Voy quel orgueil, quelle ruine: & comme
Celle qui mist le monde sous ses loix,
Pour donter tout, se donta quelquefois,
Et devint proye au temps, qui tout consomme.
Rome de Rome est le seul monument,
Et Rome Rome a vaincu seulement.
Le Tybre seul, qui vers la mer s'enfuit,
Reste de Rome. O mondaine inconstance!
Ce qui est ferme, est par le temps destruit,
Et ce qui fuit, au temps fait resistance.

is derived from this anonymous Latin epigram:

Qui Romam in media quaeris, novus advena, Roma,
    Et Romae in Roma nil reperis media,
Aspice murorum moles, praeruptaque saxa,
    Obrutaque horrenti vasta theatra situ.
Haec sunt Roma: viden' velut ipsa cadavera tantae
    Urbis adhuc spirent imperiosa minas?
Vicit ut haec mundum, visa est se vincere: vicit,
    A se non victum ne quid in orbe foret.
Nunc victa in Roma Roma illa invicta sepulta est,
    Atque eadem victrix victaque Roma fuit.
Albula Romani restat nunc nominis index:
    Quin etiam rapidis fertur in aequor aquis.
Disce hinc quid possit Fortuna. Immota labascunt,
    Et quae perpetuo sunt agitata manent.[2]

The lines of the imitation are too clear to require mention. What strikes are Du Bellay's departures from his text. Where the epigram interrupts the exposition to ask a question (vv. 5-6), Du Bellay preferred a harsh

---

[2] You, stranger, who seek Rome in the midst of Rome and find nothing of Rome amidst Rome, look at this heap of walls and broken stones and ruined theatres covered over in this frightening place. They are Rome. Do you not see how the very remains of so great a city still mightily breathe forth threats? Just as it conquered the world, it appeared to conquer itself: it conquered in order that nothing in the world be unconquered by Rome. Now defeated, that famous invincible Rome is buried in Rome and that same Rome was victor and vanquished. The Tiber now remains a sign of the Roman name. For indeed it is carried to the sea with its rushing waters. Learn from this what Fortune can do. Things immovible begin to crumble and things that are constantly in motion, remain.

statement of reality, ("*temps, qui tout consomme*"). As a result, his *pointe*, while the same as that of his source, has been carefully prepared, and the sonnet's quatrains acquire a greater unity than could have been achieved from a reproduction of the epigram's oblique allusion. With the tercets Du Bellay continues to exercise his discretion. Line 9 of the epigram obviously inspired the repetition of the word "Rome" but the French poet did not hesitate to use the technique twice, and with evident success. So, too, the *rejet* "*Reste de Rome*," where style mimics sense or the exclamation "*O mondaine inconstance!*" which translates so immediately the pent-up emotion accumulated over the period of detailed observation and awareness are traits due to Du Bellay. They were his inventions and his finished work's most poetic qualities.

Early in *Les Regrets*, Du Bellay calls his verses "*de* [*s*]*on coeur les plus seurs secretaires.*" The collection was thus conceived to be a form of journal to which the poet confided his feelings while in Rome. In fact only a part of the sonnets was composed in Italy. Several came into being during Du Bellay's trip back to France and after his return. It is also true that *Les Regrets* found their primary inspiration in the loneliness and disgust Du Bellay felt while living in a foreign city. His association with the Cardinal placed him in a perfect situation to observe the weaknesses and corruption of the Church in general; the sudden fall from favor of the Cardinal revealed that even the most powerful could become powerless. First Rome, now the Cardinal's fate forced the poet to realize how vain the trip had become, how much he was separated from the friends and the country he loved.

His reaction was not of one kind. Introducting his poems, he wrote, "*Je me plains à mes vers, si j'ay quelque regret;/ Je me ris avec eulx, je leur dy mon secret.*" To the plaintive tone belongs the first group of sonnets (I–LX). Here we find the famous "Heureux qui comme Ulysse" and "J'ayme la liberté, & languis en service." To the second tone of derisive laughter, Du Bellay devoted the next series (LXI–CXXVII), fierce in their satire of the Holy City and the Holy See. The remaining pieces deal with a return to France and the formulation of a way of life at court.

The autobiographical nature of the collection should not lead us to believe that Du Bellay had no recourse to literary sources when composing *Les Regrets*. Its title is reminiscent of the work of another poet, estranged from his native land, Ovid's *Tristia*, and on close examination, the opening work of the collection, a long poem to Monsieur d'Avanson, proves to be inspired by, sometimes even translated from, parts of the *Tristia*. The satirical verse bears the imprint of contemporary Italian poets, Alessandro Piccolomini, Burchiello, Ariosto, and especially Berni.

Les Regrets are not *L'Olive* or even *Les Antiquitez,* however. Imitation is more discreet and far less widespread. Du Bellay had tuned his lyre to the chords of his own voice. The verses were his journal. If only because of the beautiful lyric "Heureux qui comme Ulysse," *Les Regrets* have a special place in French poetry. They are also valuable as a revealing commentary on Du Bellay's concept of poetry. On the whole, the liminal poem to Monsieur d'Avanson says little about poetry that the brigade had not expressed before. The Muse is the poet's companion; he has also been ensnared by her, who since the cradle left the poet "*cest aiguillon dedans la fantaisie.*" He makes allusion to the divine "*fureur*" that is not only inspiration but comfort, especially when the poet is as unhappy as Du Bellay. At the same time, the poet, imitating Ovid, suggests that the reader may find these verses imperfect given the time, the place, and the age in which they were written. Mere modesty, we would be tempted to say, except that the introductory sonnets of *Les Regrets* echo this tone and in a more direct way announce a poetry which Du Bellay recognizes as different and special.

The *Deffence* outlined a program of elevated poetry, carefully executed. Now Du Bellay insists that he does not want to "*chercher l'esprit de l'univers*" or "*desseigner du ciel la belle architecture.*" In writing he prefers not to "*pigner et friser.*" To sing his *Regrets* he needs not Greek models, Horace, Petrarch, nor Ronsard.

> *Je me contenteray de simplement escrire*
> *Ce que la passion seulement me fait dire,*
> *Sans rechercher ailleurs plus graves argumens.*

Calling his inspiration "*plus basse,*" Du Bellay intimates that he is following the example of Ronsard in the *Continuations.* Still, Du Bellay's declaration is so much more categorical than Ronsard's petulant "A son Livre" and the context is so much more explicit in its description of the poet's subject, as compared to the mixture of material in the *Continuations,* that we may wonder if Du Bellay's announcements are more than a question of modes.

Les Regrets were to be a personal, an intimate work. Du Bellay had decided that such a work was not compatible with the great style of those distinguished models listed in the *Deffence.* He had seen beyond the mere stylistic changes suggested by a *stille bas* to the essential distinction between a personal lyricism and programmatic composing. That Du Bellay was willing to adopt so totally the implications of the *stille bas* at a time when Ronsard was merely experimenting with style defines certain basic differences in their nature—Ronsard, consciously the public figure, Du Bellay, the melancholy shadow of his giant companion—and to what degree Du Bellay saw first the pitfalls for a poet who sought intense self-expression in the very program he had outlined.

Interesting also is the adjective "*imparfaits*" in the liminal piece. No one today would criticize a poem simply because it was personal or lyrical, instead of philosophical and edifying. Du Bellay did not seem to feel this way. His sentiments demonstrate with force the classical awareness of levels in verse and rhetorical distinctions such as made Ronsard cultivate the Pindaric ode and undertake an epic poem, then, by definition, of infinitely greater poetic stature than those little odes like "Mignonne, allons voir" we treasure today. Eminently modern in his decision to create *Les Regrets*, Du Bellay belongs to his time in the apologetic compulsion to define his work with respect to the great genres and models of classical literature.

Etienne Jodelle (1532–1573)

Of the remaining members of the brigade, Jodelle occupies a very special place with regard to the impact of the *Deffence* on French letters. In 1552, Jodelle completed his *Cléopâtre captive* and fulfilled Du Bellay's wish to see the tragedy returned to its former, that is, classical dignity. In French, in five acts, replete with the three unities as they were understood by the Greeks, a chorus, and elevated language, *Cléopâtre captive* has repeatedly been termed the beginning of French classical tragedy.

It is important to recognize, however, that Jodelle's accomplishment, like the *Deffence* itself, was not an isolated event and possessed strong ties with preceding humanist activity. Renewed interest in Greek, beginning as early as the fifteenth century, very often found expression in a study and translation of Greek classical tragedy.[3] In the years just before the *Deffence*, translations of Greek tragedies were completed by Bochetel Amyot, Sébillet, Lazare de Baïf (the father of Jean—Antoine de Baïf of the brigade), and Daurat, the humanist who so inspired the brigade at Coequeret. A few even took the next step of composing tragedies, but since Muret's *Julius Caesar* (written in 1545) and Buchanan's *Jephthes sive votum* (c. 1539–44) were in Latin, manuals have tended to overlook them in favor of *Cléopâtre captive* when searching for the first French classical tragedy.

By a curious chauvinistic twist, Théodore de Bèze's *Abraham sacrifiant* (1550), too, fails to supplant Jodelle's play. It was, after all, written and

---

[3] See p. 49.

produced in Switzerland, not France. It is not divided into acts and does not respect the three unities. In addition, it depicts a biblical event, has a happy ending, and eschews elevated speech. Be that as it may, Bèze was an accomplished humanist, and behind the biblical story we find the influence of Euripides' *Iphigenia in Aulis.* Bèze used a chorus (actually two) and varied the form of his verse much as the Greeks and Jodelle did. For this very admixture of the classical and the medieval (biblical subject, no acts, a tragicomedy plot), *Abraham sacrifiant* deserves to be mentioned with the humanists' translations as a background for *Cléopâtre captive.* It shows that when humanists turned to the writing of vernacular drama, they experienced no less than Marot or even Ronsard in other genres a certain difficulty in breaking with the past. The success of *Cléopâtre captive* eclipsed momentarily but did not solve the problem.

The play was acted before the court, and Jodelle's fellow-poets greeted the event with unbounded enthusiasm and celebrated the performance with a *fête champêtre* immortalized in verse by Ronsard. On reading the play, we may suspect that they were above all heralding the realization of yet another wish of the *Deffence* rather than extolling the literary merits of Jodelle's work. The play is not of the highest quality. Its verses are sometimes obscure and unpolished. The entire third act lacks intensity both in conception and execution. *Cléopâtre captive* has been repeatedly panned by critics of French Renaissance drama, but less for frailties in isolated parts of the work than for its failure to be a dynamic rendering of classical tragedy: *Cléopâtre captive* possesses so little action that it is more properly elegiac than dramatic. The work shows only a superficial interest in the characters' psychology. There is no denying these charges; yet it is not clear whether Jodelle envisaged a psychological, Aristotelian drama when he undertook to write his *Cléopâtre.*

Dramatic theory at this time possessed few of the nuances that discussions of Aristotle's *Poetics* would impose upon the following century. Donatus, grammarian of the fourth century A.D., distinguished between tragedy and comedy in these terms: "In comedy the circumstances of the men are middling, the pressures of perils small, the outcome of the actions joyful, whereas in tragedy all things are the opposite, the characters exalted, the tenor great, the outcome calamitous." In addition, the classical texts most available and most comprehensible to Renaissance humanists, the plays of Seneca, corroborated the definition of Donatus. The simple plan of *Cléopâtre* lays bare Jodelle's evident attempt to create along the lines set by Donatus as distinguished from a psychological drama. Anthony's ghost appears to announce that before the day closes Cleopatra will die. Acts II, III, and IV are little more than a preparation for that event. Act V tells us how Cleopatra with her attendants found death.

The work relates the accomplishment of an inevitable (even announced) event. Preparation, struggle, introspection on the part of the characters are extraneous considerations. On the contrary, the role of the principals is to recognize what fate has done to them and to provide an example of human destiny about which the chorus will speak at length. Of the play's 1616 lines, 603 are devoted to the chorus, a proportion that makes patent the moralizing, sententious quality of Jodelle's drama. Fate is inconstant, power and glory are inevitably followed by ruin, the gods envy human happiness: these are the realities to which characters and chorus return again and again throughout the play.

After *Cléopâtre captive*, Jodelle wrote a comedy, *Eugène* and another tragedy, *Didon se sacrifiant* (c. 1560?). The latter work, while conceived along the same lines as *Cléopâtre*, shows Jodelle's mature treatment of a tragic subject. Its characterizations, language, and construction go far beyond their counterparts of the poet's first play and make *Didon se sacrifiant* a drama worthy of more extensive analysis than it has traditionally received. Before Henry II's reign had reached its tragic close, Rivaudeau was composing his tragedy *Aman* and Jacques Grévin, his *César*. Jodelle had shown the way; others were willing to attempt the new form. The dual source of inspiration for the two plays just mentioned (the Bible and Roman history) prove once again that the new could still be influenced by the old, but reminiscences of the medieval theatre cannot prevent us from granting Jodelle and the brigade credit for having crystallized the various humanist efforts and provided the drama with an exciting reorientation.

4

The Last of the Valois

(1559-1589)

FRANCIS II

While Henry II was succeeded by his eldest son, Francis II, the person who in reality emerged from the background after Henry's reign was Catherine de Medici. The passions of the day provoked now praise, now bitter denunciation of this woman. Ronsard, for example, described her as "*Junon de France/ Grave en royale apparence.*" But for the Protestant Agrippa d'Aubigné, Catherine was "*une femme hommace,*" "*une mere douteuse, . . . macquerelle à ses fils.*" As a result, Catherine remains to this day a figure of history whose definitive portrait has yet to be drawn. However, separated by many centuries from the violence of the Religious Wars, we are increasingly aware of the prejudicial treatment she received from her contemporaries and of the difficulties she faced from the very moment of her arrival in France.

Catherine's marriage to Francis I's second son was a political maneuver on the part of the King; everyone knew it. Everyone knew also that the origins of the Medici family hardly placed Catherine among the nobility, and the French court did not refrain from reminding the young Duchess of this fact. Her husband did not facilitate her life by taking as his mistress Diane de Poitiers, whom he loved in open defiance of his father's wishes. In addition, Catherine had no children. When Henry suddenly became the Dauphin, her childless state brought her even greater despair and anxiety. What amazes one at this point in her story is that Catherine, who loved her husband deeply, seems to have borne her problems well and even overcome them. She accepted Henry's mistress and his illegitimate children. She charmed the same court that turned up its nose at her origins and won, in time, the esteem not only of her husband but of his father. After ten years, she gave Henry innumerable children and created one of the most brilliant courts in Europe. When Henry II marched forth in 1552 to capture Metz, Toul, and Verdun, he made Catherine regent.

Her conduct appears, in general, judicious. She had had little reason to like Diane de Poitiers, but she accepted the ménage à trois with superlative grace. Even when Henry II died, Catherine checked her emotions. Diane was asked to return the crown jewels that she had received and to cede the château at Chenonceaux to the Queen Mother, a very guarded revenge for so many years of humiliation. She seems to have possessed unusual intelligence as well. She befriended the scholarly Marguerite de Navarre and Marguerite de Valois, her sister-in-law, and became a great patron of arts and letters. She was also human, that is, proud and sentimental, even to excess.

When the preliminary discussions leading to the Peace of Cateau-Cambrésis made it clear that France was about to renounce its claims to Italian territory, Catherine threw herself at the feet of her husband in protest and demanded the disgrace of Montmorency. When her son Francis II ascended the throne, Catherine accorded to the new Queen, Mary of Scots, every honor due a reigning monarch. But Mary, already "quite contrary," showed her mother-in-law all the haughtiness so ingrained in the Guise family. She is reputed even to have called Catherine "une marchande florentine." Whether the tale is true or not, it is nonetheless a fact that at the sudden death of Francis II, who had reigned but a year and a half, Catherine made clear to the widowed Queen that it was time to return to Scotland. In fairness to Catherine, it is possible that behind the female whim lurked a political sense which told her that there were already too many Guises at court. With regard to this woman's feelings toward her children, there can be no ambiguity. Catherine de Medici was a jealous and over-protective mother—her greatest blind spot and the root of much that was unwise or precipitous in her political career. Under normal conditions Catherine's failings could have remained a family matter, but given the explosive, impossible situation she inherited with the death of Henry II, they became involved in the very destiny of the French nation.

A detailed study of the records of the Geneva Company shows that Calvinist involvement in France reached its peak around 1560–1561. The first National Synod of the Reformed Church met in Paris in 1559 to mark the completion of that organizational pattern so dear to Calvin. By now the Company was handling hundreds of requests from France for pastors, money, advice, and literature. It responded so wholeheartedly that by 1562 the Company had abandoned any effort toward secrecy and the naming of pastors to French churches became an open affair.

In 1561 the Company sent a record number of books to France. It has been calculated that in the same year there were 2,150 Protestant churches and 3,000,000 Protestants in France out of a population of some 20,000,000. The numbers are impressive; they represent, however, only one aspect of the hostile forces around Catherine.

Henry II's death gave fresh impetus to the designs of the Guises. The new Queen was their relative. The King, if of age legally, was still too young to rule without advisors. The Guises swiftly took over the reins of government. Catherine, ill with grief over the passing of a man she truly loved, offered no resistance. The Bourbons did. They were poorly treated by Henry II despite their rank, and now the young and very hotheaded Prince de Condé decided to advance himself through the rights of his oldest brother, Antoine de Bourbon, King of Navarre. In view of the age of Francis II, Condé maintained that a regent should be named and by rights that regent should be the first prince of the blood—Antoine de Navarre. Given the opposing religious convictions of the two houses, it is easy to see how very dangerous for France this feud could become. The Guises, moreover, did nothing to calm religious tensions. They pursued Henry II's policy of persecution to the letter.

Even before Henry II had been buried, Condé arrived at court and convinced his brother to do likewise. The government braced itself. Condé was dispatched on an official visit to the King of Spain so that he could not be present when Antoine de Navarre arrived. Their fears had little foundation, however. The King of Navarre was a consummate failure. He did and said all the wrong things while at court. By not even pursuing the politics outlined by Condé, he eventually dashed the hopes of the Protestant party. Was he a coward? He was perhaps more wise than he appeared. The regency was a burden not worth fighting for. The cause of the Protestants did not really touch him. He had been converted by the insistence of his wife, not the conviction of his soul. In addition, Antoine had his own goal: to recapture the lands of Spanish Navarre held by Philip II. As the treaty of Cateau-Cambrésis made no mention of this question, Antoine already knew that he would not find any assistance at the French court for his claims. To become involved in Condé's plots could only engulf him in matters that took him further and further away from the only question that interested a King of Navarre. Condé, therefore, had to proceed alone. He readily accepted the challenge and formed a conspiracy.

Condé had originally hoped to place a great Protestant noble at his side but gradually came to see that so known a person could not form a plot easily. He chose in the end a young Protestant called La Renaudie. The man was a brilliant speaker and dedicated to the cause. He went about recruiting immediately. The band, or more specifically, the bands that Condé and his lieutenant succeeded in forming did not include any members of the greater nobility—they could not risk being involved. Even the majority of the lesser nobility preferred to remain aloof. This fact is best explained by the enormous system of patronage that surrounded the great families of France and the Guises and the Montmorency clan in particular. Those dependent upon the Catholic lords would not jeopardize their situation. If one considers also the lack of enthusiasm demonstrated by the King of Navarre, the absence of the lesser nobility becomes even more understandable. The troops Condé collected were mostly mercenaries. But Condé, penniless, could not pay them. Who, then, financed these soldiers—Geneva?

The Conspiracy has often been considered a religious revolt. Reasons exist for adopting such an attitude. The desire of Condé or La Renaudie to overthrow the Guises cannot be separated entirely from their respective religious positions and the fact of continued religious intolerance under the Guise leadership. Yet, when one considers the specific aims of the Conspiracy and the role played by Calvin and Geneva, the entire operation assumes a slightly different appearance. The intent of Condé was political. He saw himself and his family engaged in a power struggle with the Guises. The age of the King and the fact that Antoine de Navarre was first prince of the blood could now be brought to bear in that struggle. What Condé hoped to achieve most immediately with his Conspiracy was power, not religious freedom.

Calvin's official position with regard to civil disobedience was firm. Established authority must be obeyed; violence must be avoided. Little wonder, then, that Calvin categorically refused to lend aid to Condé's enterprise. He also had no faith in La Renaudie's ability to bring the revolt to a positive conclusion, and what catastrophe might await Geneva if a plot that she had fostered against the King of France failed! Condé would get no money from Geneva. He got some token encouragement, nevertheless, from Théodore de Bèze, Calvin's eminent colleague, who did not share all of Calvin's political views. This defection is symptomatic. What in fact Condé had begun to accomplish was a split in the Protestant community. He had offered the reformers an alternate plan of action. It was a fertile seed. It had to grow slowly as Calvin's influence in theory and fact remained enormous in France, but already at the meeting of the second National Synod on March 10, 1560, the French Protestants took a decisive step toward civil disobedience and a parting of the ways with Geneva. Pastors were now granted a certain latitude with reference to whether public speeches of an inflammatory nature would be permitted. Far more important was a decision to form a secret group of deputies to the Estates-General to spy on the court. Ironically, the failure of the Conspiracy and the gruesome retaliation it occasioned would make Condé's alternative look increasingly attractive. If Geneva would not finance the Conspiracy, the remaining possibilities were Strasbourg, a few Protestant churches in Provence, and England. Elizabeth I's participation in this rebellion, to be called by historians the Conspiracy of Amboise, was one of the first signs of those international complications surrounding the French civil crisis which put the Religious Wars in full historical perspective. With their rise to power at Henry II's death, the Guises renewed their promise to their sister Mary of Lorraine, dowager Queen of Scotland, to help her country against England. Elizabeth I knew of the French involvement but maintained her strict anti-war policy. Still, to aid Condé was to occupy the Guises and their troops at a moment when both might turn their interest toward Scotland. Moreover, she effectively strengthened her position against Catholic Scotland without the open hostilities that could provoke Philip II, self-appointed protector of all Catholic lands. When the French government conducted its investigation of the Conspiracy, England's part did not escape them.

With men and funds, the leaders met at Nantes on February 1, 1560, to plan their strategy. The attack would take place at Blois on March 10. When the King had been taken and the Guises cut off from all outside help, Condé was to lay before Francis II his grievances. If the government resisted, the Guises and their men were to be tried and punished. It was, in essence, a very curious mixture of rebellion and remonstrance. The King's person was sacred. On this point there was no doubt. He was to be seized only so that his loyal and loving subjects could place before him their cause. This double nature of the Conspiracy would make it difficult to condemn in toto.

Such an undertaking could not easily be kept secret. The Cardinal of Lorraine soon received reports from abroad of the plot. By March the Duke of Savoy was writing him of a planned massacre of the royal family and the Guises. All was to take place on the sixth. When this date had passed, the court's general panic subsided. On the eighth the King signed an edict that in effect established religious tolerance within the kingdom. In the days that followed, patrols began stopping and searching small bands in the forest about Blois. The quantity of arms and ammunition discovered left no doubt about the intention of these bands. When questioned, the men made remarks that were even more frightening. "*La Reine-Mère*," they said, "*est une putain qui nous a fait un lépreux*"—typical calumny long circulated in the most violent anti-Catholic pamphlets of the day and no worse than similar charges made against the Protestants—but spoken by armed men who were unquestionably gathering for an attack, such words produced a profound and lasting fear at the court.

Then Francis II moved to Amboise, and La Renaudie's main captains were captured. The danger seemed past. But on the morning of March 17 the enemy attacked in force. The Guises reaped a victory, and all thought of tolerance evaporated. Francis II specifically charged the Duke of Guise to punish the rebels. He worked swiftly. La Renaudie was hunted down and shot. Heads fell in rapid order with Catherine's blessing. On April 2 Condé appeared before the court at Chenonceaux. He denied that he was the leader of any seditious undertaking. He was ready to defend himself before any man who persisted in challenging him. The Conspiracy was indeed over.

Its immediate effect among the Protestants was to produce venomous documents against the Guises and the royal family. Catherine, always sensitive to what others thought of her, found in her own apartments defamatory pamphlets. Others were sent anonymously or handed to her in audience disguised as petitions. Visibly shaken by all the events of the Conspiracy, Catherine decided to intervene in the affairs of state and to put an end to the exclusive domination of the Guise family. Coligny, before leaving the court on March 20, had already advised Catherine to look at the politics of the Guises for the root of all her troubles. Jealousy, perhaps, but Catherine had enough acumen to note that many of the policies to which her son was committed definitely coincided with the interests of the Guises. The bitter pursuit of the heretics and the promises to Mary of Scotland were only two examples that could have crossed her mind. But even if Coligny had not spoken and even if these policies had not existed, the Conspiracy would most certainly have stirred Catherine to act.

The very designs of the Conspiracy shocked her and aroused her deepest prejudices. She and her family were being defamed. A group had dared to think of holding her and her family captive! Maternal sentiment and regal pride rebelled, but, it must be added, not with the fiery intolerance of the Guises. Instead of fighting the manifestations of unrest, she attacked the causes. England had helped Condé because of Scotland. One of Catherine's first acts after the Conspiracy was to cut off all further French aid to Scotland. Repression had stirred the people before the Conspiracy; it was doing the same now so Catherine prevailed upon the King to revoke this policy of hatred and hostility and to impose an attitude of tolerance until a Council should meet and examine the whole religious question.

These were immediate steps. They could meet immediate problems but not deal adequately with the position of the Guises in the government. For a family so powerful, there could be no thought of dismissal. Catherine had to devise a means whereby she alone with her son would rule. She succeeded by paying less and less attention to the institutions of the "Conseil des affaires" and the "Conseil privé" and by incarnating the recognized principle that sovereign power resided solely in the king.

Catherine was greatly aided in this thrust for control by the gradual demise of the Conseil privé even before the Conspiracy. The Conseil privé was an official body composed of persons who held their seat by birth (members of the royal family, princes of the blood) or by election (the French Cardinals, the heads of the military, and others). It was a large group, too large for effective action. The Conseil des affaires was in effect the executive body of the kingdom. One was not named to this group, however, but participated by virtue of one's intimacy with the king. It was this distinction that brought Condé to agitate for the Conseil privé and for a say in governmental affairs that rightfully belonged to him and to his brother. That he was never taken seriously shows how moribund the Conseil privé had become, but it at least had official status. For the moment, with the collapse of the Conspiracy, Catherine contented herself with retaining the Conseil des affaires from which, after all, she had little to fear since hers was the voice to which Francis II listened. But when the appropriate moment came, she would reduce the Conseil privé to a meaningless institution and abolish the Conseil des affaires. She could be a wily, practical woman, as her decision to call a national Council demonstrated.

In 1559 the Council of Trent had already been suspended for seven years. If hopes were still to be held for a reconciliation of Protestant and Catholic views, it was rather hard to continue to believe that the Church would be its sponsor. The Protestants, moreover, did not facilitate any rapprochement by insisting that they could accept only the decisions of a Council that was free from papal censure and permitted the Protestant theologians to vote with the Catholics. To create an appropriate atmosphere for the Council from which she expected much, the Queen Mother stifled all attempts by the Guises to attack Geneva and had her son sign the edicts of Amboise and Romorantin guaranteeing a pardon "à ceux qui ont failli au fait de la religion ou mal senti de la foi." For two years, in effect, persecution ceased.

The Council might take care of the religious problem, but Catherine still had to deal with Antoine de Navarre and the political overtones of the Conspiracy. She ordered him and his brother to appear at a special meeting of the Conseil privé. There she hoped they would either make public their demands or disavow the plot as Condé had done at Chenonceaux. Even if they did not come, nothing had been lost, as now the Bourbons would have consciously provoked the government. If they came, Catherine fondly foresaw an entente among the rival princes, who would have argued out their differences. At the same time, a burning debate with regard to the religious questions would show the Pope and Philip of Spain how much the government had to call a national Council.

The Bourbons did not attend the meeting of the Conseil privé held at Fontainebleau. Their absence did little to incline Catherine to be so solicitous in the future. Yet, with Coligny, she had carefully prepared a statement of the Protestant case to the assembly. The Cardinal of Lorraine and the Duke of Guise formally replied to the demands of the Protestants. The former spoke in guarded tones, the second rashly, but both made clear that the King could not recognize complete religious freedom for the Huguenots. It was decided, however, that the Estates-General should be convoked, and with that act the Conseil privé adjourned. For such an absolutist as Catherine de Medici, the convocation of the Estates-General was not welcome news. The absence of the Bourbons at Fontainebleau had begun to show its full consequences. Then, as if to efface intentionally any vestige of respect Catherine may have felt for them, the Bourbons formed a second plot. It was swiftly discovered and crushed. Francis II ordered Antoine de Navarre to present his brother Condé at court to justify himself. So strong was the emotion among the King's entourage that for the first time the government sought assistance from Philip of Spain against the Protestants.

After much delay, the Bourbons arrived at court, where they received the coldest of receptions. Condé was almost immediately arrested. But within a few weeks, Francis II was slightly, then gravely ill. When the boy died in terrible agony, Catherine had already made clear that she would be regent for the new monarch Charles IX, not yet ten years old. Her moment had come, and she felt prepared.

CHARLES IX

A woman of amazing energy, Catherine de Medici set to work immediately to insure that the situation France was facing would be dealt with as she desired. She had her bed placed in the King's chamber. She did her best to keep the notables away from the Conseil privé by suppressing the post of *premier conseiller* and the concept of a Conseil des affaires. Just before Francis II died, the Pope, infuriated and frightened at the thought of a French national Council that might settle the religious question outside the Church, reconvoked the Council of Trent. Catherine could no longer hold her own Council, yet she had no reason to believe that the new sessions of the Tridentine body would be any more effective with regard to her problems than the former ones had been. She therefore changed the name of the French body from Council to Colloquy and pursued her original plans.

Needless to say, Catherine required some time to bring her aims to fruition. England and Spain were in no mood for war, and the Queen Mother was determined to foster that attitude. Having stopped all French intervention in Scotland, she refused to let the family interests of the Guises compromise her country. With Spain, a suitable tactic was hard to find. Facts here spoke louder than intent. France and Spain were natural enemies, locked in an overt struggle to control Europe. France and Spain were supposedly both Catholic countries; yet, Henry II's repression had stopped. Protestant insurrection in the Spanish Netherlands had repeatedly been traced to French influence. Catherine did all she could to keep the Crown above suspicion, but Philip II was a suspicious man and clever enough to see that until France put down the Protestants, his control over the Netherlands could not be complete. What, in fact, Catherine's politics entailed was a refusal to aggravate the tensions surrounding the major international feuds, that is the rivalry of France and Spain, of Catholic and Protestant, until she had settled the domestic ills that confronted her. Unfortunately for Catherine, such a policy was virtually impossible. To bring internal harmony meant catering to the Protestants, meant seeming to side with the Protestants against Spain. At the same time Catherine protested against all rumors that France was the secret leader of a Protestant League. But if this were so, why did she not form a Catholic League against the Protestants? So went the vicious circle which Catherine pretended did not need to be broken.

She fought on, meeting crisis after crisis with her unfailing energy. The night of Francis II's death, she obtained Antoine de Navarre's renunciation of the regency. She flattered him and cajoled him so thoroughly that when the Estates-General met at Orléans and Catherine's right to the regency was in question, Antoine refused to support his own rights and all opposition to the Queen Mother collapsed. The tenor of the discussion held at Orléans proved, however, that Catherine's personal victories could not efface the desperate problems facing her country.

The Chancellor, Michel de l'Hospital, delivered a long speech at the opening session of the Estates-General. He warned the delegates of the dangers that militant religious sentiment represented to the order of the state and to the very concept of loyalty to one's country. He did not suggest that the Huguenots be driven out but did condemn most soundly their acts of sedition. De l'Hospital, a voice that would long cry out for moderation, had in essence sketched the program that France would later have to follow, but in 1560 he spoke in vain. The government could not condone and condemn the Protestants at the same time.

From the outset Catherine's attempts at appeasement proved disastrous. She had Condé released. She permitted the Princesse de Condé, Coligny, and Renée de France, Duchess of Ferrara, all converts to Protestantism, to hold services in their apartments. The Catholics were scandalized. Montmorency, the Duke of Guise, and the Marshal of Saint-André formed a Catholic League to uphold their faith: the Triumvirate of April 6, 1561. It was, as J. E. Neale has said, "a turning point" in the religious struggle. "For now a party existed . . . whose object was to defend the Catholic faith, apart from the King and if need be against him."

Catherine's Colloquy, held at Poissy five months later, produced very similar reactions. She invited Théodore de Bèze to speak for the Protestants and received him well. The Catholic theologians were less polite. From the very first exchange, it became evident that the Cardinal of Lorraine and his kind had no intention of attempting a reconciliation. The arrival of the papal legate did not relieve the tension. The Colloquy of Poissy ended on October 18, a resounding failure that had succeeded only in angering further the Catholics and disquieting the King of Spain, who believed more and more in fact (the Reform movement had made great strides in France) and less in declarations (the French government was master in its own house). A few overtures to Antoine de Navarre by Philip II concerning Antoine's lost lands in Spain succeeded in bringing this titular leader of the Protestants into the camp of the Triumvirs. Alarmed, Catherine worked in even closer concert with Coligny and Condé. On January 17, 1562, a royal edict granted Protestants the right to worship outside the cities and to meet inside them if the meetings were held in private houses. The fruit of this final gesture in Catherine's policy of moderation was the Massacre of Vassy.

The Duke of Guise, passing through Vassy one Sunday, decided to hear Mass. The church was very near a barn where a group of Huguenots had gathered, illegally, for prayer. The order of events is not entirely clear, but it would seem that the frightened Protestants, after an initial conversation with Guise, barricaded themselves in the barn and threw stones at the Duke and his soldiers as they approached. When the battle was over, the Catholics had killed 23 of the Protestants and wounded over 100 more. The Duke, upset by the event, rushed to Paris, where he was greeted as a hero. Condé fled the city after receiving four letters from the Queen Mother, who put herself and her family in his hands. Condé did not seize the opportunity. Consequently, when the troops of the Triumvirs arrived at Fontainebleau to escort the royal family back to Paris, Catherine cursed the Protestants for having abandoned her. She abandoned their cause and joined the Triumvirs.

Massacres by both sides took place. The Parlement ordered the people to arm against the Protestants, who, by their numerous raids on churches to destroy the idolatrous statues, incensed the Catholics. The first Religious War had broken out. Elizabeth of England, believing that France was about to destroy herself and eager to share in the spoils, signed a treaty with Condé (Treaty of Hampton Court), according to which she would furnish him men and arms in return for Le Havre to be traded for Calais at the end of the war. Religion could be stronger than nationalism in the sixteenth century. Condé agreed to Elizabeth's demands, just as the Catholics would later deal with Spain, France's mortal enemy, when aid was needed.

Only Catherine gained from the war. Antoine de Bourbon and Saint-André were killed, Montmorency, captured, the Duke of Guise, assassinated. At the time Coligny was implicated in Guise's death. The Duke's heirs would remember his name and later reap their revenge. Thus, with a few strokes, the war had made Catherine the official head of the Catholic forces. She concluded a peace with Condé called the Peace of Amboise (March 19, 1563). It was an ignominious document. Religious tolerance was granted only to Huguenots of the higher nobility, and the list of privileges diminished greatly as one moved down the social ladder. Condé could sometimes forget he was French to recall only that he was Protestant. He could never forget that he was a prince of the blood. That Catherine thought it was a peaceful solution reveals, as did the Colloquy of Poissy, that she had no grasp of the deep-seated passions involved in the Religious Wars. This was a fatal failing.

If events at home were not enough to reveal to Catherine the force of religious convictions, she could have looked at the situation in the Spanish Netherlands. By 1567 Protestant strength there had gathered such momentum that Philip II decided to dispatch the ruthless Duke of Alba to exterminate his enemies. Not only did Catherine disappoint the Protestants by refusing to help a revolt in a country that France had long eyed with envy, but the Queen Mother went to Bayonne to talk with her daughter, the Queen of Spain, and Philip's emissary, the

Duke of Alba. The Protestants could not know how neutral Catherine tried to remain; she even refused to permit the Duke's troops to cross France to reach the Netherlands. When Alba seized the Dutch leaders Egmont and Horn, the Protestants waited no longer. They thought that the Catholic uprising against them, too, was only a matter of time and decided to strike first.

The second Religious War began with an abortive plot to seize the King at Meaux. Furious, Catherine vented her anger on De l'Hospital, whose disgrace was not long in coming. Montmorency died at the battle of Saint-Denis and was replaced at the head of the army by Catherine's third and favorite son, Henry of Anjou. On March 23, 1568, the Treaty of Lonjumeau ended the war. Condé had no money to pay his troops and yet held Chartres, a position too close to Paris to suit Catherine.

Although a treaty had been signed, hostilities continued as if nothing had transpired to end them. Alba put Egmont and Horn to death. Huguenots were known to be fighting against the Catholics in the Netherlands. Catherine's entire foreign policy was being threatened. She decided to act against Coligny and Condé, as Alba had done with his opposition. These Protestant leaders barely managed to escape, and the third Religious War began. Its horror was indescribable. It was not a war, but a slaughter. Neither side could claim the least exemption from a brutality that defies the imagination. At the battle of Jarnac, Condé was murdered after having surrendered. The battle of Moncontour brought another Catholic victory and more glory for Henry of Anjou, whose popularity was beginning to annoy his brother the King. On August 8, 1570, the Peace of Saint-Germain quelled the butchery.

Out of the carnage of the Religious Wars emerged two new policies, one political, the other personal. Many of the finest minds of France had seen too much fighting to believe that either party could ever win a decisive victory. These men, called the *Politiques*, looked for a diversionary activity beyond the frontiers of France, that is, war with Spain. France hardly needed a specific reason for such a war, and it would unite the country and end civil discord. The personal intrigue belonged to Catherine, who now decided to embark on an alliance with England via a royal marriage between Elizabeth and the Duke of Anjou. To make the match, Catherine needed the support of the Protestants, who understandably were very cool to the Queen Mother. A second marriage was proposed, then, between Henry of Navarre and Marguerite de Valois, sister of Charles IX. As Catherine pursued her plans, so did the *Politiques*.

Coligny, without the knowledge of Catherine, captured the imagination of Charles IX with his scheme to attack Spain. Preparations were well-advanced when Catherine, to her horror, discovered that another was advising her son and in a project of which she did not approve. No doubt this possessive woman was angered to think that Coligny had wrested Charles away from her; she, nevertheless, knew France would have to fight Spain alone and France was tired and without funds. What was to be done? Catherine de Medici decided upon an old Italian solution. She would have Coligny assassinated and chose the forthcoming wedding of Henry of Navarre and Marguerite de Valois as the moment. The Guises were willing accomplices in a plot to kill their most hated enemy. What Catherine did not count upon was that her plan would fail, Coligny would merely be wounded, not killed, and that this would take place when she was surrounded by the flower of the Protestant nobility who had gathered in Paris for the wedding of their leader. The Protestants threatened revenge; the Guises prepared to defend themselves. If they talked, Catherine saw herself implicated. What was she to do? The answer came on St. Bartholomew's day (August 24). At a given signal Paris began to massacre all the Protestants within its walls. The fearsome pursuit lasted for days and spread into the provinces. Coligny and nearly all the Protestant nobles were murdered. Henry of Navarre and Condé, princes of the blood, were allowed to convert, and Montgomery and Jean de Ferrières escaped. Thousands died in the massacre. Charles IX never fully recovered. He grew solemn and melancholy. There is no reason to believe that Catherine was even disturbed by what she did. The congratulatory notes she received from Catholic powers convinced her of her cleverness. She even continued to bargain with the Protestant states as if nothing had happened.

In truth enough had happened to inspire the most violent and most significant Protestant tracts of the conflict: Hotman's *Franco-Gallia* (1573) and the *Réveille-Matin des François* (1573–1574). Although Calvin's strict theories of passive resistance had long been undermined by the French Huguenots, these men nonetheless maintained until the Massacre of St. Bartholomew that they were fighting on the side of the King against the influence of the Guises. After 1572 the Huguenots, led more and more by the towns and not the nobles, abandoned their constitutional position to attack the King personally. The *Réveille-Matin* hinted that revolt by a people was a valid reaction to tyranny. Hotman stated specifically that sovereignty resided with the people and their representatives (the Estates-General). He singled out the institution of the regency for attack. Only regencies admitted by the Estates-General could be accepted, and a female regent should be avoided at all costs. The cases of Isabeau de Bavière and Blanche de Castille were cited as examples in the text, but no one could escape the contemporary implications of his diatribe.

In addition to reaping this mountain of abuse, Catherine discovered that she had definitely not crushed the Huguenots. The town of La Rochelle not only refused to open its gates to her agent but also resisted a formidable siege. The entire Midi, too, refused to recognize her authority. With her violent revenge, Catherine alienated the *Politiques* as well. She had renewed the conflict they had hoped to stifle with their war on Spain. Their designs against the Queen Mother merely reopened within the court circle the internal wounds that Catherine had wanted to heal with one barbarous stroke. At this juncture, Charles IX died, haunted, it is said, by vivid memories of the massacre. He was only twenty-four; his death was the second proof of the decadent blood that flowed in the veins of the Valois.

HENRY III

Charles IX's successor was the former Duke of Anjou, since 1572 King of Poland, now Henry III. In the time necessary for him to return home, Catherine again assumed power. She needed control to finish some business begun just before Charles IX's death. To rob the *Politiques* of their leaders, Catherine had seized upon tales of a new plot to arrest François de Montmorency, head of that house and a great force behind the *Politiques*. The Queen Mother also counted on catching Montmorency's brother Damville in her trap, but she failed. Damville, governor of Languedoc, joined the Huguenots, who formed with him a veritable republic independent of the central government. Without money, Catherine was doubly helpless. When Henry III returned to be crowned on February 13, 1575, he found himself master of only part of his kingdom.

In the months following his coronation, matters worsened considerably. Only capitulation remained for the Crown. On May 6, 1576, Henry III signed the Peace of Monsieur. The King officially regretted the Massacre of St. Bartholomew; freedom of worship was accorded the Protestants everywhere but in Paris and in the town where the court was residing (but only for as long as the court remained). Damville was made vice-roy of Languedoc, a clear recognition of his established powers in the Midi. The capitulation must be understood not only in terms of the strength of the Huguenots and *Politiques* but of the immense disfavor with the Crown that Henry III had been able to create in so short a time.

Headstrong and whimsical, the new King loved formality and all means of demonstrating his authority. He had favorites, his *mignons* as they would eventually be called, to whom he was willing to give some of the most important court posts. In doing so, he disregarded entirely the service and perquisites of the incumbents. The price of his frivolity was great disaffection among the nobility. His dissolute ways, unpredictable personality, and effeminate favorites hardly made the situation any easier. When the Catholics, especially the Guises, witnessed the concessions given to the Protestants in the Peace of Monsieur, they were determined to take matters into their own hands. Henry of Guise called upon the nation to form a League against the heretics. Henry III hurried to head off the ambitious Guise by making himself the leader of the League. Still, the very act of the Duke of Guise showed how weak the Crown was both in fact and in the thoughts of its subjects. The League of 1576 reaped a healthy victory in the North and by the Edict of Poitiers reduced significantly the privileges granted by the Peace of Monsieur.

Henry III did little that satisfied his subjects. All efforts to raise money turned against him. First the money was spent for the most dubious of reasons—earrings and lapdogs for the King, lavish gifts for his *mignons*. Secondly, there seemed no end to the rise in taxes. Between 1576 and 1588 the *gabelle*, for example, had risen from 1,000,000 livres to 3,400,-000 livres. By 1583 there were 12 offices for every original one—all because the sale of offices had proven so profitable a source of revenue. More serious yet was Henry's failure to produce a male heir. With the death of his last brother (1584), the crown had to pass to Henry of Navarre, a Protestant! (Once free from Catherine after the St. Bartholomew massacre, Henry had quickly returned to his original faith.)

Merely three months after the death of Henry III's brother, the Guises, as ambitious as ever, formed a new League financed with Spanish money. They even had their own pretender to the throne, the Cardinal Bourbon, Henry of Navarre's aged uncle, whose candidacy offered a thin veil of decency and legitimacy behind which Henry, Duke of Guise, hid his own aspirations. Again the Crown stood between two hostile forces, but now the country liked even less its King, whose impotence is testified to by his Edict of July 18, 1585. It forbade the Protestants to hold services, ordered their ministers to leave the country, and gave them the choice of conversion or exile. It was war again, the War of the Three Henries—Navarre, Guise, and Henry III.

As Philip II was contributing money to the League, he naturally watched its activity with great interest. At the same time, his interests were concerned with a much broader area than France, which in Philip's mind could prove to be a useful pawn in a game that centered on the conquest of Europe. With France reduced to such catastrophic straits, only England remained as a major problem in Philip's bid to dominate the continent. Time and again he had rejected all suggestions of an invasion of England on the basis that it was impossible. Now a series of events was making that invasion seem almost sensible. First, in 1587, Elizabeth I put Mary of Scots to death. Mary was a Catholic, and Philip would have risked placing her on the English throne if his invasion were successful. That contingency was past. The French King, so weak and ineffectual, could not be expected any longer to have the means to second England were she attacked by Spain. Philip II waited for his moment.

It was arranged by the Spanish ambassador in Paris, Don Bernardino de Mendoza. He and the League plotted a triumphal entrance into the city of Paris by the Duke of Guise. The Duke, ordered specifically by Henry III not to enter, disobeyed and arrived on May 9, 1588. As he approached, barricades were set up, immobilizing the King's army. Henry III was a virtual prisoner in his own capital. Within the month the Spanish Armada set sail.

As the Spanish galleons had sailed toward defeat, so in the final days of 1588 the Duke of Guise went forth to meet his King (who had escaped from Paris by an unguarded gate) at Blois, where he and his brother the Cardinal were speedily assassinated. Henry III knew of the defeat of the Armada. The news, which inevitably meant that an attack on the Guises would no longer run the risk of bringing Spain into war with France, must have encouraged the pitiful monarch to make one last desperate gesture toward recovering his sovereignty.

Once again Henry III proved a failure. The fanaticism of the Leaguers turned against the King with renewed vigor. The preachers who had so recently whipped the Paris mob into a frenzy of admiration for the Duke of Guise now brought the people to open revolt. Henry III had little choice but to unite with Henry of Navarre. The war was going well for them when Jacques Clément, a young priest, begged the King for a audience concerning a most urgent matter. The King received him and, as he bent forward to receive the latest news from Paris, was stabbed. He died the following day (August 2, 1589). Catherine de Medici had died only seven months earlier. The Valois dynasty was at an end and France, a sorry sight. Still, the defeat of the Spanish Armada had checked Philip's bid for mastery of Europe. The Counterreform, too, had been stopped at a strategic point. As France lay torn by civil strife, England had determined that France could again become the pivotal state in

European politics. It remained for Henry IV to rebuild his kingdom and claim that power.

THE WARS AND A DEVELOPING LITERATURE

No facet of French life escaped the trauma of the Religious Wars. Throughout the years 1559–1589 drama, poetry, and prose were each in turn to feel the preoccupation of the literary world with this national crisis. Some works, such as Ronsard's *Discours des Misères de ce temps* (1562), deal entirely with the religious question. In others, including Montaigne's *Essais* or Jean de La Taille's tragedy *Saül le furieux*, reference to the wars is less central. Yet present where unexpected, the wars reveal all the more their impact on contemporary thinking.

It would be unfair to speak of this period solely in light of the Religious Wars, however. Du Bellay died in 1560, but Ronsard, who in the same year published the second book of his *Amours*, had yet to compose his epic or many other projects dear to the hearts of the Pléiade. The drama, just recently returned to prominence by Jodelle's *Cléopâtre captive*, had to be developed, and so too did several intellectual currents on the periphery of the literary world. All humanists were not primarily interested in religious reform. The spirit of critical examination of ancient texts gradually spread to students of law and history. By mid-century the fruits of such activity were beginning to mature. It is one of the tragedies of the sixteenth century that this general flowering coincided with the grimmest of civil wars. By the same token, the realization of so many works during this time testifies to the great inner strength of their authors.

Ronsard

With the death of Saint-Gelais in 1558, Ronsard became the official court poet. This title alone was sufficient to draw Ronsard into the political debate, and in his first major work written after the passing of Henry II, the poet chose to outline for young Charles IX the principal attributes of a good king. Much in the *Institution pour l'Adolescence du roi* (published in 1562) could have been written at any period and applied to all kings. But two lines of advice, 'Et garder que le peuple imprime en sa cervelle/ Le curieux discours d'une secte nouvelle," speak bluntly of the religious crisis and of Ronsard's position. It was, of course, an official position, on the side of the established faith and the established government upon which Ronsard depended for patronage. To assume that the poet's declaration stemmed from simple expediency would do considerable violence to the depths of Ronsard's feelings. He never quitted this position. The several long poems he subsequently wrote to Catherine de Medici, to the people of France, and to the Protestants who had attacked his poetry as pagan and impious show Ronsard's attitude to be a complex admixture of religious, political, and literary sentiments that go far beyond a simple apology for the status quo.

Ronsard realized the need for reforms within the Catholic Church and said so. But he also feared schism and the dissolution of the Church's hegemony. He saw that for all their claims to simplicity with respect to the idolatrous, rite-loving Catholics, the Protestants were neither better people nor more in harmony with the Christian tenet of love. He realized that authority flaunted in the religious sphere could quickly undermine respect for authority in the political sphere. Protestantism had to be seen as a threat to state as well as Church. "Les enfants," he wrote in his first *Discours* to the Queen Mother, "sans raison disputent de la foi/ Et tout à l'abandon va sans ordre et sans loi." In addition, Ronsard could not escape the fact that many Protestants looked with disfavor on his art. Théodore de Bèze had already expressed this hostility to worldly poetry in his introduction to *Abraham sacrifiant*: "A la verité il leur seroit mieux seant de chanter vn cantique à Dieu, que de petrarquiser vn Sonnet, & faire l'amoureux transi, digne d'auoir vn chapperon à sonnettes . . ." In 1563 three pamphlets against Ronsard branded him a pagan and claimed that he had even sacrificed to Bacchus on the occasion of Jodelle's successful staging of *Cléopâtre captive*. Ronsard's *Réponse aux Injures et Calomnies de je ne sais quels prédicants et Ministres de Genève* (1563) denied the charge and went on to attack their allegation that his poetry "va par fantaisie" and that, ceding to the disorganization of the poetic *fureur*, he had produced verse without order. His Muse, he retorted, has more art than his critics see, but they must realize that poetry is not a sermon, where the speaker has to present an ordered argument. The poet "se promène/ D'une libre contrainte où la Muse le mène," and indeed, Ronsard's tone is not always restrained in dealing with the Protestants. Satire, elaborate prosopopoeia, invocation of the Muses, lyric outbursts, all appear in these works. His description of the poetic experience is, in fact, quite applicable to a number of works Ronsard composed both before and after the *Réponse*—the *Hymnes* of 1555-1556, the *Poësies* of 1563 and *Poëmes* of 1569. For this reason, Ronsard's contemporaries looked upon this poetry as a veritable genre, and its influence was to last much beyond the issues that occasioned it.

The poems in response to France's religious troubles are conspicuously grouped about the year 1562 and testify to Ronsard's awareness that disaster was near. After the wars had broken out, he soon ceased to harangue his enemies and warn his country. The die was cast. The Crown looked with disfavor on all inflammatory literature, and Ronsard had a greater project to complete: his epic. From the outset, the brigade dreamed of writing an epic poem to rival those of Homer and Virgil. As early as 1549 Ronsard spoke of such a project, and by 1552 he had worked out his subject in some detail. Then, for lack of money, he abandoned the poem, but not its style. Among the hymns of 1555–1556 can be found clear attempts to create an epic style on a much more limited scale. In 1566, thanks to encouragement from Charles IX, Ronsard took up his epic again to publish in 1572 *Les Quatre Premiers Livres de la Franciade.*

The poem was a failure, and Ronsard never completed the remaining books. Much time has been devoted to an analysis of this failure. It has been attributed to the choice of verse form (decasyllabic lines, rather than the alexandrine), to the subject (a concocted legend Ronsard read in Lemaire de Belges' *Illustrations de Gaule,* according to which Francus, son of Hector, survived the fall of Troy and founded Paris—a story without historical veracity, divorced from the lore of France). More fruitful, perhaps, is a consideration of Ronsard's conception of the epic and the point at which he abandoned his poem.

In a long essay on the *Franciade* published with the posthumous collective edition of 1587, Ronsard gave specific advice on how to write "le Poëme Heroïque." "*Tu embelliras de braves circonstances tes dons, et ne les presenteras tout nuds ny sans ornement, comme le present du Roy Latin à Aenée*" is a typical phrase. Again and again we return to the example of the ancients—"*Tu imiteras les effects de la nature en toutes tes descriptions, suyvant Homere. . . . Suy Virgile qui est maistre passé en la composition et structure des carmes.*" Homer and Virgil had become more than models; they were molds into which the poets' inspiration must flow if the resulting poems were to be worthy additions to the epic genre. No free play of the imagination was encouraged. On the contrary, in his first preface to the *Franciade* (1572), Ronsard judged the body of Ariosto's epic as "*tellement contrefaict et monstrueux qu'il ressemble mieux aux resveries d'un malade de fievre continue qu'aux inventions d'un homme bien sain.*" And despite a number of impressive passages, the *Franciade* reads as a cold, imitative poem in which the

appropriate conventions are observed but without the slightest suggestion that the poet wrote with excitement. There is no doubting Ronsard's wish to write the poem or the sincerity of his conviction that the
work would gain from an imitation of antiquity, but neither sentiment
proves an adequate substitution for sustained inspiration.

The example of Homer and Virgil posed the general problem of
imitation. Given the point at which the fourth book of the *Franciade*
ends, Ronsard may well have abandoned the work because of a more
specific difficulty. Hyante, daughter-priestess of King Dicée, Francus'
host, has agreed to reveal the future to the Trojan hero and already
begun to relate the story of the kings of France. It was Ronsard's
announced plan to cover all the monarchs up to his patron Charles IX.
As the fourth book closes, he had advanced only to Charles Martel.
It is hard to blame Ronsard for retreating in the face of so laborious
a task as lay before him.

The *Franciade* demonstrates to what degree respect for antiquity
could stifle as well as fire the brigade's imagination. It shows, too, how
much the success of the brigade in adapting classical forms may be
related to the amount of definition these forms had received. Tragedy
and epic poetry were the best delineated of classical genres, and here
the brigade failed most noticeably. Not being able to declare with
precision what they understood imitation to be, the brigade was often
saved from disasters on the order of the *Franciade* by the freedom
they enjoyed in working with less codified genres, such as the ode.

In an adjudication of Ronsard's final works, the failure of his epic
is more than offset by the brilliant collection of love sonnets first
published in 1578 under the title *Sonnets pour Hélène*. This group of
poems represents a dramatic return to the love sonnet. The collective
edition of 1560 had presented Ronsard's last sonnet cycle, the so-called
Marie poems, most of which were not new but borrowed from the
Continuations. Indeed, the only new poems included in the cycle of
1560 were not sonnets but long works of an eclogue-elegy variety,
imitated in part from Theocritus and yet another aspect of Ronsard's
experimentation with form and style. As we have seen, Ronsard's
official post as court poet was to take him even further from a personal
lyricism into the passions of religious and political conflict.

It would be a mistake, however, to conclude from these facts that
Ronsard had abandoned the love theme or his desire to become the
Petrarch of France. The seasonal hymns of 1563, for example, relate
in allegorical form the cycle of nature by describing the union of first
Flora and Spring, then Summer and Ceres, Autumn and Bacchus to
bring forth life. The pairs are hardly well-versed in the art of loving.

Union takes place in a sudden, passionate way that is justified by the recognized need to accomplish Destiny's designs. Ronsard preceded two of the hymns with long introductions devoted to a definition of the poet, who, also, is a man marked by Destiny. As the hymns advance, Ronsard develops in particular the concept that these couplings must take place, that the creative process must be maintained, and that all situations contrary to such cannot be tolerated. There is a patent parallel here with Ronsard's objection to a fidelity as demonstrated by Petrarch, who loved without being loved (or gratified), and the next adventure related by Ronsard, the elegies to Genèvre, show that he was not unaware of the possibility of applying his general remarks on the seasons to his private life.

Genèvre pines for a dead lover. Ronsard entreats her saying that *"Dieu ne fait une femme si belle/ Pour estre contre amour de nature rebelle."* Genèvre is still young; to insist on preserving a love that runs counter to all natural desires is unthinkable. When the lady is at last won over, the poet rejoices in their pleasure and makes a significant discovery:

> *Lors vous trouvant aussi douce & traitable*
> *Qu'auparavant vous n'estiez accostable,*
> *L'aspre fureur qui mes os penetra*
> *S'esvanouit, & Amour y entra:*
> *La difference est grande & merveilleuse*
> *D'entre l'amour & la rage amoureuse.*
> *Adonc la vraye & simple affection*
> *Loin de fureur, de rage & passion*
> *Nourrit mon coeur, passant de veine en veine,*
> *Qui ne fut point ny frivole ny vaine.*

This contrast between *"la rage amoureuse"* and *"la vraye et simple affection,"* as well as Ronsard's greater awareness of the role of love in the fulfillment of a poet's destiny, form the essential innovations that separate Cassandre and Marie from the *Sonnets pour Hélène.*

For the heroine of this final cycle, Ronsard chose a lady-in-waiting to Catherine de Medici, Hélène de Surgères. Contemporary reports suggest that Hélène was not a great beauty—a fact which has caused modern critics to attribute the choice to Ronsard's appreciation of the many associations with Hélène's name (Homer, Troy, and so forth). Whatever lay behind the choice, Ronsard produced for Mlle. de Surgères some of his most perfect sonnets, including the famous "Quand vous serez bien vieille."

Less well-known is this poem:

> De voz yeux, le mirouer du Ciel & de Nature,
> La retraite d'Amour, la forge de ses dards,
> D'où pleut une douceur, que versent voz regards
> Au coeur, quant un rayon y survient d'aventure,
> Je tire pour ma vie une douce pasture,
> Une joye, un plaisir, que les plus grands Cesars
> Au milieu du triomphe, entre un camp de soudars,
> Ne sentirent jamais: mais courte elle me dure.
> Je la sens distiller goutte à goutte en mon coeur,
> Pure, saincte, parfaite, angelique liqueur,
> Qui m'eschaufe le sang d'une chaleur extrême.
> Mon ame la reçoit avec un tel plaisir,
> Que tout esvanouy, je n'ay pas le loisir
> Ny de gouster mon bien, ny penser à moymesme.

Everything in the first quatrain betrays Petrarch's continued influence over Ronsard. Petrarchist conceits were still the model for love verse in an elevated vein. At the same time, taken as a whole, the sonnet bears little resemblance to Ronsard's early style. The structure is firm. Although the poet wishes to describe a strong emotion ("eschaufe," "extrême"), he juxtaposes an accent on sweetness (vv. 3, 5) and renders the invasion of her "pasture" in verses 9–10 by a slow, steady rhythm. Very little is being said in this poem that cannot be found in innumerable Petrarchist sonnets. The poet's tone, however, is quite unusual. It is one of remarkable sobriety and introspection. He does not develop his comparisons in an extraordinary way. The ending is not a surprise or smart remark. Such traits, in addition to the balancing of tones and consciousness of form as contrasted with the élan of many Cassandre sonnets, point to a decided evolution in Ronsard's love poetry toward what might be termed a classical aesthetic. The poet's indictment of Ariosto's Orlando furioso quoted earlier suggests the same evolution. In one aspect the fruit of Ronsard's contemplation of "la vraye et simple affection" and the role of love in poetic creation, this evolution could also be interpreted as the final coming to grips with those classical models demanded by the Deffence. In either case, Ronsard's ideas had changed, and the span of his work now contained the widest variety of style, genres, and attitudes. That variety determined much of the confusion and complexity of French poetry well into the seventeenth century.

Desportes (1546–1606)

Well before his death (1585), Ronsard saw his glory challenged and precisely in the realm of love poetry. Both King and court had found in Philippe Desportes a more agreeable, more comprehensible proponent of the Petrarchist style.

This poet was taken into the household of Henry III even before that strange personality became King of France. Desportes accompanied his master to Poland only to return with him to France and fame upon the death of Charles IX. The French courtier had never been completely enamoured of Ronsard's love sonnets. The criticism occasioned by the *Amours* of 1552–1553 was a fact that Ronsard hid from no one, and if we are to believe the initial sonnet of the *Continuation des Amours,* the *stille bas,* too, was not an unqualified success. Was it Ronsard's mythological allusions, his sensuality that brought about this reaction? In part perhaps, but the eventual movement in his style as compared with the rapid rise of Desportes suggests that Ronsard and the court were simply of two minds regarding the nature of love verse. Ronsard sought to produce an artistic achievement worthy of him and his vocation; the courtiers wanted an entertaining style, easy to understand, and well-grounded in the language and conventions of their circle. Whereas Ronsard combined the Petrarchist mode with lessons learned from the classics, the court doted on the Italian style.

Desportes' love sonnets have nothing new to say. The first 11 lines of this sonnet, for example, contain the most traditional ideas, simply expressed:

> Quand quelquesfois je pense à ma premiere vie
> Du temps que je vivois seul Roy de mon desir,
> Et que mon ame libre erroit à son plaisir,
> Franche d'espoir, de crainte, et d'amoureuse envie:
> Je verse de mes yeux une angoisseuse pluye,
> Et sens qu'un fier regret mon esprit vient saisir,
> Maudissant le destin qui m'a fait vous choisir,
> Pour rendre à tant d'ennuis ma pauvre ame asservie.
> Si je lis, si j'escry, si je parle, ou me tais,
> Vostre oeil me fait la guerre, et ne sens point de paix,
> Combatu sans cesser de sa rigueur extreme:
> Bref, je vous aime tant que je ne m'aime pas,—
> De moymesme adversaire—ou si je m'aime helas!
> Je m'aime seulement pource que je vous aime.

The final tercet is another matter. It is complicated and willfully so. But once the game is understood, we are again within the world of the simple and the trite. Such a technique is typical and underlines the traits so pleasing to the courtier mentality. All humanist baggage, whether mythology or neologisms, has disappeared. (When Desportes used myths, they tended to be the best known.) The poem is immediately grasped except perhaps in its final lines which require more thought. Here Desportes exhibits his "originality," that is, wit, subtle enough only to give us the smile of surprise when we understand, but never so subtle as to tax our mind. Desportes' better verse has won just praise for its musical qualities, but if this sweetness of style represents a positive borrowing from the Pléiade and a positive legacy for the seventeenth century, so many concessions to the public's taste paved the way for that surge of *précieux* poetry which virtually eclipsed Ronsard, the love poet.

Du Bartas (1544–1590)

Characteristic of the attitudes toward Ronsard among the poets who followed him are these two statements: "*En ses amours, il est quasi ridicule, et il y a quelquefois du galimatias*" and "*son esprit n'était porté qu'à représenter des guerres, des sièges de ville, des combats.*" Both remarks were made by Cardinal Du Perron, who, as an avowed admirer and disciple of Ronsard, wrote numerous encomiastic poems and *pièces de circonstance* along the lines of Ronsard's Pindaric odes of 1550. He is a rather unfaithful disciple, however. The remarks just quoted show to what degree much of Ronsard's work had lost its appeal. What in 1550 had been innovation and revitalization of language and literature was "*ridicule*" and mere "*galimatias*" to later generations. Du Perron's odes, like Desportes' sonnets, avoid the recondite at all costs. The form is regularized; the diction, adjusted even to the point of banality.

Not all poets at the end of the sixteenth century had such divided feelings about Ronsard. Many who lived in the provinces, away from the Italianate court, still revered in particular the Ronsard of the hymns, that inspired poet who gave in to the poetic *fureur* and described the cosmos with a fiery lyricism which was in no way *ridicule*. Prominent among such poets was Guillaume de Salluste Du Bartas.

His major work, published in 1578, is the *Semaine*, a poem in seven cantos, each devoted to one day in the week of the Creation. The scope is immense. Scarcely an element of the Creation is omitted. No less amazing is the style. At a moment when mythology, neologisms, and other humanist trappings had ceased to inspire many poets, Du Bartas published such verses as:

> *Les froidureux Trions ne couvrent de verglas*
> *Les bois Phoeniciens, l'Autan ne daigne pas*

> Passer le bord Lybique, et l'autre Hyperboree
> Retient dans ses prisons captif le froid Boree.

He uses words like *arreste-nef*, *flo-flotant*, and *porte-luth*. A study of Ronsard's variants would show that even the master had repudiated these terms when the *Semaine* was published, but the hymns remained behind to inspire those who did not know of changing tastes in Paris or who did not want to change their tastes. These partisans of Ronsard's virile diction could only scoff at the Italianate sweetness of a Desportes. Subject, too, separated them from the court trends. Profoundly religious and erudite, Du Bartas and his emulators had little use for a poetry that did not seek out the epic Muse or shunned "difficult" verse.

Thus the lines were drawn. A more polished, courtly group admired Ronsard in both his light and serious poetry but saw both through a critical eye that in essence copied Ronsard only to transform him. It is this mentality that led to Malherbe. The second group of admirers were, in a sense, archaic at the very moment of their blossoming. But the wars and the arrival in Paris of Henry IV (1594) interrupted the movement of the Valois court toward a more regular, if banal, poetry. In addition, the spirit of the hymns and of Ronsard's *fureur* was loath to die. Only many years after the prince of poets died did the satire of his *Discours* and the gravity of the *Franciade* find eager imitators. But the imitators did come, and, in this way, from the one great fertile mind of Ronsard emerged a poetic spectrum as varied as the talent that inspired it.

The Drama

If the development of light and serious verse during this period points both ahead and back, what can be said of the drama, that literary form recast by the Pléiade and destined to reach unequalled perfection in the seventeenth century?

In the years following Jodelle's success signs of the early humanist treatment of classical tragedy can still be found. Seneca's *Agamemnon* was translated in 1556 and 1561. La Péruse adapted the story of Medea as it appeared in Seneca and Euripides, preserving in the main all the violence of the ancient texts. Gradually the poets tried their hand at original plays. Jacques Grévin published his *César* in 1561, Des Masures, a David trilogy entitled *Tragédies saintes* in 1563, Rivaudeau, his *Aman* in 1566. Jean de La Taille published his *Saül le furieux* in 1572, although the play was certainly composed much earlier, probably before 1563. It is interesting to note that all these dramatists are Protestants and that only Grévin's play does not have a biblical source.

The author of *César* explained his intentions in a *Bref Discours pour l'intelligence de ce théâtre.* He remarked, "*Aussi je diray ceci sans arrogance, que je suis encores à voir Tragédies et Comédies Françoises . . .*" *César* was designed to correct this state of affairs. The inspiration behind the other plays is more complex. All make reference to the Religious Wars and accentuate to varying degrees those aspects of the biblical material which paralleled the Protestant plight. *Aman's* allusions to the afflictions of the Jews, victims of tyrannical, idolatrous princes or Des Masures' insistence upon the rewards awaiting those who suffer yet put their faith in God contain unequivocal allusions to contemporary problems. Freer than the Catholics to read and study the Bible, Protestant writers promptly recognized the theatre as a means of dramatizing their situation, in addition to comforting the faithful. But even here, in nearly every case, the general humanist effort to bring about a classical French drama continued to be an important stimulus.

When we read the plays of Rivaudeau, Des Masures, and La Taille, we discover that significant differences in form separate Des Masures' *Tragédies saintes* from the other plays. If in his liminal "Epistre," he spoke of representing "*à l'ancienne mode,/ Quelques tragiques traits,*" Des Masures did not mention Aristotle or any attempt to make his play conform strictly to the definition of tragedy given in the *Poetics.* Grévin, Rivaudeau and La Taille, on the contrary, introduced their plays with remarks on the nature of tragedy and specifically mentioned Aristotle. As a consequence, their plays are tighter in construction and more rhetorical in tone than Des Masures'. The *Tragédies saintes* were written for the "*décor simultané*" of medieval drama and share with that drama as well a formless, rambling plot and innumerable characters, including Satan. What then are the "*tragiques traits*" to which Des Masures referred in his "Epistre"? The same document provides an answer. "*Le Tragique, induisant à la fin de la Scene/ Un spectacle piteux et miserable à voir,*" can be found in these plays, says the poet, since throughout David leads a "*vie agitée.*" There is, moreover, a reversal of fortune in the portrait of Saul, although Des Masures referred in his "Epistre" only to God "*qui abbat la hautesse, et renverse les forts.*" In other words, Des Masures conceived of tragedy in terms of content, not form.

His contemporaries had read Aristotle and knew better. It was not sufficient to take a medieval form and add suffering to create a tragedy. Rivaudeau insisted upon the unity of time. Jean de La Taille's *De l'Art de la Tragédie* (written after *Saül le furieux,* but published with it) added that the hero must not be too wicked or too virtuous. The plot should be well-constructed, in five acts, devoid of allegorical figures and theological arguments. La Taille's remarks seem aimed particularly at discrediting the persistent medieval influence and show a greater awareness of the essentials of the *Poetics* than the comparable writings of Grévin or Rivaudeau. Whichever dramatist we read, however, the general lines of development are similar. Caesar's assassination, Aman's thwarted ambitions, Saul's fall from grace all represent a piteous spectacle, based on the reversal of fortune.

More correct (by Aristotle's dicta) than Des Masures' *Tragédies saintes*, these plays are still radically different from the great works of Corneille or Racine and much closer in concept to the justification given by Des Masures for his choice of "tragedy" to describe his trilogy. Separated by a divergence in form, all these playwrights preserved the pattern for tragedy defined by Donatus, executed by Jodelle, and reaffirmed by their reading of Aristotle. With the French Classical theatre behind us, we see in this phrase from the *Poetics*, "it is from such traits [of character and thought] that a man's actions and hence his eventual success or failure springs, whether in drama or in real life," a clear reminder that psychological depth and motivation must accompany the tragic spectacle. The sixteenth-century dramatist did not share this view of tragedy. He should not be too severely censured. After all, Aristotle also said that "while there cannot be a tragedy without action, there may be one without character." What is essential here is to recognize that the works of Donatus, Aristotle, and Seneca pointed to a drama of lament based on the reversal of fortune of a great personage, and on these grounds the sixteenth-century poet wrote and continued to write tragedies. Even Robert Garnier (c. 1544–1590), a Catholic playwright of greater talent than any other in these years, brought no fundamental changes to the form. He did write the first important French tragi-comedy (*Bradamante* in 1582) and borrowed his love plot from Ariosto, not the Bible or ancient history, but in working out his plot, he used the most standard techniques.

The discovery of Aristotle, while heightening the differences between medieval and classical forms, contributed relatively little to the formulation of a tragedy as Racine practiced the genre. Too much had to transpire in French literature—new sources, new styles, new attitudes—before one can see the Senecan pattern give way to a sophisticated psychological drama. Furthermore, as the prefaces and introductions quoted above reveal, the sixteenth-century dramatist did not look deeply into the dicta he found in Donatus and Aristotle. The Italian Academies, the salons, and finally the French Academy would have to intervene before these rules could take on greater and, in a sense, less meaning.

Michel de Montaigne (1533–1592)

While the new dramatists battled with all-too-healthy manifestations of the medieval theatre, other struggles of a related nature were progressing in the realms of law and historiography, struggles that were to effect a break not only with medieval but with humanist attitudes as well.

Even before Ronsard began contemplating an epic poem or Grévin, a French tragedy, the humanists had begun to develop an inordinate attachment to classical culture. Stunned by the discoveries of such men as Valla and Budé, firm proponents of exegesis based on original documents, certain jurists discarded the scholastic texts and, even more, the mountain of commentary—so often erroneous—that scholastic teaching had accumulated. Led by the great Jacques Cujas (1520–1590), these jurists returned to the *Corpus juris* and looked upon their predecessors and contemporaries with scorn for having propagated ignorance and confusion. They went even further. Exegesis was placed above practical knowledge in the training of new lawyers, and Roman law came to be considered a universal law, applicable to all lands at all times.

Similarly, Italian humanists of the Renaissance, after having read the great classical historians, decided that only history as written by Sallust and Livy or as described by Cicero in his *De Oratore* was worthy of consideration. Sallust had written of a single war, so Rucellai composed his *History of the French Invasion* (referring to the descent of Charles VIII into Italy). Livy's main work studied the founding of a single city, Rome, so Bruni wrote a history of Florence. The format, too, was standardized according to the classical models. The narration proceeded chronologically, year by year, with extensive descriptions of the military campaigns and geographical areas of battle, and invented speeches sprinkled throughout to express the characters' motivation. Although Cicero had said that history should be true, the humanists permitted these invented speeches not only because the ancients had done so, but because the ultimate aim of history was moral. It should preach and correct men's acts by showing examples of past wisdom and folly, a view of history not unrelated to the jurists' desire to use the *Corpus juris* to establish laws for modern man.

As the sixteenth century advanced, a reaction set in against both jurists and historians who possessed such an attitude toward antiquity. Italian historians, in an attempt to find an explanation for the collapse of city-state diplomacy and the subsequent French invasion, came to realize that the codified format of historical writing was inadequate to deal satisfactorily with such a problem. Girolamo Borgia and after him Francesco Guicciardini (1483–1540) grew convinced that the French invasion had to be studied as a European question, not as part of the history of Florence, as a subtle interplay of diplomacy, not as just a series of military campaigns. The result of Guicciardini's reflection was his monumental *Historia d'Italia*. Published posthumously in 1541, the work contains 20 books of which the last four were completed by Guicciardini's nephew. The traditional division into books must not fool us. Guicciardini put aside some of the most sacred conventions. He doubted the possibility of judging modern acts by their classical counterparts and employed a chronological narration quite unlike any used by other Italian historians. Within a single chapter, even page, Guicciardini changed focus innumerable times. Now we are in Milan, now Rome, with individuals, with armies, listening, judging, contemplating at a rate that often taxes the imagination but conveys, as the writer must have hoped, a firm sense of the complexity of his subject, the instability of institutions, and the varieties of human character and action.

In France, by mid-century, Ramus, Hotman, Baudoin, and, most importantly, Jean Bodin (1530–1596) had decided that law must have as its basis a wider range of information and precedents than the *Corpus juris* could provide. Intensive study of common law showed repeatedly that Roman law was not easily adapted to the requirements of the modern French state and that many of its principles even ran counter to the traditions of French jurisprudence. To be valid as a universal standard the *Corpus juris* had to encompass universal experience, and, as Hotman pointed out, the *Corpus juris* did not even contain the best of Roman law. Baudoin boldly asserted that history alone could provide for the jurist such a universal basis, since it alone could supplement the knowledge of customs and institutions contained in the law. Bodin took up these arguments and in his *Methodus ad facilem historiarum cognitionem* (1566) sought to outline a method whereby such a universal history could be compiled, something Bodin himself achieved, in part, later in the *De Republica libri sex* (1576).

Since Bodin was to deal with history as a source, he had to confront the problem of historiography and questions such as what is history and what is reliable history. A great admirer of Guicciardini, Bodin expressed in the *Methodus* many ideas already put into practice in the *Historia d'Italia*. History, despite Cicero's discussion in *De Oratore*, is not rhetoric: "Ce serait en effet une grande sottise de n'admirer dans l'histoire que la force de l'éloquence, l'invention du discours ou l'agrément des digressions. . . ." Both men show marked interest in insuring that their work and profession related to reality, not conventions.

Guicciardini revamped the chronological narrative to conform to the complexity of real events; Bodin broke with Cujas' purely exegetic approach to learning law and insisted, regarding history, that

ceux qui abandonnent la considération des choses humaines et naturelles pour commencer par l'histoire sacrée et qui exposent aux enfants et aux ignorants les questions ardues touchant les choses divines sont déçus dans leur espoir et ils ne font que détourner le plus grand nombre de cet objet trop élevé. . . . Si l'esprit humain, sous la touche de l'esprit éternal et divin, peut bien oublier dans une très large mesure ses tares terrestres, il n'en reste pas moins . . . profondément immergé au sein de la matière impure, affecté par sa contagion . . .[1]

Throughout runs a reassessment of the humanists that was definitely related to the reaction in court poetry to the learning of the brigade, yet of much wider significance. Bodin, Guicciardini, Hotman, and others had not only taken the humanists to task; by accentuating the practical and the human, by recognizing the complexity of human events, and the difficulty of dealing with absolutes, they had thrust the sixteenth century even further away from the Middle Ages and closer to the modern world. At this crucial moment we encounter Michel de Montaigne, whose *Essais* reflect such a reassessment of ideas, perfect it in a sense, and, above all, give it an expression that charms and arrests the mind even today.

Since his early career revolved about the law courts, it is not surprising that Montaigne should know of Bodin. We are not sure where Montaigne studied law, but it is very probable that he was a student at Toulouse, the great law faculty that included Jacques Cujas. From 1554–1557 Michel occupied a seat in the court in Périgueux, which his father had originally bought for himself. This court was soon dissolved and its judges absorbed by the Parlement of Bordeaux. Montaigne rarely alludes to these years in the *Essais* except to extol his friendship with Etienne de La Boétie. When occasionally Montaigne does speak of French laws and judges, his remarks are caustic enough to assure us that during this time Montaigne witnessed more corruption, stupidity, and injustice than their opposite. In 1571 Montaigne retired from the Parlement, disappointed that he had not been able to accomplish great things, depressed by the deaths of his father, his infant child, his relatives, and La Boétie.

---

[1] All quotations are from Pierre Mesnard's French translation of the *Methodus* (Paris: Société d'édition "Les Belles lettres," 1941).

In his tower at Montaigne, he read voraciously both the classics and his contemporaries, including Bodin and Guicciardini. Montaigne speaks well of these two authors. In particular he praises Guicciardini for his impartiality and reliability as a historian and remarks that Bodin has best expressed to what degree we are ignorant of our own affairs, a fine demonstration of Montaigne's sympathy for the iconoclastic ways of Bodin and Guicciardini and his ability to grasp the essence of his reading. Montaigne had a mind of his own, however, and did not hesitate to criticize these same authors. He disliked Guicciardini's excessively dark portrait of human motivation and Bodin's excessive rationalism (criticisms that are worth pondering with respect to the general message of the *Essais*). Montaigne's early education, directed by a private tutor and an enlightened father, certainly contributed to the formation of so independent a mind. So did the skepticism gleaned from his years in the Parlement and his particular social position.

Montaigne's family name was Eyquem. Both his parents were of merchant stock, and it was only in 1477 that the Eyquems secured a title and the property of Montaigne. By entering the law, Michel formalized the distinction already present in his origins between himself and the noblesse d'épée.[2] Bourgeois, jurist, nobleman, Montaigne had access to several worlds in which he might move with authority and, therefore, with freedom. Indeed, although he dropped the name Eyquem, coveted the order of St. Michael, and repeatedly spoke of his writings in deprecating terms, lest one consider this aristocrat a serious author, or worse, a pedant, Montaigne was also quick to criticize the unlettered aristocracy whom he recognized as more concerned with sport than with the development of their being, that *cultura animi* so important to the ancients. A learned man, he also reviled those whose heads were full of matter that ignored or conflicted with the art of living. So varied an experience convinced Montaigne that this art was not easily mastered. Yet he knew his goals, and out of his own intelligence and that of the men he studied, Montaigne fashioned a new social ideal which the seventeenth century was to term the *honnête homme*.

As we might expect, this independent mind was not likely to let itself be circumscribed by existing literary forms. Not the least of Montaigne's accomplishments was to create for the expression of this particular ideal a new form: the essay. Its models were the letters and dialogues of antiquity. In discussing Plato's *Dialogues*, Montaigne makes clear the attraction of these two informal, unstructured genres. "*Platon me semble avoir aymé cette forme de philosopher par dialogues, à escient, pour*

---

[2] See p. 146, n. 1.

loger plus decemment en diverses bouches la diversité et variation de ses propres fantasies. Diversement traicter les matieres est aussi bien les traicter que conformement, et mieux: à sçavoir plus copieusement et utilement." He would have chosen to express himself through letters, he tells us elsewhere, except that he had no one to whom he could write. And so he devised a new form, consciously preserving that all-important possibility of treating a variety of subjects and presenting his material in a variety of ways.

The essay form developed slowly. Evidence exists to suggest that Montaigne did not come upon the title of his work until six or seven years after his retirement (1571), and even when he used the word essai in his text, it was with the primary sense of a "test" of his judgment. Moreover, the very earliest essays bear the mark of more traditional pursuits. Such essays as 3, 7, 8, 14, 15 of the first book, all composed between 1572 and 1574[3] and noticeably shorter than most, contain little reference to the person Montaigne but present instead examples from the lives and works of others, selected because of their relevance to certain general questions Montaigne found interesting. These characteristics have earned for the early essays small praise. Villey saw them as representative of the period's enjoyment of sententia and exempla. At the same time, the particular questions Montaigne chose to treat are not without importance. Problems of human judgment (how do men act in certain circumstances; how do we judge certain acts) and human emotions (what is the effect of fear, ambition, anger upon us) are perhaps the most conspicuous. They show Montaigne's immediate preoccupation with man and his nature. They also reveal the influence on Montaigne of Stoic philosophy, which deals at length with the passions in order to show their nefarious effect upon the mind.

"De la Solitude" and "Que Philosopher C'est Apprendre à Mourir," two rather long essays in the earliest group, develop to considerable degree Stoic concepts. The importance of solitude derives from the sage's necessary withdrawal from the temptations, the passions of the world in an attempt to achieve the true introspection and state of tranquillity which is the object of all Stoics. At the same time Mon-

---

[3] Books I and II of the Essais were published in 1580. In 1588 Montaigne added not only the essays of Book III but also innumerable passages sprinkled throughout the essays already published. Montaigne continued this procedure even after 1588. In 1595 a posthumous edition of the Essais incorporated still more additions found in the so-called Bordeaux copy, where Montaigne had written his afterthoughts. These three stages of the text are usually designated by the letters a (1580), b (1588), and c (1595). It is understood that when we say "composed between 1572 and 1574," the reference is to the a stratum only.

taigne, like Seneca, took pains to explain that the solitude he is speaking of is more an attitude than a physical retreat. "Que Philosopher C'est Apprendre à Mourir" echoes Seneca's preoccupation with death. Inevitable, death is, therefore, a source of fear, which, like all strong emotions, must be controlled. Montaigne adopted Seneca's solution, to wit, the realization that we must familiarize ourselves with death and live as if each moment might be our last.

Despite the evidence of these essays, not enough has been made of Montaigne's reliance on Seneca throughout the creation of the *Essais*. Recognized as a more urbane form of Stoicism, Seneca's philosophy is, in fact, highly eclectic. He borrowed from Epicurus, admitted that certain aspects of Stoicism, such as excessive love of the syllogism and dialectical subtleties, might best be left aside while others (the sage's self-reliance, for example) should be rethought and redefined. Life in Seneca's eyes was a compromise between the ways of the sage and those of the world, between an inordinate attraction to and hatred of life. His *Epistulae morales* (translated as *Letters to Lucilius*) deal with much more than solitude and death. Friendship, habits, religion, custom, education are talked about and in a manner quite comparable to their treatment in the *Essais*. In addition, Seneca possessed a definite sense of the fragility of all things and the vagaries of human intelligence.

The latter consideration is of particular interest, given Montaigne's most impressive writing between 1573 and 1578: the "Apologie de Raimond Sebond." Probably composed in part with no thought of Sebond but rather as an attack on human presumption, the "Apologie" took final form only in the two years preceding the edition of 1580. Asked to write an apologia for Sebond, Montaigne created a superstructure to that end around the earlier passages on reason and produced the longest, most perplexing of his essays.

It contains the famous motto, "Que sçay-je," which for so long has been considered Montaigne's final message to his reader. Today, the attribution of such importance to the "Apologie" appears to many excessive. Though the composition of the essay is definitely related to Montaigne's brush with the more skeptical writings of Sextus Empiricus and Plutarch, "Que sçay-je" can be said to represent the totality of Montaigne's philosophy only by doing extensive violence to the text.

The essays written between 1578 and 1580, for example, contain one of Montaigne's most constructive, "De l'Institution des Enfants." Addressed to Diane de Foix, who was expecting her first baby, the essay discusses the kind of education Montaigne would recommend for the child-to-come in conjunction with those practices which Montaigne overtly deplored. A man's education should lead to what is most profitable for him, that is, in Montaigne's eyes, the creation of a firm ability to judge, one independent of others' views and capable of turning upon itself to admit its own mistakes. Memorization, *récitation*, these standbys of scholastic pedagogy, Montaigne abhorred. They instill in the student an uncritical attitude toward authority and contribute in no way to the formation of a free mind. After Gargantua's encyclopedic curriculum, Montaigne's seems shockingly narrow. But Montaigne knew what he was about. Depth, not breadth, was his prime concern. When we have learned the *"sens et substance"* of what we read or study, then we have achieved something truly significant.

Equally interesting is the famous essay "Des Cannibales." The impact of overseas expansion at last begins to be seen. With a satirical flair that would blossom throughout the eighteenth century, Montaigne used a description of the New World to impose upon the old a disquieting objectivity. He makes the reader rethink the concept of *"barbare,"* his practices in war, even the institution of royalty. With the same finesse, he studies in detail the traits of a civilization still ruled by nature. The spectacle of the cannibals is best summarized by one word—*vertu*—which describes their attitude toward their enemies (*"Leur guerre . . . n'a autre fondement parmy eux que la seule jalousie de la vertu."*), the success of their polygamous marriages (*"Estans plus soigneuses de l'honneur de leurs maris que de toute autre chose, elles cherchent et mettent leur solicitude à avoir le plus de compaignes qu'elles peuvent . . ."*), and the tenets of their religion (*"Il y a quelqu'un des vieillars qui . . . presche en commun toute la grangée . . . Il ne leur recommande que deux choses: la vaillance contre les ennemis et l'amitié à leurs femmes."*) As this assemblage of contexts suggests, *vertu* in Montaigne means more than "virtue." Its more accurate translation would be "valor" in that valor connotes physical as well as moral strength.

Taken together, "De l'Institution des Enfants" and "Des Cannibales" are as positive in orientation as the "Apologie" appears negative. "Des Cannibales" demonstrates Montaigne's faith in an inner strength given to man by nature but weakened by society. "De l'Institution des Enfants" shows that Montaigne was convinced of the efficacy of a proper education to a sufficient extent to spell out its necessary components. Neither essay has a place in the work of a man whose final word on human capabilities was a negative "Que sçay-je."

How is it possible, then, that within so short a time and within the same work, Montaigne could exhibit such varying opinions on the capacity of human intelligence? The traditional answer has been to insist on the evolution of Montaigne's philosophy. First a Stoic, he underwent a crisis after exposure to Sextus Empiricus. In his third phase, beginning about 1578, Montaigne adopted an Epicurean philosophy whose finest expression appears in the last book of the *Essais*. Formulated by Pierre Villey, in his *Les Sources et l'Evolution des Essais de Montaigne*, this theory held sway for many decades. In recent years, it has lost considerable ground. We have been shown, for example, that skepticism in Montaigne appeared before the "Apologie," but it is equally important to note that the "Apologie" stands out among the essays because of its perspective, rather than its philosophy.

Montaigne will put down Sebond's critics, he says, by making them "*mordre la terre soubs l'authorité et reverance de la majesté divine. C'est à elle seule qu'apartient la science et la sapience.*" The last sentence is quite absolute, and the essay has often been spoken of as if Montaigne meant it to be so. When we look at the examples that the author gives of those subjects of which man has foolishly claimed knowledge—the nature of God, the soul, the sky—the sentence takes on a more specific application. We are assuming to penetrate the subtlest mysteries of life whereas, Montaigne reminds us, "*C'est à Dieu seul de se cognoistre et d'interpreter ses ouvrages.*" This restriction still leaves open much more than the earlier quotation from the "Apologie" would intimate, and, as Donald Frame has so wisely seen, "What he mocks is our claims that we know what we cannot know. Never does he suggest that we know too much or think too much about ourselves and our behavior." [4] The essays composed between 1578 and 1580 return to man and his behavior and to the perspective Montaigne had begun with in 1572, a perspective that was not hostile to Montaigne's view of man in the "Apologie," but simply its complement. Morever, from this interplay of perspective (what man cannot do versus what man can do) derives one of the major themes of the *Essais*: moderation. A basic Stoic principle, it appears even in the "Apologie." "*Je vous conseille, en vos opinions et en vos discours, autant qu'en vos moeurs et en toute chose, la moderation et l'attrempance,*" he remarks to the Princess who commissioned the work. The final pages of the third book's last essay will in no way contradict this word of advice.

There are changes, of course, in this long work which spans so many years of Montaigne's life. But how many of them are of philosophical rather than biographical and literary origins? If in the third book Montaigne speaks more lightly of death, we know that an accident recorded in "De l'Exercitation" and an attack of kidney stones proved to him how much imagination could create more pain than actual illness and

---

[4] Donald M. Frame, *Montaigne's Discovery of Man* (New York: Columbia University Press, 1955), p. 77.

that in any event nature, through sleep, provided man with a continual rehearsal of that ultimate moment. If the essays in the third book are longer and franker than the others, certainly the great success of the 1580 edition, coupled with the experience gained in its composition, had given Montaigne more confidence and candor, but not necessarily a new view of life.

If we leave aside the thorny questions of interpretation when we read the *Essais*, it is difficult not to be struck by Montaigne's pithy remarks, show-stealing in their ability to condense his wisdom and grasp of the truth about human acts. Yet neither these phrases nor the questions of interpretation should hide from us the uniqueness of the total work that Montaigne wrote.

Both Montaigne and Rabelais, for example, treat the subjects of religion and education. Both have pronounced affinities with Stoic doctrine. But ultimately the Good Life for Rabelais is conceived in religious terms: *"il te convient servir, aymer et craindre Dieu, et en luy mettre toutes tes pensées et tout ton espoir; et par foy formee de charité, estre à luy adjoinct, en sorte que jamais n'en soys desamparé par peché."* From Montaigne's formula, *"Les plus belles vies sont, à mon gré, celles qui se rangent au modelle commun et humain, avec ordre, mais sans miracle et sans extravagance,"* God and sin are noticeably absent. This is not to say that Montaigne had lost sight of Rabelais' religious ideal; he had not. He knew, however, that in most cases a man's profession of faith was as fortuitous as his nationality. He saw God as a mysterious, impenetrable force, not the protective and paternal being of Rabelais' novel, who even possesses his analogy in the numerous father figures Rabelais created. Like Bodin, Montaigne considered theological questions unfruitful and tried to help us get on with the immediate problem of living.

Rabelais, too, mocked human pretentiousness and scourged the jurists. Through Pantagruel, he censures Panurge for wanting to know God's designs. Judging by the "Apologie," Montaigne would not disagree, but he did not possess Rabelais' Evangelical convictions. Hypothadée can tell Panurge, *"Pour sçavoir sur quel est son [de Dieu] plaisir, ne fault entrer en desespoir. . . . Le bon Dieu nous a faict ce bien qu'il nous les a revelez, annoncez, declairez et apertement descriptz par les sacres bibles."* Montaigne insists that while, *"il a pleu à la bonté de Dieu de nous esclairer, il est bien besoin qu'il nous preste encore son secours, d'une faveur extraordinaire et privilegée, pour la pouvoir concevoir et loger en nous; et ne croy pas que les moyens purement humains en soyent aucunement capables . . ."* In the face of man's limitations, Montaigne invites us to explore other paths to knowledge—the self and, in his final essay, experience. The two have in nature a common denominator. The final essay shows a sharp awareness on Montaigne's part that the self's needs and limits are synonymous with what nature has prescribed for us. Similarly, the experience of a phenomenon (immediate contact as opposed to any intellectualizing about it) will undoubtedly bring us closer to seizing its true (natural) form. But, of course, for the *Essais* to bear fruit, we must be able to grasp both what Montaigne says and the truth he asks us to seek. Herein lies the complexity of the *Essais*: they are an appeal for the intelligent restraining of the intellect. Herein lies the unity of the *Essais*: with the judgment that education can form, the awareness that solitude can provide, plus the realization of our mind's failings, we can begin to live as nature and her Creator designed.

This network of ideas shows, too, how far the French had diverged in their search for values from the principles of the Reform movement. There was still much protest against the dry prattle of the pedagogue, but criticism had led not to simple piety but to man himself, not to the Bible but to Seneca and the wisdom of other men. A critic of the intellect who will also uphold man's ability to know himself, Montaigne looked forward where Rabelais looked back by believing in God, yet building on man.

5

𝕳𝖊𝖓𝖗𝖞 𝕴𝖁

(1589-1610)

THE STRUGGLE FOR RECOGNITION

Few kings of France ever faced, upon assuming the throne, such difficulties as confronted Henry of Navarre. Fortunately for the King and his country, it is also true that few French monarchs possessed his ability to deal with adversity or had a more splintered opposition. Huguenots and Catholics, Gallicans and Ultramontanes, noblesse d'épée and noblesse de robe[1] were involved, throughout Henry's reign, in a series of bitter quarrels from which the Crown eventually profited. That Henry IV remained King of France until his death represents an immense personal victory. His assassination in 1610 shows that such a victory had its price, that the monarchy could be strengthened only at the expense of irritating its rivals and opponents. The image of a happy, prosperous France in the years of Henry's rule must remain a legend that was greatly aided by the emotional impact of his death. The King knew of the dissension within his country. An attempt on his life occurred as early as 1594. He predicted that only when he was gone would his people realize his accomplishments. Time proved him right. Time proved also that Henry's efforts to establish his position had laid the foundations of an absolutism that would stand long after 1610. In that his assassination contributed directly to make the throne firm and all-powerful, even in death Henry IV maintained his fight to bring

---

[1] The Gallicans agitated for a strong national church; the Ultramontanes, for strong papal control over the Church. The terms "noblesse d'épée" and "noblesse de robe" distinguish between the old families of nobles whose function in the kingdom was to bear arms and those magistrates who had earned nobility through their service or their family's service in those offices.

the monarchy out of the gloom of the Religious Wars and into a glory that would be Versailles.

Henry III had recognized the King of Navarre as his successor when on his death bed. This did not suffice to reconcile his circle to the idea that they must accept as their king a Protestant and a man whom the Pope had excommunicated. (When seized the night of the St. Bartholomew Massacre, Henry and Condé were spared with the announcement of their conversion. No sooner released, they abjured this conversion. In 1585 Pope Sixtus V retaliated by excommunicating them and excluding them from succession to all titles in France.) After Henry III's death, a small group of the Catholics from his entourage went to Saint-Cloud to inform Henry of Navarre that should he convert, he would be recognized as King of France.

Henry met them with firmness and eloquence. He would not convert; he would be advised only by a national Council. The Catholics relented somewhat and so did Henry (compromise and arbitration were to play large roles in Henry's strategy). On August 4, 1589, Henry was given temporary recognition in return for a promise to convert within six months. The agreement disgusted the Huguenots and failed to placate the more radical Catholics. Both groups abandoned the new King in large numbers.

Henry's faith did not create the only objection raised against him. For many Frenchmen, Henry's very claim to the throne was a moot question, if not a breach of the laws of succession. Navarre was Henry III's cousin but only *au vingt-deuxième degré*—a distance far greater than in the case of the succession of either Louis XII or Francis I. Henry had no legitimate claim; he was a usurper. Moreover, this Protestant was descended from yet another usurper, Hugues Capet. The Guises, on the other hand, traced their lineage back to Charlemagne. Thus, when the Duke of Mayenne, a Guise, countered the agreement signed at Saint-Cloud by proclaiming Henry's aged uncle the Cardinal Bourbon, Charles X, and himself, Lieutenant General of France, it was not difficult to sense Mayenne's overall scheme.

Navarre would not be discouraged. He intended to seize Rouen with his remaining troops, but Mayenne advanced and Henry fell back to Dieppe. The armies battled at Argues, and Henry carried the day. The victory was enough to win Henry new friends, but he needed more. He needed Paris as well.

All of those who opposed the new King did not live in France. The Hapsburg empire followed very closely the developments that occurred after Henry III's death. Long rivals of France, the Hapsburgs still tended to think and act as protectors of the Catholic faith. The Austrian

House defended Catholicism against the infidel Turks. Spain watched over the Church's interests in western Europe. Philip II could hardly have viewed without alarm the prospect of a Protestant King of France! In addition, whether Protestant or Catholic, France played hob with Hapsburg aspirations. It divided their possessions; it made difficult the transportation of troops from Spain to the North and from Germany to the West, where the Netherlands constantly created rebellions and unrest. Since the new King of France had a disputed claim to the throne, Philip decided to end all his troubles (and those of France) with one ingenious blow. He conspired with Mayenne to have himself named "Protector of the State and of the religion of the kingdom of France" in return for the troops and supplies Mayenne needed to defend Paris. Philip's intentions were even easier to see through than those of Mayenne. He would help defeat Henry, become King of France, and make France a fief of the Empire. Astute, Henry IV was also lucky, and here Navarre's luck became evident for the first time. Mayenne, already hesitant, was dissuaded from putting himself in the ignominious posture of a tool of Philip of Spain. He accepted instead to be helped by Sixtus V and rode out to destroy Henry IV's army.

The clash took place at Ivry on March 14, 1590. Henry crushed his enemy and laid siege to Paris. The siege was long and painful, but each day new nobles rallied to Henry's cause, now sweet with the odor of victory. At this point, Cardinal Bourbon died. Without money to pay his troops, Henry had to raise the siege and contemplate how little he had accomplished. "If only you would convert," his friends and family told him. Henry was adamant, but when 1591 brought no change in the position of either side, such advice began to impress even Henry as the only solution. He sent a delegation to the new Pope, Gregory XIV. Feeling his support in danger of collapse, Mayenne called the Estates-General, only to learn that the Pope had refused to see Henry's delegation.

The Estates-General met in Paris on January 26, 1593. Few delegates appeared. The *Satyre Menippée* ridiculed the meeting unmercifully. In truth, it showed remarkable judgment—another stroke of luck for Henry of Navarre.

Mayenne openly thought that the Estates would elect him King of France. They made no effort to do so. They dealt rather with the more serious problem of Spain. Philip II had devised a new plan. He made his daughter Clara Isabella Eugenia, a granddaughter of Henry II of France, a claimant to the throne. Of course her election would have meant putting aside the Salic Law, but these were desperate times. The French Catholics needed Philip's aid. Would they need it enough to put his daughter on the throne? When it became clear that Philip did not even intend that the Infanta should marry a Frenchman but had chosen an Austrian Archduke for her, the Estates temporized no longer. Their patriotism won the day, and Philip's proposals were summarily dismissed.

Then the long-awaited event took place: Henry recanted. On July 25, 1593, Henry asked before the doors of Saint-Denis to be received into the Catholic church. The populace rejoiced, but Henry soon discovered that he had failed to silence all the opposition. The Pope's representative thundered that only the Pope himself could raise the state of excommunication placed by Sixtus V. Rabid Catholic preachers maintained that Henry's recantation was without any meaning whatsoever. Clement VIII, who had succeeded Gregory XIV, paid no attention to the King's envoys. At the same time the Catholic League saw that further opposition made little sense. The various district governors asked to retain their posts upon recognition of the Catholic monarch. Henry wisely consented. He had his enemies still, but he was King. The final touch came on February 27, 1594, at Chartres where amid the traditional pomp, Henry IV was crowned King of France.

HENRY'S REIGN

Within a month of his coronation, Henry IV entered Paris. His predecessor had been dead for nearly five years, and only now did Navarre possess the crown and the capital of France. This lapse of time is symbolic of the general struggle Henry IV would continue to wage until his death. With each gain, old questions remained (in 1594 the problem of Henry's relations with the Holy See had yet to be solved), and new ones rapidly replaced those he solved. Spain, debts, social and religious tensions rushed to confront the monarch. He dealt with each carefully, never provoked crises, but when they occurred, he acted with force. When force was not possible (for lack of money), he used diplomacy and arbitration.

It was often doubted during his rule that Henry IV's conversion had been in any way sincere. Once a Catholic, he did not turn away his Protestant friends. He even made a Protestant Marshal of France! But Henry had learned the lesson of the Religious Wars well: the Huguenots and the Catholics had to learn to live together. To this end the King worked steadily for both his country and his continent.

No less tense than the conflict between Huguenots and Catholics was the split within the Catholic group between the Gallicans and the

Ultramontanes. The Parlement of Paris was strongly Gallican. The old Leaguers were predominantly Ultramontane and welcomed, to the displeasure of the Gallicans, the growing influence of the Jesuits. The problem of the Jesuits afforded Henry his first major crisis after the coronation.

On December 27, 1594, a young man named Jean Chatel, who was studying with the Jesuits, attempted to assassinate the King. The Parlement fixed the blame on the order and decreed that the Jesuits were banished from Paris, Rouen, and Grenoble. The country needed a good war, Henry decided. Victory in battle had begun his rise to power; it could serve again to divert the country from its internal tensions. Henry declared war on Spain. The act did not help to convince the ardent Catholics that Navarre's conversion was serious, but it did rally all Frenchmen around a common cause. In this way Henry effaced the remnants of opposition among the League and made known to Philip II that France had not forgotten his treacherous designs. Despite the superior numbers of his enemy, Henry IV won a victory at Fontaine-Française. It was in truth a small rout, but the country treated it as a great success. More important, it produced not only the surrender of Mayenne, but an agreement with the Pope.

The issues surrounding Henry IV's relations with the papacy at this time had begun to take on a desperate and dangerous air. The new King knew perfectly well that papal recognition would further consolidate his hold on the country, but other groups were now pressuring the Pope to act. The Gallicans long hoped that a French king would follow the example of Henry VIII of England and create a national church, independent of the Holy See. Henry IV seemed their man. Married early to Marguerite de Valois, daughter of Catherine de Medici, Henry IV had already been separated from his wife for some time when he became king. Their temperaments and their infidelities made any reconciliation unlikely. Worse still, they had no children, and the kingdom would be left to a Protestant heir, the Prince de Condé. Clearly Henry IV needed to divorce his wife and marry again. The Gallicans saw the drama of Henry VIII and the Anglican Church being reenacted in their own country. Everything seemed in their favor. How was the Pope to grant a divorce to a King whom he refused even to recognize? And the King was given to understand that what the Pope was unwilling to do, members of the French church would agree to in a moment. The Ultramontanes and the Jesuits contemplated the situation with alarm and pressed the Pope to recognize Henry IV, if only to keep France within the Church. These pleas, coupled with Henry's victory at Fontaine-Française and the complete disintegration of the League, convinced the Pope. On September 17, 1595, Clement VIII granted Henry IV his absolution. The Gallicans had been routed, and Henry IV could thank this little internal quarrel for bringing him the formal allegiance of all French Catholics.

Clement VIII had no intention of letting his precious recognition be given without the strings that mattered so much to him. If he was about to aid Henry IV in securing the support of his flock, he fully intended that Henry IV help the Holy See maintain its position in France against the Protestants. Absolution was granted to the King of France *on the condition* that he establish Catholicism as France's only religion, that he adhere strictly to the Concordat of 1516, that he discontinue naming Protestants to any ecclesiastical benefices and apply all the reforms of the Council of Trent, that he obtain the conversion of the Prince de Condé, and that he build monasteries throughout the realm.

Henry IV was caught in a bind. France had just spent 30 years in battle to prove that a single religion could not be established. Moreover, Henry IV was at war with Spain. He needed the Protestants to help him fight. Each rapprochement of King and Pope drove the Protestants farther from the throne. The Gallicans were not about to rejoice either. Only a year before one of the members of this group had written *Les Libertés de l'église gallicane*. Henry IV paid little heed to any of these radical outbursts or to any of the radical demands of the Pope. He accepted gratefully the absolution, but when Henry IV died in 1610, almost none of the Pope's conditions had been carried out. Henry IV's refusal to embrace a policy of extremes alone marks him as one of France's greatest kings. That the policy he did adopt furthered the interests of the Crown as well as those of the nation cannot detract from Henry's genius. This was no accident, but given the alternative he faced (so brilliantly sketched by Clement VIII), it was evident that just as war and the triumph of a single party or foreign power went together, so internal peace, compromise, and the subordination of private interests to the will of the Crown had to form an interlocking series of objectives.

Henry IV's reaction to the Pope's gesture was characteristic. He made full use of his gains, chose to procrastinate in the application of the conditions, and went about ruling his country. The war with Spain dragged on with no startling event until suddenly on March 10, 1597, the enemy seized Amiens. This act laid open the route to Paris. Henry IV rushed to horse and laid a siege that was to last six months, but he prevailed. Within seven months Spain signed the Peace of Vavins (May, 1598). In September Philip II died, exhausted by the pursuit of ambitions that—as far as France was concerned—had failed completely.

Had Henry possessed more money in his coffers, he might never have signed the Peace of Vavins, but finances plagued him as they had his predecessors. As it was, the Peace merely ended open hostilities. Although Philip III was not the man his father had been, Hapsburg strategy could hardly change, and Henry was as committed by his position as King of France to stay the Spanish dreams as Philip III was to pursue them. In the absence of the funds to maintain a war, Henry IV devised a diplomatic campaign that proved even more successful than his military victories.

From the North Sea to the Adriatic a series of minor states stretched along the border between French and Hapsburg territory; singly these states could be of little importance in the battles of the two great powers, but collectively they could decide whether Hapsburg troops might move easily or slowly about Europe. Henry IV's attempt to unite the Italian states against Spain failed. His dealings with Geneva, the United Provinces,[2] and certain small states along the Rhine had remarkable consequences. Toward the United Provinces, so long a trouble-spot for Spain, Philip III adopted a more lenient attitude than his father had possessed. He was willing to grant them independence on the condition that freedom of worship for the Catholics be granted. The Protestant Provinces would not accept this condition. In 1608 Henry IV allied himself with the Provinces and sent 10,000 men. The following year Philip III signed an agreement with the Provinces that established a twelve-year truce. The Provinces were independent; the religious question did not even come up. It has been said that at this moment in history, Spain's dominance over European affairs passed to France.

As we might expect, Henry IV's most difficult problem, the problem which would cost him his life, was the religious tensions from which France still suffered. In the days before the Religious Wars, Catherine de Medici had been hard pressed to explain her country's inconsistency in condemning the Protestants abroad and courting them at home. As good a case as she might have made in terms of France's internal situation, the Queen Mother eventually had to end this strategy. Henry IV also pursued a policy that appeared to many to be fraught with inconsistencies. While certain implications may have given the King pause, again the Crown persisted and laid the foundation for a prosperous country and a strong monarchy.

Henry IV's conversion shocked the Huguenots into refusing to lend aid to the King against Spain. In 1593 they even re-formed the firm organization of the days of the Religious Wars. When the Pope gave

---

[2] In 1579 the northern provinces of the Netherlands formed a confederation dedicated to ending Spanish rule.

Henry absolution and demanded that Catholicism be established as France's only religion, the Huguenots seemed even more justified in their distrust of the man who had abjured their faith to take the throne. Henry IV not only ignored the papal conditions, but in 1598 he issued the Edict of Nantes which guaranteed religious freedom to the Huguenots. The document was not very different from others on the subject that had been proclaimed before. Its importance lies in the fact that it lasted, thanks to Henry IV's insistent efforts to bring about peace between the warring factions. By favoring the Huguenots, he of course angered the militant Catholics, but Henry always knew how to parry. He obtained a divorce from Marguerite de Valois without so much as hinting at a schism à la Henry VIII. He married a good Catholic, Marie de Medici, and produced a Catholic heir. The child was named Louis, and his godfather was the Pope. The Catholics could not have asked for more.

But they did. Throughout the years of the Council of Trent, the Gallican church remained aloof from the proceedings. It and the Crown felt that many of the reforms interfered with the established workings of the Church and neither would permit such interference from without. Still, constant pressure was applied to force Henry IV to make the decrees of the Council French law in accordance with his promises to Clement VIII. The King in 1600 persuaded his ministers to accept the principles set down by the Council of Trent. He was warned that the Gallican Parlement of Paris would never accept to register the decrees. Henry did not force the issue. He had made his gesture to the Church. The Pope, angry that Henry would not go further, thought the King in error to fear the Parlement, but Henry knew his people too well to provoke needless crises.

His manner of dealing with important political questions throughout his reign continually points up this fact. A burning issue of the day was raised by the absolutist James I of England, who attempted to turn the tables on the Holy See's claim to temporal and spiritual powers by attributing to himself spiritual as well as temporal dominion. Henry IV steered a clear path between the two sides. He had no intention of accepting the Pope's claims but recognized, too, that to adopt the extreme position of James I would renew difficulties between the Crown and the Holy See, between the Crown and the Ultramontanes. At the same time, he hoped to lure England into an alliance against Spain. He chose to arbitrate, to keep on good terms with both sides, and to bring the dispute to a close.

A similar situation arose when the Venetian republic imprisoned two ecclesiastics on civil charges and refused to recognize any immunity the

Church claimed for itself and its members. To support the Pope meant alienating the only Italian state that could successfully defy the Hapsburgs. On the other hand, Henry IV knew of a determined effort behind the scenes to bring Venice into the Protestant camp. He saw many dangers in making Venice a Protestant state. A strong Protestant coalition among the European complex of nations would inevitably lead to new wars. Again Henry chose to arbitrate with the result that, without angering either side, he secured the release of the Jesuits and the restoration of peace.

What Henry IV accomplished abroad is only a shadow of his accomplishments within the realm. The debts incurred by the Crown both within and outside of France had risen to staggering proportions by the time Henry III died. They had to be paid. One source of money throughout the sixteenth century had been the sale of offices—a practice which over the years created two sets of noblemen. The noblesse d'épée belonged to the old families of France whose function had always been to defend the country. The noblesse de robe were upstarts. Sons of wealthy bourgeois would hold offices which had been bought and, if held by three successive generations and still held at the death of the latest possessor, granted nobility to the family. Documents of the day show how much scorn the established noblesse d'épée heaped upon their competitors, but competitors they were nonetheless. Wealth opened to the middle class functions previously held by the old nobility. Worse, their participation raised the price of offices to a point where the spendthrift noblesse d'épée could no longer afford to compete.

All these problems and tensions Henry IV met with his usual aplomb. His appointment of Sully to oversee state finances proved a brilliant stroke. By clever, often by brutal, means Sully paid debt after debt and turned an empty treasury into a storehouse of funds. Henry IV knew that he was being well served and followed Sully's advice even in rather ruthless measures. Sometimes, the solution had its compensations. When Henry IV married Marie de Medici, her dowry virtually effaced the immense debt owed the Duke of Tuscany, without doubt a major consideration behind the match.

Henry IV's relationship to Sully characterizes his attitude toward the crown servants in general. He wished to be surrounded by men he could trust and was willing to protect them. In the end, this meant a victory for the ennobled functionaries, whom Henry IV saw as being more intimately tied to the king's service than the noblesse d'épée could ever be. In 1604 the King institutionalized his protection of the state servants by relieving them of the "règle des quarante jours." Originally, if a man resigned his office (in favor of one of the family, of course), his wishes would be carried out only if he were still living 40 days after his resignation. At a time when few were safe from epidemics and assassinations, this clause had become the final stumbling block in a system of state offices that was otherwise automatically hereditary. In return for the repeal of this provision, the officers would pay the Crown an annual fee, called the *annuel*. This change disconcerted the rival nobility who had no funds with which to compete as inflation hit the *annuel*. It also disconcerted the more conscientious members of the noblesse de robe, who predicted a decline in the quality of officers since money alone was now the basis for the awarding and retention of a government post. Henry IV no doubt foresaw both problems and welcomed them. The *annuel* became a prime source of revenue, and the decline in competence of the functionaries provided him with an excuse to exercise greater and greater control over the country.

The noblesse d'épée fought back, but they did not really have the means to wage a successful campaign. To reduce the number of individuals exempt from paying taxes, the government demanded proof from a noble seeking such a privilege that three generations of his family had borne arms for the king. In the chaos and destruction of the Religious Wars, such documents were lost, and many new names appeared on the tax rolls. Furthermore, the noblesse d'épée was never known for conservative budgeting. The old nobility was always in debt and more and more to the wealthy bourgeois and ennobled crown servants. By 1614 matters had reached a critical point, and the nobles succeeded in convoking the Estates-General to lay their grievances before the young Louis XIII.

The situation was potentially most dangerous. Any united action among the three estates would have made it impossible for the King to refuse redress. Fortunately, the old rivalries remained, and no significant coalition was formed. The *annuel* had so won the Third Estate to the sale of offices that they were prepared to block any attempt by the other estates to suppress it. Such an action was proposed, and the Third Estate concurred but only if the royal pensions (enjoyed by the nobility and the clergy) were also suppressed to balance the loss in revenue. This countermove effectively killed the attempt by the First and Second Estates to destroy a system that was rapidly depriving them of their privileged positions in the kingdom. The Crown was safe and the path to absolutism open. It would be paved with books, tracts, and pamphlets that flooded the country after Henry IV's assassination, the second that France had known within recent memory. Regicide was condemned, the inviolability of the king's person proclaimed. The Ultramontanes resented such an upsurge of feeling, and the Jesuit Cardinal

Bellarmine wrote his *Tractatus de potestate summi pontificis in temporalibus* to reaffirm the Pope's position. It was directed mainly against James I, but French feeling ran so high that the Parlement of Paris quickly banned the book and forbade all teachers to discuss it. Absolutism could not be far away.

NEW TRENDS IN ART AND LETTERS

Just as the complexity of France's emergence from the Middle Ages during the early years of the century was mirrored in the works of Lefèvre, Marguerite, or Rabelais, so, now, as Henry IV created a new state out of the ruins of the Religious Wars, a state that was to form the foundation of the Ancien Régime, the artistic production of these years between 1589 and 1610 reveals both the confusion of Henry's situation and the signs of a reorientation that announced the Classical period. These years are, in brief, a period of transition. The previous techniques in painting and poetry continued to be practiced, but new attitudes came into prominence, as well as new subject matter. Since, by definition, a period of transition lies between two rather clearly defined movements, it is inevitable that the crisscrossing currents—the old forms which continue and the emerging elements of the new school—will not always present an easy subject for analysis. In the case of the transition from the world of Ronsard and Du Bellay to French Classicism, the picture is one of an inordinate complexity, created in part by the critics, but due also to the very nature of the era. Needless to say, such a situation renders this moment one of the most fertile for study.

The Second Ecole de Fontainebleau

For reasons to become clear later, it is best to introduce this period through its art. The second Ecole de Fontainebleau, dominated by three names, Toussaint Dubreuil (c. 1561–1602), Martin Fréminet (1567–1619), and Ambroise Dubois (1543–1614), cannot be called a milestone in western or even in French art. Extremely derivative since many of its painters had worked under the direction of Il Primaticcio and others of the first school, the second is interesting primarily because of its historical position and its ability to indicate tastes in subject and technique at the close of the sixteenth century.

In that this school counts among its major works a portrait of Angelica and Medoro from the workshop of Dubreuil and a "Clorinda" by Dubois, there is no mistaking the extent of interest in Italian literature among French writers and artists of the time. The former subject comes from Ariosto's *Orlando furioso*, the same poem in which Garnier found material for France's first important tragi-comedy (*Bradamante*). The Dubois canvas portrays a character in Tasso's *Gerusalemme liberata*. Both the Italian poems, called epics, derived their plot from the crusade theme in the *chansons de geste*. Yet the love stories these poets wove into the epic fabric have more in common with Desportes' poetry than with the *Franciade*. Indeed, the mythological world, so fertile for the Italian painters who first arrived at the court of Francis I and for the young poets of the brigade, tended to recede well into the background— another indication of waning interest in the culture of the humanists.

In their technique, the second Fontainebleau school continued Michelangelo's nervous, agitated style, already present in the works of some of their teachers and readily available to those of the new school, such as Fréminet, who had travelled to Italy. Fréminet's "Fall of the Rebellious Angels" and Toussaint Dubrueil's "Giantomanchia" illustrate this tendency. In the latter painting, Jupiter (Henry IV) is shown casting down the Giants (the Leaguers). This celebration of an historical event of note became a grand subject which permitted the artist to give free rein to his imagination. Movement, even violence, struck their fancy as do large scenes in which the individual, so much an object of study for the first Fontainebleau group, now tends to contribute to the composition only on the level of mass and ornament.

These tendencies of the painters at the court of Henry IV have had an increasing influence on literary analysis of the poetry of the same period. Scholars have come to recognize that in the works of Jean de Sponde or Agrippa d'Aubigné, for example, just such movement and violence often dictated the course of the poet's imagination. We find in a sonnet by Sponde on death this startling series of images:

> J'ay veu ces clairs esclairs passer devant mes yeux,
> Et le tonnerre encor qui gronde dans les Cieux,
> Où d'une, ou d'autre part, esclattera l'orage.
> J'ay veu fondre la neige, et ses torrents tarir,
> Ces lyons rugissans je les ay veus sans rage,
> Vivez, hommes, vivez, mais si faut-il mourir.

D'Aubigné, who in his *Stances* (composed probably between 1570 and 1573) had already written,

> J'ayme à voir de beautez la branche deschargée,
> A fouller le feuillage estendu par l'effort
> D'autonne, sans espoir leur couleur orangée

> *Me donne pour plaisir l'ymage de la mort.* . . .
> *Si quelque fois poussé d'une ame impatiente*
> *Je vois precipitant mes fureurs dans les bois,* . . .
> *Milles oiseaux de nuit, mille chansons mortelles*
> *M'environnent, vollans par ordre sur mon front.*

began in 1575 his famous poem, *Les Tragiques* (published in 1616), in which the horrors of the Religious Wars and an apocalyptic vision of the Last Judgment appear. In the world of the theatre, Raymond Lebègue has demonstrated that after 1580 the tragedy departed from Horace's precept that violent acts should not transpire on stage but be narrated. The year 1585 saw the publication in a French translation of an Italian tragedy *Orbecche*, which offered a patricide, a suicide, and five bodies to the public. Hays' tragedy, *Cammate* (1598), ends with a poisoning and three suicides. Adultery and rape round out the list of violent subjects suddenly in prominence among French dramatists. Having proved the existence of this bizarre, "Shakespearean" element in French tragedy, Lebègue concludes that this literary current was less strong and of shorter duration in France than in other European countries.

The subtle procedure of recognizing, yet minimizing, the character of this literature has a long history. Its finest expression appears in Lanson's *Histoire de la Littérature française*, Part IV. After discussing in general terms the reign of Henry IV, Lanson embarks on an analysis of the *"La Préparation des Chefs-d'oeuvre."* Unfortunately, such writers as d'Aubigné, instead of participating in this transition, balk, and Lanson finds around Malherbe's classical ideal *"des résistances, des reculs, des contradictions, des aberrations de toute nature."* To introduce his discussion of them, he devised the phrase *"Attardés et Égarés"* and counterbalanced that chapter with its successor *"Trois Ouvriers du Classicisme."* He saw that there were writers who resisted the coming of a classical aesthetic, but the rival spirit worked on and carried the day.

The Baroque

Despite these remarks, and, in some measure, because of them, a number of literary critics felt obliged to rehabilitate the literature in question. As Marcel Raymond put it:

> *Des oeuvres de "transition"* . . . *vont acquérir ce qui leur manquait: une espèce de légitimité. A des faits de style, a des traits de nature, à des beautés isolées, on va pouvoir attribuer une valeur. On ne rangera plus des oeuvres importantes parmi les exceptions, on ne les definera*

plus par négation. Certaines d'entre elles . . . symboliseront pour nous une vision du monde qui eut une raison d'être.[3]

The background for such a "*valeur*" and a "*raison d'être*" came from several sources. Undisputed priority goes to the German art historian, Heinrich Wölfflin. In his *Renaissance und Barock* (1888), this scholar first suggested that one could apply these art terms to an examination of literary works. A second book, *Kunstgeschichtliche Grundbegriffe (Principles of Art History)*, published in 1915, outlined a series of categories to be used in distinguishing between the two art styles. The terminology was immediately applied to literary analysis, and in the ensuing 30 years a Baroque literature was identified and accepted by all the major European countries save France. By the 1950s renewed efforts with French literature had made it appear that France, too, could be brought into the fold. Jean de Sponde had been edited, reprinted, and his work, along with that of others of his generation, compared to trends in English poetry of the same period. Wölfflin-inspired critics such as Imbrie Buffum and Jean Rousset brought common traits in art and letters of the sort outlined above to bear in establishing the salient features of the Baroque sensibility (metamorphosis and ostentation for Rousset; theatricality, exaggeration, horror, moral purpose, movement and metamorphosis, and acceptance of life for Buffum). Despite an evident overlap of results in the work of these two scholars, continued analysis has not yet brought agreement on many basic points. Is the Baroque a general, ahistorical phenomenon, or is it the product of a concatenation of events that can occur but once? Can it be explained in purely stylistic terms, or does it use images that properly belong to other traditions, imparting to them a Baroque nature through the intervention of a particular vision?

At the present time, moreover, the question of the Baroque grows more complicated with the recent introduction of new terms such as "mannerist" and "metaphysical." Since these words have not acquired any greater precision than the word "Baroque" enjoys, they do not shed much more light on the general problems raised by the initial use of the concept of the Baroque to describe a particular moment in French literature. This is not to say that writers on the Baroque have accomplished nothing. The renewed interest in Sponde, La Ceppède, or d'Aubigné has justly helped re-evaluate a number of texts too long ignored. This literature demonstrates that Classicism did not capture

---

[3] Marcel Raymond, *Génies de France*, p. 84. Quoted in Sponde, *Poésies*, ed. Ruchon and Boase (Geneva: P. Cailler, 1949), p. 95.

France as swiftly and as simply as had once been believed. On the other hand, how possible or desirable is it to discuss literature in terms of a critical vocabulary borrowed from the arts? Is it not also difficult to believe that any general line of criticism that over the years has led primarily to greater discord and confusion can provide a firm basis for understanding the nature of the phenomenon it discusses? Of course, the ultimate judgment of the reader will be a personal one, based on whether or not Baroque criticism opens all doors for him. But before he judges, he may want to consider the results of an examination of these poets viewed in historical perspective.

Jean de Sponde (1557–1595)

Brought up in a strict Calvinist environment, Jean de Sponde converted to Catholicism in 1593. Educated to be a humanist, the translator of Homer and Aristotle's *Pythagoreorum fragmenta,* Sponde is recognized today as a great talent because of his poems on love and death. Such contrasts and perhaps tensions (he was censured for his conduct by no less a personage than Théodore de Bèze long before his conversion) appeal to partisans of the Baroque aesthetic. They have discovered throughout Sponde's poetry evidence of contrasts and a dislocated vision which, when added to the violence of certain Sponde images (see above), give ample evidence of Sponde's Baroque qualities.

In the third sonnet on love, for example, Sponde begins by noting that to contemplate the earth from the sky would be to realize its smallness, whereas to station oneself on earth and view the firmament produces an awesome sight of immensity. As the poet then passes on to talk of love, it has been said that Sponde never resolves this contrast and never arrives at a unified perspective to embrace both extremes. But is the poem really about perspective, and can we pass so lightly over the second part of the poem dealing with love? Let us reread the entire poem:

> Qui seroit dans les Cieux, et baisseroit sa veuë
> Sur le large pourpris de ce sec element,
> Il ne croiroit de tout rien qu'un poinct seulement,
> Un poinct encor caché du voile d'une nuë:
> Mais s'il contemple apres ceste courtine bluë,
> Ce cercle de cristal, ce doré firmament,
> Il juge que son tour est grand infiniment,
> Et que ceste grandeur nous est toute incognuë.
> Ainsi de ce grand ciel, où l'amour m'a guidé,
> De ce grand ciel d'Amour où mon oeil est bandé,

Si je relasche un peu la pointe aigue au reste,
Au reste des amours, je vois sous une nuict
Du monde d'Epicure en atomes reduit,
Leur amour tout de terre, et le mien tout celeste.

The tercets are introduced by the word "*Ainsi*," the same *ainsi* of the normal comparison pattern "just as . . . so," and on close reading we can observe that Sponde's original contrast of perspectives is but the first part of a comparison whose second half appears in the tercets. The possibility of arriving at two views of the earth is comparable to the poet's realization that when he contemplates other loves, they seem small and insignificant whereas his own appears to him grandiose. The poem is very carefully constructed, and within the tercets Sponde takes care to reproduce key elements of the initial contrast. He situates himself in love on a level with "*ce grand ciel*" and uses in the closing line those words "*terre*" and "*celeste*" which, though pertaining to the contrast in loves, also succinctly reproduce the distinction of the quatrains.

Whatever Sponde may be referring to when composing this contrast, there can be little doubt that he wished to praise his love and compliment it. In fact, if we are quite objective about the imagery and structure of the sonnet, we find that despite the elaborate nature of Sponde's expression, the idea he wishes to convey is not new, unusual, or especially philosophical. His close has the inescapable qualities of a *pointe*, first because it is unexpected and secondly because it is a clever restatement of what precedes. (In both "*terre*" and "*celeste*" Sponde is, to a degree, playing with words.) Compliment, *pointe*, playing with words, these phenomena bring Sponde close to the dominant love tradition of his day: Petrarchism. Granted, this sonnet does not read like those of Desportes, but if we move on to the opening quatrain of Sponde's fifth poem on love,

Je meurs, et les soucis, qui sortent du martyre
Que me donne l'absence, et les jours, et les nuicts
Font tant, qu'à tous momens je ne sçay que je suis,
Si j'empire du tout ou bien si je respire,

the Petrarchist affinities grow much clearer. Certainly there is nothing here to distinguish the poet's sentiments from those of many works by Scève, Ronsard, even Desportes.

Interestingly enough, Sponde's sonnets on death reveal a technique quite similar to the style of his love poems. The first sonnet on this subject, "Mortels, qui des mortels," recalls to men that they live from what was once the possessions of persons now gone, yet manage to forget the reality of death. The poem appears to be developing into a sermon, but Sponde does a sudden about-face and pardons man his forgetfulness since "*Un oubly d'une mort/ [N]ous monstre un souvenir d'une eternelle vie.*" Again the end can be properly termed a *pointe*, and again that *pointe* depends in part on a game of words. Forgetting and remembering have been the terms on which Sponde constructed his poem, somewhat as he had done with the contrasts of the love poem. Suddenly they reappear like the words "*terre*" and "*celeste*" to acquire unexpected meaning.

Instead of admonishing man for treating his earthly life as eternal, Sponde reveals the particular cast of the mortal mind by turning our failing into a paradox of positive import. We are pardoned, not chastised, because our forgetfulness with regard to death demonstrates our awareness of eternal life. We are wrong; we are confused. But Sponde is less interested in rendering this prosaic fact than the startling realization that our incorrect imaginings make manifest the ultimate truth we slight. Paradox, too, it must be remembered, is a fundamental trait of Petrarchist thought. Living and dying, loving and hating, absence and presence are only the more obvious antitheses on which Petrarchist paradox is built. Naturally paradox has its role in Christian thought as well, but what occurs in Sponde's poetry is the use of Christian concepts as if they were Petrarchist commonplaces. He has done this in the first sonnet on death; he does so again in the eighth sonnet:

> Voulez-vous voir ce traict qui si roide s'eslance
> Dedans l'air qu'il poursuit au partir de la main?
> Il monte, il monte, il perd: mais helas! tout soudain
> Il retombe, il retombe, et perd sa violence.
> C'est le train de noz jours, c'est ceste outrecuidance
> Que ces monstres de Terre allaittent de leur sein,
> Qui baise or des monts le sommet plus haultain,
> Ores sur les rochers de ces vallons s'offence.
> Voire ce sont noz jours: quand tu seras monté
> A ce point de hauteur, à ce point arresté,
> Qui ne se peut forcer, il te faudra descendre.
> Le traict est empenné, l'air, qu'il va poursuyvant,
> C'est le champ de l'orage: hé! commence d'apprendre
> Que ta vie est de Plume, et le monde de Vent.

The beginning is an allegory glossed by the rest of the poem. Each element is identified much as happens in a poem of Petrarch ("E qual cervo ferito di saetta"), imitated by Bembo, who inspired both Ronsard and Baïf to try their hand at comparing the wounding of a deer to the lady's attack with her eyes. From technical similarities we can proceed to thematic resemblances. The basic message of Sponde's poem—the vanity of our earthly efforts to attain greatness—has a counterpart in the Petrarchist awareness of the vanity of the lover's pursuit of so insensitive a woman, while the Petrarchist concept that the poet seeks this end wittingly recalls Sponde's seventh sonnet on death where man is presented as consciously spending his life in harmful pursuits. Thus, whether we are dealing with Sponde's thoughts on love or death and whatever their interrelation, it can be argued that the cosmic imagery and the love of paradox and contrast do not constitute a new general aesthetic, but merely one poet's handling of basic poetic material in vogue at the time he was writing. Sponde admittedly appears quite different from Desportes, but Desportes was not the humanist we know Sponde to be. Desportes did not have Sponde's sense of construction or density. Whereas Desportes was content to reproduce the Petrarchist conceits and themes, Sponde enjoyed grappling with their potential within the sonnet form and discovering alternate images for the rendering of the more tired commonplaces. In this, he greatly resembles the mature Ronsard; he shows the qualities of a serious poet but not necessarily that he can be placed in a category fundamentally different from that of other sixteenth-century Petrarchists of merit, Maurice Scève and Pierre de Ronsard.

Agrippa d'Aubigné (1552–1630)

The violence of d'Aubigné, flaunted by the poet very early in his preface to *L'Hécatombe à Diane* (written c. 1570–1573), too, has a precise historical context. He first makes reference to the fact that his verse emerged from a world of "orages," "guerres" and 'voiages." (D'Aubigné, a militant Protestant, participated in the Religious Wars, beginning in 1568.) But, on reading farther, we discover that d'Aubigné's general attitudes concerning poetry have an equal, if not greater, bearing on the nature of his verse. Like the brigade, d'Aubigné subscribed to Horace's "Odi vulgus":

> *S'il t'[his book]est force de desplaire*
> *Au plus rude populaire*
> *Pour n'estre d'eux entendu,*
> *Di leur qu'ilz aillent aprendre*
> *La raison à le reprendre*
> *Aux ignorans deffendu.*

Simplicity was not his main aim. He wrote for the learned and intended to use a learned diction. He eschewed "*proverbes emmanchez*" to enrich his style and would be displeased to hear chambermaids singing his rhymes. Above all, he despised the ignorant courtiers and their tastes.

> Ces sotz bronchent à toute heure
> Sur la rime la meilleure
> Et le vers le mieux polly;
> En fin, toute leur sentence
> Ce sera que monsieur pence
> Que cela est bien jolly.

It is hard not to think of Desportes when reading this stanza, and given that Desportes in 1573 had also published a collection of poems for a lady named Diane, d'Aubigné may have had precise as well as general reasons for opposing this favorite of the court. The general reasons are strong enough, however. Before the close of the poem, d'Aubigné vilifies "*l'ignorant*" to praise "*le docte.*"

D'Aubigné's stand was both a conscious attempt to perpetuate the early designs of the brigade and to counteract the influence of simpler, lighter poetry whose vogue must have appeared a distinct threat to the advances urged and accomplished by the brigade. In a word, the poet accepted unequivocally the views on poetry of Du Bartas, not Desportes. To the prattle of fawning amateurs, d'Aubigné opposed the virile, yet difficult fruits of the learned imagination. It could not be bothered with prettiness and frills. Great poetry was made of other stuff. Admittedly, such attitudes as d'Aubigné expressed in the preface to *L'Hécatombe à Diane* do not give a direct explanation of the apocryphal vision this poet sometimes exhibits. At the same time, they definitely shed light on that point from which he entered into the poetic experience. Erudition and obscurity belong to that experience; so, too, avoidance of facility and simplicity. Such an attitude, incited further by the poet's militant religious sentiments and the horrors of civil war, could not produce a poetry too different from the verse of *Les Tragiques*. Moreover, just as a penchant for paradox can be attributed to the wave of Petrarchist poetry or d'Aubigné's excesses related to serious literary quarrels of the day begun even before Ronsard died, so one could point to the long-standing popularity of such violent subjects as Medea and Electra among students of classical drama when confronted with the current of blood and gore plays during this period.

Naturally, literary history will not explain everything about a work of art or a writer's personality. Still, knowing a literature in depth can

prevent us from seeing novelty where it does not exist and from subordinating the many talents at work to any single intent when differences among writers were not only inevitable but cultivated. To divorce
Jean de Sponde's love poetry from the Petrarchist tradition is as dangerous as to expect that he or d'Aubigné would write exactly like Ronsard.

Malherbe (1555–1628)

Between the poets of Coqueret and the great French Classical writers
stands François Malherbe, whose reform of poetic techniques inspired
these famous verses from Boileau's *Art poétique*:

> Enfin Malherbe vint, et le premier en France,
> Fit sentir dans les vers une juste cadence:
> D'un mot mis en sa place enseigna le pouvoir,
> Et reduisit la Muse aux regles du devoir.

The reform, if we read what precedes, would seem to have been
directed against practices introduced by Ronsard:

> Reglant tout, [Ronsard] broüilla tout, fit un art à sa mode:
> Et toutefois long-temps eut un heureux destin.
> Mais sa Muse en Francois parlant Grec et Latin,
> Vit dans l'âge suivant par un retour grotesque,
> Tomber de ses grands mots le faste pedantesque.
> Ce Poëte orgueilleux trébuché de si haut,
> Rendit plus retenus Desportes et Bertaut.

Doubtlessly too much has been made of Malherbe's reform in terms
both of its relationship to the poetry of the day and to his own work.
(We know, as Boileau suggests with "*plus retenus*," that many of
Malherbe's rules were already in practice before he arrived in Paris.
Also, Malherbe regularly broke his own rules when composing.) But
most revealing with respect to an appreciation of his reform is the
attempt made by Malherbe to discredit Desportes, not Sponde or
d'Aubigné or Du Bartas. These proponents or practitioners of a vigor-
ous, if somewhat obscure and excessive, verse would appear far more
worthy of Malherbe's diatribes than Desportes. In truth time and
change had already begun to discredit them when Malherbe launched
his campaign.

Here again Boileau's remarks are telling. Between Ronsard and
Malherbe come two names only: Desportes and Bertaut. The latter,
forgotten, has not been found in need of review. The former has not

caught the fancy of even lovers of the Baroque, but Desportes and Bertaut, together with Du Perron, ruled the poetic world when Malherbe arrived in Paris in 1605. Sponde or Du Bartas had not been forgotten, but they were not in vogue either. Du Bartas' greatest success was in England, not France. Sponde's poems appeared less and less frequently in the anthologies of the day; when *Les Tragiques* appeared in 1616, it read (to the very few who bought the volume) like a poetic curiosity out of the past. By 1605 language, style, and tone were already so removed from those contained in Ronsard's works that Vauquelin de la Fresnaye could write "*on n'écrit point à cette heure, comme on écrivait quand elles furent écrites.*" However, if even before Malherbe came, French poets were rejecting the grandiose, erudite verse of Ronsard and his admirers, why did Malherbe, partisan of rules and logic, attack Desportes, who himself had been attacked by such proponents of the old style as d'Aubigné?

The complexity arises from the fact that Malherbe was both a disciple and opponent of Ronsard. He, too, appreciated the poetry of antiquity, its forms, its language, its expression, and for that reason deplored the limpid, shallow verse of Desportes. At the same time, Malherbe inherited and accepted the prejudices of Bertaut and Du Perron. He thundered against Desportes' unpolished composition, extravagant metaphors, and illogical developments and condemned similar excesses in Ronsard. He stands out from the general group of Ronsard's critics because, as Boileau's verses indicate, Malherbe went deeply into the question of prosody. He shared with the brigade a keen awareness of the relationship between music and poetry and insisted on reforms regarding caesura, stanzaic patterns, and grammatical constructions that go much beyond his predecessors' condemnation of the "*galimatias*" in Ronsard's love verse.

Of course, placing such considerations at the forefront of poetic practice was guaranteed to annoy the more imaginative bards and it did. The battle could hardly be a fair one, however. The fate of Du Bartas, Sponde, and d'Aubigné shows that their diction was by 1600 already too archaic to rival that of Malherbe successfully. Their fate also demonstrates to what degree it is difficult to see the Baroque aesthetic as the dominant view of artists throughout this period. Even those who protested indicate that ultimate victory lay with Malherbe.

In the years during which Malherbe fought to impose his reform, no one opposed him with more vigor than Marie de Gournay. She admired Ronsard and defended him. But when she published his "Harangue du duc de Guise aux soldats de Metz" in 1624, she produced a text significantly different from the original. She reworked at least 159 lines out of 291, changing vocabulary, syntax, caesura, very often along the lines of Malherbe's reform. One is led to believe that Mlle. de Gournay never intended to betray her favorite poet. She very likely hoped to prove that, with a few corrections, Ronsard's text would reveal its worth and give the lie to Malherbe. Neither her corrections nor the handsome edition of Ronsard's works published in 1623 rescued the poet. The sentiments on Ronsard expressed by Cardinal Du Perron early in the seventeenth century were not to be countered. To that period in French literature Ronsard remained a poet of remarkable scope but little refinement.

Marie de Gournay's liberties with the original text intimate that even she could not be saved from the advance of time and a recognition that in certain ways Ronsard was passé. To the end she feared that Malherbe's rules would obscure the necessary ingredient of imagination in poetry (a not unfounded worry as Voiture proves) and insisted that Ronsard was France's greatest poet. But Ronsard was now great despite the archaic words, imprecise caesura, and fuzzy syntax, and even Mlle. de Gournay could not pretend any longer that clarity in expression was of little importance. By the 1620s Malherbe had made his point.

Conclusion

The preceding pages have shown that the sixteenth century is neither simple nor homogeneous. As a series of events, the hundred years from 1500 to 1599 are more properly appreciated not as a single period but rather as the prolongation of efforts already set into motion in the preceding century (the rise of the monarchy, the Italian Wars, the Reform movement), and after 1559, when exhaustion and the religious situation turned France away from a conquest of Italy, as the breeding ground of those concepts which culminated in the institutions and culture of French Classicism. In intellectual developments, too, the century defies any facile definition. The surge of the early thirties, built on the shifting sands of royal self-interest and ideals incompatible with basic realities, corresponded to what men hoped more than to what they accomplished. The classical revival of the forties proved a young, ebullient, and somewhat ill-fated phenomenon. The threat and then the reality of war doomed the flourishing arts by exiling their talent (Goujon) or emptying the patrons' treasuries. A decided break with older modes of expression accompanied this revival to contrast the period with earlier developments in the literature of this century, but it was a luxuriant production, overextended in imagination and erudition and not likely to become as such a cultural heritage even for the educated classes. As the century wore on, familiarity with the great works of antiquity brought some Frenchmen to associate education and culture not with the capacity to memorize or use mythology but with a doubting of the old authorities and the creation of a faculty of judgment, free from the pretensions of the pedant as well as the stupidity of the illiterate. This view, so firmly expressed by Montaigne, has in Malherbe's literary doctrine an adaptation of obvious parallels.

Throughout the century a distinct critical spirit was at work, animating the Reform movement and spreading eventually to literature, education, law, and history. It was distinctly related to an appreciation of antiquity and scholarship, but that same spirit in time turned on itself. The sixteenth century in France is both the triumph of humanism and its reevaluation. Once the brigade had advanced beyond the enthusiasm of the *Deffence*, they recognized the excesses and limitations of their manifesto. A greater understanding of Roman law and its texts eventually unmasked its insufficiencies for a modern state. Once the concept of a *cultura animi* had been grasped by Montaigne, it became a lever to foist from a seat of honor the very pedants and scholars who had made the treasured ancient texts available.

In what sense is the sixteenth century a renaissance? Contact with Italy, contact with antiquity did not begin with the year 1500. The progress of ideas and forces within France from 1500 to 1599 followed the dictates of national problems, not the evolution of the Italian city-states in earlier decades. Rather than a clear movement toward a single goal, the century continued to build upon the work just accomplished. Now it enriched itself with the ideals of Erasmus or Rabelais; now it reviewed with circumspection certain products of that enrichment as when Montaigne turns on the pedant, Bodin criticizes Cujas, or Malherbe, Ronsard. Its history is a continuum, punctuated, to be sure, by moments of demarcation such as the Peace of Cateau-Cambrésis, but composed in the main of protracted efforts to deal with immediate problems more than with the advancement of western civilization. When the century opened, the fight for a Reform had begun; when it closed, the introduction of classical models had been effected, and voices were heard speaking for moderation—that nuance which led directly to the principles behind French Classicism. And so the continuum ran.

It did not run wild, however. If the early humanists sought neither schism nor heresy, they did believe in reform, new sources of inspiration, and new methods of investigation. The sixteenth century is a renaissance because the seed of revolt inherent in such protest did not die but took root and prevailed. Basically religious, legal, and linguistic in orientation, the humanists' spirit of criticism had by the time of Bodin and Montaigne brought such writers to conceive of man's relation to himself and to society as well as to history in terms unacceptable to the medieval ethos. To say that the century always meant to arrive at such an end fails to take into account the piety of Rabelais and Marguerite, the erudition of Ronsard; at the same time the evolution in ideas did transpire.

While the value of this evolution in the formation of modern society should be patent, an appreciation of the story told in the preceding pages need not end with the beginnings of the contemporary world. In many ways that story continues. The drama of the Council of Trent and the Catholic Church's effort to survive its critics is but a chapter in a chronicle that includes Vatican II and Pope John XXIII's call for an "aggiornamento." The story may repeat itself. The emergence of the Fifth Republic under General De Gaulle is not without parallels to the drift of French public sentiment after the Religious Wars, and, more particularly, after the assassination of Henry IV. Above all, that story makes a statement about the human condition. The sixteenth century knew persecution and violence, civil war, and foreign threats. In all instances, the intensity of emotions unveiled the animal in man. It was also a period of hopes, of attempts to realize such hopes. Many, like the Meaux experiment, hardly outlived their conception. And, still, despite these setbacks, certainly no less painful than the world wars of the twentieth century or the frustrations of those who believed in the League of Nations, the sixteenth century did not conclude that human existence was absurd. The later writers could not escape a sense of insecurity, an awareness that change surrounded them at every turn, but their sentiments merely provoked a greater effort toward an equilibrium between order and chaos. Although Montaigne, in analyzing the particular yet universal *moi* in the *Essais* quickly saw the pernicious force of ambition, he did not surmise that man must go as society wills any more than that we are forever what custom dictates because custom's influence is so strong. He preserved a firm conviction that man can discern what is best for him within the limits set by nature. The sage acquiesces to what is inevitable and immutable, no more. Even Montaigne's realization that he was himself far from the ideal in question did not bring him to denounce it. All times in modern history have succeeded in trying men's souls, but not all have shaken man's faith in himself. The willingness of the sixteenth century to nurture and proclaim such faith should give us pause today and make us reflect, if not act.

A Selected Bibliography

I. HISTORY AND HISTORY OF IDEAS

ALLEN, J. W., *A History of Political Thought in the Sixteenth Century.* London: Methuen & Co. Ltd., 1928.

BAKER, HERSCHEL, *The Dignity of Man.* Cambridge, Mass.: Harvard University Press, 1947. Reprinted in paper as a Harper Torchbook under the title *The Image of Man.* Offers challenging thoughts on the world view of men such as Erasmus.

FAGUET, EMILE, *Le Seizième Siècle.* Paris: Lecène, Oudin, 1894. Dated but with provocative introduction.

FERGUSON, WALLACE, *The Renaissance in Historical Thought.* Boston: Houghton Mifflin Company, 1948. *The* study of the concept of the Renaissance through the ages.

FRANKLIN, JULIAN, *Jean Bodin and the Sixteenth Century Revolution in the Methodology of Law and History.* New York: Columbia University Press, 1963. Short, clear, informative.

HAUSER, H., "De l'Humanisme et de la Réforme en France 1512–1552," *Revue historique,* 64 (1897), 258–97. Studies the shifting of views among humanists of the period indicated.

HUIZINGA, JOHAN, *The Waning of the Middle Ages.* London: Longmans, Green & Co. Ltd., 1924. Available in paper as a Doubleday Anchor Book. Best for appreciating the context of late French, Burgundian, and Dutch art and literature.

IMBART DE LA TOUR, J., *Les Origines de la Réforme en France.* Paris: Hachette, 1905–35. Very long and scholarly but rewarding.

KINGDON, ROBERT, *Geneva and the Coming of the Wars of Religion in France (1555–1563).* Geneva: Droz, 1956. Lucid, careful analysis of Geneva's relationship to France in these years.

LAVISSE, ERNESTE, ed., *Histoire de France depuis les origines jusqu'à la Révolution.* Paris: Hachette, 1900–1911. The standard history of France.

MAJOR, J. RUSSELL, *Representative Institutions in Renaissance France 1421–1559*. Madison: Wisconsin University Press, 1960. One man's view but stimulating and informative.

MATTINGLY, GARRETT, *Renaissance Diplomacy*. London: Jonathan Cape Limited, 1955. Available in paper as a Peregrine Book.

————, *The Armada*. Boston: Houghton Mifflin Company, 1959. Like his other work, a classical study, elegantly written.

MOUSNIER, ROLAND, *L'Assassinat d'Henri IV*. Paris: Gallimard, 1964. A magnificent review of Henry IV's reign.

NEALE, JOHN E., *The Age of Catherine de Medici*. London: Jonathan Cape Limited, 1947. Available in paper as a Harper Torchbook. A must: short, lively and lucid.

PANOFSKY, ERWIN, "Renaissance and Renascences," *Kenyon Review*, VI (1944), 201–36. A great art historian explains why the Renascences of the Middle Ages are not the Renaissance.

RENAUDET, A., *Préreforme et Humanisme à Paris (1494–1517)*. Paris: E. Champion, 1916. Reprinted in 1953. Definitive work on the subject but long and tough going.

ROMIER, LUCIEN, *Les Origines politiques des guerres de religion*. Paris: Perrin, 1913–1914.

————, *Le Royaume de Catherine de Médicis*. Paris: Perrin, 1925. Not easy to read but intelligent and informative.

SIMONE, FRANCO, *Il Rinascimento francese: Studi e Richerche*. Turin: Società editrice internazionale, 1961. A good survey of past and present views on the subject.

WADSWORTH, JAMES, *Lyons 1473–1503*. Cambridge, Mass.: Medieval Academy of America, 1962.

II. LITERARY CRITICISM

Rhétoriqueurs:

FRAPPIER, JEAN, "L'Humanisme de Jean Lemaire de Belges," *Bibliothèque d'Humanisme et Renaissance*, XXV (1963), 289–306.

GUY, HENRY, *Histoire de la poésie française au XVIᵉ siècle*. Paris: H. Champion, 1910–1926.

Marot:

MAROT, CLÉMENT, *Oeuvres*, ed. C. A. Mayer. London: Athlone Press, 1958—. Four volumes published to date. The introductions and notes

provide the most accurate discussion of Marot's bibliography available.
MAYER, C. A., *La Religion de Marot.* Geneva: Droz, 1960. Highly debatable conclusions.

Marguerite de Navarre:

JOURDA, PIERRE, *Marguerite d'Angoulême.* Paris: H. Champion, 1930. More informative than critical.

MARGUERITE DE NAVARRE, *Théâtre profane,* ed. V.-L. Saulnier. Paris: Droz, 1946. Each play is preceded by an excellent introduction.

Rabelais:

BRAULT, G. J., " 'Ung Abysme de Science': On the Interpretation of Gargantua's Letter to Pantagruel," *Bibliothèque d'Humanisme et Renaissance,* XXVIII (1966), 615–32. A provocative attempt to reassess traditional views on Gargantua's letter.

FEBVRE, LUCIEN, *Le Problème de l'incroyance au XVIᵉ siècle: La Religion de Rabelais.* Paris: Editions Albin Michel, 1942. Reprinted 1962.

GILSON, ETIENNE, "Rabelais franciscain," *Revue d'histoire franciscaine,* I (1924), 257–87.

KRAILSHEIMER, A., *Rabelais and the Franciscans.* Oxford: Oxford University Press, 1965.

SAULNIER, V.-L., *Le Dessein de Rabelais.* Paris: Société d'édition d'enseignement supérieur, 1957. Controversial effort to describe the "plan" of Rabelais' works.

SCREECH, MICHAEL A., *The Rabelaisian Marriage.* London: Edward Arnold (Publishers) Ltd., 1958. A milestone in modern criticism on Rabelais.

———, "Some Stoic Elements in Rabelais' Religious Thought," *Etudes Rabelaisiennes,* I (1956), 73–97.

Scève:

COLEMAN, DOROTHY, "Les Emblesmes dans la 'Délie' de Maurice Scève," *Studi francesi,* VIII (1964), 1–15. *The* introduction to this subject.

SAULNIER, V.-L., *Maurice Scève.* Paris: C. Klincksieck, 1948–1949. General survey of man and works.

SCÈVE, MAURICE, *The Délie,* ed. Ian McFarlane. Cambridge, England:

Cambridge University Press, 1966. Contains the best introduction to Scève's poetry to date.

Drama:

LEBÈGUE, RAYMOND, *La Tragédie française de la Renaissance*. Brussels: Office de Publicité, 1944. Reprinted in 1954.

Pléiade:

CASTOR, GRAHAME, *Pléiade Poetics*. Cambridge, England: Cambridge University Press, 1964. Insightful study of the theoretical side of the Pléiade's work.

CHAMARD, HENRI, *Histoire de la Pléiade*. Paris: Didier, 1939–1940. Reprinted Paris, 1961–1963. Contains essential historical information about the Pléiade's works.

DU BELLAY, JOACHIM, *Oeuvres poétiques*, ed. H. Chamard. Paris: E. Cornély, 1908–1931. Invaluable introductions and notes.

————, *La Deffence et Illustration de la Langue françoyse*, ed. H. Chamard. Paris: Didier, 1948. Excellent edition.

GADOFFRE, GILBERT, *Ronsard par lui-même*. Paris: Editions du Seuil, 1960. Excellent introduction to Ronsard.

BALMAS, ENEA, *Un Poeta del Rinascimento francese: Etienne Jodelle*. Florence: Olschki, 1962. *The* study on Jodelle's life and plays.

Montaigne:

FRAME, DONALD, *Montaigne's Discovery of Man*. New York: Columbia University Press, 1955.

————, *Montaigne: A Biography*. New York: Harcourt, Brace & World, Inc., 1965. The most complete studies in English on Montaigne.

FRIEDRICH, HUGO, *Montaigne*. Berne: Francke, 1949. Reprinted in 1967. Most comprehensive study of Montaigne, but in German. Translated into French in 1967.

VILLEY, PIERRE, *Les Sources et l'Evolution des Essais de Montaigne*. Paris: Hachette, 1908. More reliable for its erudition than for its interpretations.

Baroque:

BUFFUM, IMBRIE, *Agrippa d'Aubigné's Les Tragiques*. New Haven: Yale University Press, 1951.

————, *Studies in the Baroque from Montaigne to Rotrou.* New Haven: Yale University Press, 1957.

MOURGUES, ODETTE DE, *Metaphysical, Baroque and Précieux Poetry.* Oxford: Oxford University Press, 1953. An intelligent effort to define and understand these terms.

RAYMOND, MARCEL, "Les Poésies d'amour d'Agrippa d'Aubigné," *Mélanges Abel Lefranc.* Paris: 1936. Pp. 436–47.

ROUSSET, JEAN, *La Littérature de l'âge baroque en France.* Paris: Corti, 1953.

SPONDE, JEAN DE, *Poésies*, eds. François Ruchon and Alan Boase. Geneva: P. Cailler, 1949. The introduction by Sponde's two editors constitutes the most complete study on the poet to date.

WELLEK, RENÉ, *Concepts of Criticism.* New Haven: Yale University Press, 1963. Contains a history of the term "baroque."

III. ART AND ARCHITECTURE

BLUNT, ANTHONY, *Art and Architecture in France 1500–1700.* London: Penguin Books, 1953.

GÉBELIN, FRANÇOIS, *Les Châteaux de la Renaissance.* Paris: Les Beaux-arts, 1927.

Index